ACCOUNTING
ESSENTIALS

More than 100 Wiley Self-Teaching Guides teach practical skills on everything from accounting to astronomy, from microcomputers to mathematics.

STGs FOR MATHEMATICS

Accounting Essentials, 2nd Edition, Margolis & Harmon
Finite Mathematics, Rothenberg
Geometry and Trigonometry for Calculus, Selby
Linear Algebra with Computer Applications, Rothenberg
Management Accounting, Madden
Math Shortcuts, Locke
Math Skills for the Sciences, Pearson
Practical Algebra, Selby
Quick Algebra Review, Selby
Quick Arithmetic, 2nd Edition, Carman & Carman
Quick Calculus, 2nd Edition, Kleppner & Ramsey
Statistics, 3rd Edition, Koosis

Look for these and other Self-Teaching Guides at your favorite bookstore!

ACCOUNTING ESSENTIALS

A Self-Teaching Guide

Second Edition

Neal Margolis

N. Paul Harmon

in consultation with

Joseph Peter Simini, C.P.A.

*Department of Accounting
University of San Francisco*

A Wiley Press Book

JOHN WILEY & SONS, INC.

New York · Chichester · Brisbane · Toronto · Singapore

Library of Congress Cataloging-in-Publication Data

Margolis, Neal.

  Accounting essentials.

  Includes index.
  1. Accounting. I. Harmon, Paul. II. Title.
HF5635.M3 1985   657   85-12332
ISBN 0-471-82721-5

Printed in the United States of America

85 86 10 9 8 7 6 5 4 3 2 1

Preface

Accounting Essentials has been so well received that we have been encouraged to prepare a second edition. The book's strength is its systematic coverage of the basic accounting concepts and techniques, and we have resisted the urge to add material that would make it less straightforward. We have updated various examples so that they reflect the economic realities of the mid-Eighties. In addition, we have provided an overview of how computer-based accounting systems work.

Accounting is a body of theory and technique used to record, sort, summarize, and analyze the "raw data" of business transactions and produce condensed information which managers can use in planning the future course of business activity.

In even the simplest business, information is too complex to analyze without summaries. If we were to ask someone what a business was worth, we wouldn't expect him to tell us about each piece of merchandise, the cash register, buildings, and so forth. We would expect him to express those possessions in terms of money and just give us a total sum. If we wanted to know how a business was doing, we might be satisfied to simply know its income during the last year. Similarly business managers don't always need to know exactly what sums of money were received across which counters by which clerks, but they want a general picture of the state of the business on which they can base their actions and decisions during the coming days and months.

In keeping with the nature of accounting, we stress both theory and practice, although practice varies in particular situations. In Chapter One, "Fundamental Concepts of Bookkeeping and Accounting," we present a bookkeeping model to be used as a framework for later knowledge of accounting.

In the next four chapters, we discuss various parts of the bookkeeping model in greater detail. In these chapters, we follow the route of business transactions as they are documented, recorded, sorted, summarized, and finally reported to managers.

Once we master the basic record-keeping procedures, we illustrate how to use these techniques in particular applications, including protection of assets, inventory, payroll, and special record-keeping devices. To get a taste of decision-making in accounting, we touch on some basic techniques for analyzing important business statements. Finally, to prepare the student for the use of computer-based accounting systems, we have included an Appendix that provides an overview of how the principles covered in this book are represented in computer software.

San Francisco, California
May, 1985

Neal Margolis
N. Paul Harmon

To the Reader

The purpose of <u>Accounting</u> <u>Essentials</u> is to give you a strong, general overview of the basic concepts and techniques of bookkeeping and accounting. You need little or no experience with processing business events or working with the common records of a business to use this book. <u>Accounting</u> <u>Essentials</u> is called a <u>Self</u>-<u>Teaching</u> <u>Guide</u>, because you should be able to learn the subject matter with little or no difficulty if you follow the instructions. This guide has been designed to allow you to skip portions of the text that you already understand and to pinpoint concepts that you need to review.

To make the main concepts clear from the beginning, we have often simplified examples and procedures. Many of the forms, for example, do not require that cents be included when entering amounts of money--$5 is sufficient, rather than $5.00 or $5.76. As you progress through the guide, more details will be included and the forms will be closer to those used in actual practice.

To make the best use of this book, you should know how the book is put together and what it can do for you. Read the following description carefully. Each of the ten chapters contains the following:

1. A TITLE PAGE that states the learning objectives of the chapter. If you feel you already know the material, you will be directed to the chapter self-test, to see if you can skip all or part of the chapter.

2. A CHAPTER OVERVIEW that gives a short description of what the chapter is about. This will give you the approach that you will need to work efficiently through the chapter.

3. SELF-TEACHING SECTIONS composed of a series of learning units called <u>Frames</u>. Most of your learning will take place in these sections. Each frame presents information and then asks you a question using the information you were given. After answering each question, check your answer with the answer below the dashed line immediately following. It is a good idea to use an index card

or a folded piece of paper to cover the answers until you have answered the question yourself. In this way you can be sure you understand the information at least well enough to answer a question about it. If your answer does not agree with the one given, be sure you understand why befor you go on.

Frames are arranged so that they build on one another. To fully understand the frames at the end of a section, you must first have completed all of the preceding frames. It is important that you do not skip any frames within a Self-Teaching Section. Doing frames out of order will usually slow down, rather than speed up, your progress.

4. A SELF-TEST, which will tell you how well you learned the material in the chapter. After you have taken the test, compare your answers with the answers given. If you miss any questions, review the frames listed at each answer--to be sure you have mastered all the material before you go on to the next chapter.

To assist you in rapid study and review, we have included an Index-Glossary at the end of the book.

This guide has been thoroughly tested on students, like yourselves, and where confusion or error was found, the book was revised or corrected until it is as close to perfection as we could manage. However, no testing procedure can be 100 percent effective. And while we may be "experts" in designing teaching materials, you are the expert on how you, as an individual, can best learn this material. So we welcome suggestions about how to improve this guide. Should you have any comments about Accounting Essentials, please address them to:

Editor, Self-Teaching Guides
John Wiley & Sons, Inc.
605 Third Avenue
New York, New York 10016

One final note: Even accountants and bookkeepers make mistakes, so use a pencil. Now begin to teach yourself Accounting Essentials.

N. M.
N. P. H.

Contents

CHAPTER ONE

Fundamental Concepts of Bookkeeping and Accounting

OBJECTIVES

When you complete this chapter, you will be able to

- define <u>bookkeeping</u>,
- differentiate between <u>bookkeeping</u> and <u>accounting</u>,
- classify transactions according to whether they affect assets, liabilities, or owner's equity,
- state the Fundamental Accounting Equation,
- recognize and give examples of business documents,
- use a model of bookkeeping to specify how information flows through the bookkeeping system.

If you feel that you have already mastered these objectives and might skip all or part of this chapter, turn to the end of this chapter and take the Self-Test. The results will tell you what frames of the chapter you should study. If you answer all questions correctly, you are ready to begin the next chapter.

If this material is new to you, or if you choose not to take the Self-Test now, turn to the Overview and Self-Teaching Sections that follow.

CHAPTER OVERVIEW

BOOKKEEPING AND ACCOUNTING

Depending on one's purposes, there are many good definitions of accounting and bookkeeping, but for our purposes perhaps the best way to define accounting and bookkeeping is to first describe very generally what it is that accountants and bookkeepers do.

A bookkeeper records those events (expressed in dollars) which affect the financial condition of a business. A bookkeeper or accountant will then classify, sort, and summarize these events to give a concise, condensed picture of the financial condition of the business. Since thousands of events may affect a business, bookkeepers and accountants must exercise great care to be sure that their records are both complete and accurate. To help them ensure the accuracy of their records, they use recordkeeping techniques such as those you will learn in this book.

With this general idea of what bookkeepers and accountants do, we can give a definition of bookkeeping:

> Bookkeeping is the systematic recording, sorting, and summarizing of events (expressed in dollars) that affect the financial condition of a business.

The definition of accounting is as follows:

> Accounting includes and goes beyond bookkeeping. Accounting is also concerned with the analysis and interpretation of financial data, and with setting up bookkeeping systems.

In general, accounting emphasizes analysis, while bookkeeping emphasizes recording.

THE BUSINESS ENTITY

The principles and techniques of bookkeeping regard any business as an entity separate from its owners. This means, for example, that the business, not the owners, purchases supplies; the business, not the owners, pays wages to employees. The distinction between the business and its owners is of paramount importance in understanding the way bookkeeping records are kept.

The Fundamental Accounting Equation

Assets. As a separate entity, one conceives a business as owning property and rights. All of a business's possessions and rights that have money value are called the assets of that business--cash and land are two such assets.

Liabilities. Being a separate entity, a business may borrow money from individuals or from other businesses. It may also purchase goods or services with a promise to pay at some future time. The debts of a business-- the amounts owed to its creditors--are called its liabilities.

Owner's Equity. The owner's claim against the assets of a business after liabilities have been deducted is called the owner's equity. Owner's equity is also commonly called capital, proprietorship, or net worth.

The Accounting Equation. The Fundamental Accounting Equation states that the total assets of a business are equal to (1) the total liabilities of the business added to (2) the total owner's equity of the business. This may be expressed as follows:

ASSETS = LIABILITIES + OWNER'S EQUITY

Another way of stating this relationship is that the total assets of a business represent claims by the creditors and by the owners.

BUSINESS TRANSACTIONS

We stated that bookkeepers and accountants record events (expressed in dollars) that affect the financial condition of a business. These events are called business transactions. Sale of merchandise, payment of a debt, and purchase of supplies are all types of business transactions which affect the assets, liabilities, and owner's equity of a business.

Rarely will a record of a transaction be made unless some kind of paper exists to prove that the transaction has in fact taken place. These papers are collectively called business documents. Examples of business documents include invoices, vouchers, cash register tapes, and adding machine tapes.

A BOOKKEEPING MODEL

We regard bookkeeping as a system through which information flows. Disorganized information "enters" the system in the form of daily transactions represented by business papers. The system "processes" this information by recording it, sorting it, and summarizing it. The processed information "exits" the system in the form of statements which summarize the events that have affected the business. A bookkeeping model is shown in the following diagram:

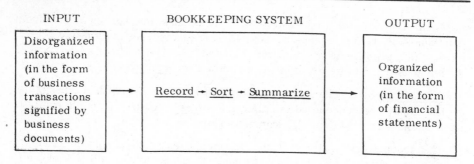

The output of the bookkeeping system is organized information contained in the financial statements. The two most important financial statements are the Balance Sheet and the Income Statement. The Balance Sheet reports the financial condition of the company in terms of its assets, liabilities, and owner's equity as of a certain date. The Income Statement reports on how the financial condition of the business has changed over a given period of time.

These financial statements are read and used as a basis for making decisions by various people, including managers, owners, creditors, investors, the government, and the public.

Self-Teaching Section A

BOOKKEEPING AND ACCOUNTING

1. The Clothes Call manufactures theatrical costumes and sells or rents them to actors and acting studios. Charles P. Adams is the bookkeeper for The Clothes Call. It is his job to keep track of the events (expressed in dollars) that affect the financial condition of the business. These events may be very important to The Clothes Call or they may be relatively minor. On April 21, for example, Adams was made aware of the following two events which had an effect on the financial state of The Clothes Call:

(a) $200 in cash was received for the sale of costumes
(b) a new typewriter was purchased for $290

There are many ways in which bookkeepers keep track of these events. For clarity's sake, let's assume that Charles P. Adams simply writes the events down as follows:

April 21: cash sales of costumes $200
office equipment purchase (typewriter). 290

The first thing a bookkeeper will do to keep track of events that affect the financial condition of a business is to _____ the events.

- - - - - - - - - - - - - - - -

record, or write down

2. Over a period of time, Adams records many events of various types. After a week, his record of events looks like this:

    April 21: cash sales of costumes $200
               office equipment purchase (typewriter). 290
    April 22: cash sales of costumes 100
    April 23: office supplies purchase 50
    April 24: cash sales of costumes 150
               office supplies purchase 20
    April 25: cash sales of costumes 50
    April 26: cash sales of costumes 70
               office supplies purchase 10

As bookkeeper for The Clothes Call, Adam's next job is to combine the records of similar events. He does this by writing the amounts under headings that describe the events. This <u>sorting</u> or <u>classifying</u> procedure is shown below. Complete the procedure by filling in the blanks:

Cash Sales of Costumes	Office Supplies Purchases	Office Equipment Purchases
$200	$50	$290
100	20	
___	—	
50		
___		

- - - - - - - - - - - - - - -

Cash Sales of Costumes	Office Supplies Purchases	Office Equipment Purchases
$200	$50	$290
100	20	
<u>150</u>	<u>10</u>	
50		
<u>70</u>		

3. In addition to <u>recording</u> events that affect the financial condition of the business, a bookkeeper also _____ those events.

- - - - - - - - - - - - - -

    sorts, or classifies

4. At the end of the week, Adams summarizes all the events that affected the financial condition of The Clothes Call. He does this by totaling the amounts under each heading in his classification. Go back to Frame 2 and do this. Then, fill in the blanks below to show the summary of events.

Cash Sales of Costumes	Office Supplies Purchases	Office Equipment Purchases
$_____	$_____	$_____

- - - - - - - - - - - - - -

$570	$80	$290

5. In addition to recording and sorting events that affect the financial condition of a business, a bookkeeper also _____ those events.

- - - - - - - - - - - - - -

   summarizes

6. This brief study of the techniques and practices used by the bookkeeper of The Clothes Call should give you enough of an idea of what bookkeepers do so that you can tell what bookkeeping is. Complete the following definition:

   Bookkeeping is the _____, the _____,

   and the _____ of events that affect the

   _____ of a business.

- - - - - - - - - - - - - -

   Bookkeeping is the recording, the sorting, and the summarizing of events that affect the financial condition of a business.

7. Most people draw a distinction between bookkeeping and accounting. Accountants know how to do everything that a bookkeeper does. In addition, they do much more. Next to each of the following activities, write a "B" if it is done by both a bookkeeper and an accountant; write an "A" if the activity is done only by an accountant.

   ____ a. making a record of daily cash sales
   ____ b. interpreting and analyzing the results of a weekly
            summary of events affecting the business
   ____ c. classifying events affecting the business according
            to type of event
   ____ d. setting up a bookkeeping system

- - - - - - - - - - - - - -

   (a) B; (b) A; (c) B; (d) A

8. In addition to dealing with the recording, sorting, and summarizing of events affecting the financial condition of a business, <u>accounting</u> also deals

with _____

_____

_____.

— — — — — — — — — — — — — — —

analyzing the events, or interpreting the events, or setting up bookkeeping systems (or equivalent answer)

Self-Teaching Section B

THE BUSINESS ENTITY

9. It is of the utmost importance in bookkeeping and accounting to regard any business, no matter how large or small, as a <u>separate</u> entity--apart from its owners and apart from its creditors. In this sense, a business can do almost anything a person can do; for example, it can

> (a) borrow or lend money,
> (b) pay wages,
> (c) sell merchandise,
> (d) rent office space.

From a bookkeeping standpoint, who pays the wages when John Crack, the floor manager of Shop-Fair Market, receives his weekly paycheck:

> _____ a. the owner of Shop-Fair
> _____ b. the bookkeeper of Shop-Fair
> _____ c. Shop-Fair itself

— — — — — — — — — — — — — — —

(c)

10. A bookkeeper must be able to distinguish between those events that have a direct effect on the financial condition of the business and those events that do not. Which of the following events would the bookkeeper for Shop-Fair <u>not</u> record?

> _____ a. Shop-Fair's floors are waxed at a cost of $40
> _____ b. Mr. Martin, the owner of Shop-Fair, spends $900 to send his wife to Acapulco for a vacation
> _____ c. Mr. Martin repays a <u>personal</u> loan of $500
> _____ d. Shop-Fair takes in $1000 in cash sales

— — — — — — — — — — — — — — —

(b); (c)

11.   A business usually owns some property, which may be in one of many forms--such as land, cash, equipment, buildings, or supplies. Taken together, all of these properties or rights that have money value are known as that company's <u>assets</u>. If you add up the money values of every individual thing a company owns, the sum would be the total value of that company's assets. Shop-Fair owns the following things:

      (a) cash in the amount of $5000
      (b) merchandise that cost $7000
      (c) a building that cost $10, 000

The total value of Shop-Fair's assets is $_____.

— — — — — — — — — — — — — — —

    $22, 000

12.   Marvin Vain is the principal owner of The Clothes Call, Inc.   He has a personal savings account of $3500, a car worth $4000, a new home worth $45,000, and 98% of the stock in The Clothes Call.   From these figures, what can you say about the amount of the total assets of The Clothes Call?

_____. Why ? _____

_____

_____.

— — — — — — — — — — — — — — —

    Nothing; because we have enumerated only Mr. Vain's possessions and have said nothing about the possessions (assets) of The Clothes Call, Inc.

13.   A business may borrow money; it may also make purchases "on account" (this means <u>with a promise to pay in the near future</u>).   When a company borrows money or makes a purchase on account, it acquires a <u>debt</u>.   The debts a business owes are called the <u>liabilities</u> of the business.   The Clothes Call, Inc. has the following debts:

      (a) It owes Harold Stark, an employee, wages in the amount of
          of $100
      (b) It owes the Neighborhood Loan Co. $1000
      (c) It owes Tape Measure Fabric Distributors $500 for fabric
          purchased on account

The amount of $1600 gives the total of The Clothes Call's _____.

— — — — — — — — — — — — — — —

    liabilities

14.   The Clothes Call, Inc. owes the Neighborhood Loan Co. $1000. Should The Clothes Call fail to pay the amount, the Neighborhood Loan Co. would probably decide to sue:

     _____ a.   the owner, Marvin Vain
     _____ b.   The Clothes Call

- - - - - - - - - - - - - - -

(b).   (If the law suit disclosed that The Clothes Call did not have sufficient assets to pay the debt, there is a possibility that the Neighborhood Loan Co. could sue the owner.)

15.   If the Neighborhood Loan Co. sued The Clothes Call and won, the money would be paid out of The Clothes Call's _____.

- - - - - - - - - - - - - - -   (assets/liabilities)

assets

16.   For each of the following write an "A" if the item is an asset, and an "L" if it is a liability:

     _____ a.   wages owed to an employee in the amount of $30
     _____ b.   a company car that cost $3000
     _____ c.   a loan payable to a bank in the amount of $4000
     _____ d. $60 owed for purchases on account
     _____ e.   a gross of paper clips worth $2
     _____ f.   an office building with an appraised value of $500,000
     _____ g. $7500 in cash

- - - - - - - - - - - - - - -

(a) L; (b) A; (c) L; (d) L; (e) A; (f) A; (g) A

17.   We said earlier that if a creditor won a law suit against a company he would be paid out of the assets of that company.   Another way of stating this is that "a creditor has a claim on the assets of a business to which he lends money."   The amount of the claim is equal to the amount the company owes the creditor.   The owner of a business also has a claim against the assets of that business after liabilities have been deducted.   His claim is called the owner's equity in the business.   The amount of owner's equity is given by:

     _____ a.   the total assets of the business minus its total liabilities
     _____ b.   the total liabilities of the business
     _____ c.   the total assets of the business

- - - - - - - - - - - - - - -

(a).   (It would not be the amount the owner invested in the business, because the business may have either gained or lost assets in the course of operations.)

18. When Marvin Vain established his business, he invested $5000 of his own money and the business borrowed $3000 from a bank.

    (a) The owner's equity in the business was $_____.

    (b) The liabilities of the business were $_____.

_ _ _ _ _ _ _ _ _ _ _ _ _ _ _ _

  (a) $5000; (b) $3000

19. In general, the creditors of the business and the owners of the business are the <u>only</u> persons who have claims against the assets of the business (though the government has claims for taxes, as we'll see later). Therefore, the total assets of the business equal the claims of the creditors plus the claims of the owners. This relationship can be stated mathematically in the following equation (fill in the blanks):

    ASSETS = _____ + _____

_ _ _ _ _ _ _ _ _ _ _ _ _ _ _ _

  ASSETS = LIABILITIES + OWNER'S EQUITY, or ASSETS = the claims of the creditors + the claims of the owners

20. The relationship,

    ASSETS = LIABILITIES + OWNER'S EQUITY

is called the <u>Fundamental Accounting Equation</u>. It is fundamental because this relationship <u>always</u> exists from a bookkeeping or accounting standpoint.

At any point in time, creditors have claims on the assets of the business entity and the remainder is claimed by its owner or owners. Thus, while the total assets of a business may increase or decrease, the change will always be accompanied by a corresponding change in liabilities or owner's equity, keeping the fundamental equation in balance.

If a business has total liabilities of $5000 and total owner's equity of $8000, what must the assets of the company be?

    $_____

_ _ _ _ _ _ _ _ _ _ _ _ _ _ _ _

  $13,000

21. Sandy's Auto Supplies has the following <u>assets</u>:

   (a) $2000 in cash
   (b) $1000 in store supplies and equipment
   (c) $10,000 in merchandise for sale

Sandy's has the following <u>liabilities</u>:

   (a) a loan of $5000
   (b) purchases on account totaling $800

What is the <u>owner's equity</u> in Sandy's? $_____

- - - - - - - - - - - - - - -

   $7200 (total assets of $13,000 - total liabilities of $5800)

Self-Teaching Section C

BUSINESS TRANSACTIONS

22. We know that bookkeepers record events (expressed in dollars) that affect the financial condition of a business. These events are called <u>business trans-actions</u>. In Chapter 2 we will fully define what is meant by business transactions, but for now, a business transaction will be thought of as any event

_____ by a bookkeeper.

- - - - - - - - - - - - - -

   recorded

23. Some examples of business transactions are making a sale, borrowing or repaying money, purchasing supplies, and investing money in a business. Some businesses conduct thousands of transactions daily. In order that each transaction be accounted for, a bookkeeper will usually require some kind of proof that it has in fact taken place. For this reason, whenever a transaction takes place, some type of paper is prepared. There are many types of papers to prepare for different transactions. These papers are all known as <u>business documents</u>. Some kind of business document must be shown to a bookkeeper or an accountant:

   ____ a. before he records a business transaction
   ____ b. after he records a business transaction
   ____ c. after he summarizes all business transactions

- - - - - - - - - - - - - -

   (a)

24.   Here is one type of business document:

RENT RECEIPT

Received: *Three Hundred Dollars* $ *300 $\frac{00}{100}$*

As payment of rent for (dates): *10/1 to 10/31*

Date received: *October 1$\underline{st}$, 19—*

Payer: *The Clothes Call*

Payee (signed): *Fern Realty (Adam Smith)*

This document is used to show the payment of rent by The Clothes Call. The bookkeeper for The Clothes Call will record the transaction:

_____ a. when the cash is paid
_____ b. on the date that payment is required
_____ c. when the owner tells him that the rent was paid
_____ d. when he sees the receipt

– – – – – – – – – – – – – – –

   (d)

25.   There are many other kinds of business documents, such as sales receipts, register tapes, adding machine tapes, and invoices, but they all have the same purpose. What is this purpose?

_____

– – – – – – – – – – – – – – –

   they show that a business transaction has taken place (or equivalent answer)

Self-Teaching Section D

A BOOKKEEPING MODEL

26.   We have seen generally how bookkeepers become aware of business transactions; how they "act upon" these transactions by recording, sorting, and summarizing them; and how, using these techniques, they produce concise pictures of the effects of business transactions on the financial state of a business. It is convenient to regard the entire practice of bookkeeping as a system that processes or organizes <u>information</u>. Before a bookkeeper begins to process information (i.e., before it "enters" the system), it is in a relatively disorganized state. The disorganized information (called the <u>input</u> to the system)

is in the form of _____ validated by business documents.

– – – – – – – – – – – – – – –

business transactions

27. The bookkeeper acts upon the disorganized information (business transactions) by organizing it with the techniques of recording, sorting, and summarizing. This process results in concise summaries of the financial condition of the business. These financial statements, then, must constitute the

_____ of the bookkeeping system.
— — — — — — — — — — — — — —

   output, aim, results, or product (or equivalent answer)

28. Here is a diagram of the bookkeeping system:

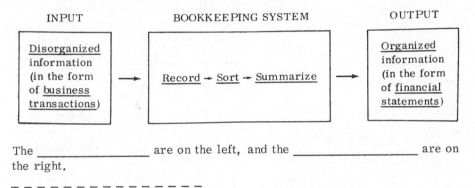

The _____ are on the left, and the _____ are on
the right.
— — — — — — — — — — — — — —

   inputs (business transactions); outputs (financial statements)

29. The input to the bookkeeping system is disorganized information in the
form of business transactions. The output of the bookkeeping system is
organized information in the form of summaries. This situation is somewhat
analagous to the preparation of a meal by a great chef. You would probably
never consider eating the "raw information" of the meal: vanilla, pepper,
cooking oil, flour, and so forth. Similarly, a business owner or a potential
investor could not hope to understand a list of hundreds of different transactions. Thus, given the application of appropriate techniques, you will be able
to enjoy your "organized" meal, just as the concerned individual will be able
to comprehend the condition of a particular company by reading the organized

outputs, the _____.
— — — — — — — — — — — — — —

   financial statements, or summaries

30. The outputs of the bookkeeping system are called <u>financial</u> <u>statements</u>. There are many kinds of financial statements, but the two most important and widely used are the <u>Balance Sheet</u> and the <u>Income Statement</u>. Given below is the simplified Balance Sheet of a manufacturer of printing supplies, Ink, Inc.

```
┌─────────────────────────────────────────────────────────────────────┐
│                         INK, INCORPORATED                             │
│                                                                       │
│                           Balance Sheet                               │
│                         December 31, 19--                             │
│                                                                       │
│   ASSETS                            LIABILITIES                       │
│     Current Assets                    Current Liabilities             │
│       Cash . . . . . . . . $ 5,000      Accounts payable . . . $   500 │
│       Supplies . . . . . .     700      Notes payable. . . . .   1,000 │
│     Total Current Assets . $ 5,700    Total Current Liabilities $1,500 │
│     Long-Term Assets                  Long-Term Liabilities           │
│       Equipment . . . . . . $ 1,000     Mortgage payable. . . $8,000   │
│       Factory . . . . . . .   9,000   TOTAL LIABILITIES  . $9,500      │
│     Total Long-Term Assets $10,000                                    │
│                                       OWNER'S EQUITY                  │
│                                         Initial investment. . . $5,000 │
│                                         Profit for the year . . 1,200 │
│                                       TOTAL OWNER'S                    │
│     TOTAL ASSETS . . . . $15,700      EQUITY . . . . . . . . $6,200    │
└─────────────────────────────────────────────────────────────────────┘
```

Many of the terms in the Balance Sheet may be unfamiliar to you at this point. Don't worry, because they will be discussed in later chapters. For our purposes now, it is important to note that the Balance Sheet gives the financial

condition of a business by listing that business's _____,

_____, and _____.

– – – – – – – – – – – – – – –

     assets, liabilities, and owner's equity

31. The Balance Sheet gives the financial condition of a business in terms of its assets, liabilities, and owner's equity <u>as</u> <u>of</u> <u>a</u> <u>certain</u> <u>date</u>. Look back to Ink, Inc.'s Balance Sheet. What can we say about the financial condition of

the company on December 1? _____

– – – – – – – – – – – – – – –

     nothing (because the Balance Sheet only gives information as of the 31st of the month)

32.   What information <u>is</u> given by the Balance Sheet of a company ?

_____

_____

_____

– – – – – – – – – – – – – – – –

   it gives the financial condition of a business in terms of the business's
   assets, liabilities, and owner's equity as of a particular date (or equivalent answer)

33.   The other important financial statement is called the <u>Income Statement</u> (also called
the Profit and Loss Statement or the Statement of Revenue and Expense, though these
terms are not so common).   This statement tells the nature and the amounts of expenses
that the business has had <u>over a period of time</u>.   It also describes the nature and amounts
of revenue, or income, that has come into the business for the same period of time.   A
simple form of an Income Statement, that for Ink, Inc., is given below:

INK, INCORPORATED

Income Statement
for the year ending December 31, 19--

Sales (revenue) $17,000

Expenses
     Supplies expense   3,000
     Mortgage expense   2,000
     Salaries expense   10,000
     Miscellaneous expense   800

Total Expenses $15,800

Net Income for the year (revenue
     minus expenses) $1,200

The Income Statement also gives the difference between revenue and expense,

or the _____.

– – – – – – – – – – – – – – – –

   net income (if income is greater than expense) <u>or</u> net loss (if expenses are
   greater than income)

34. Match the following:

     ____ a. Income Statement   1. Gives the financial condition of a business in terms of assets, liabilities, and owner's equity as of a certain date

     ____ b. Balance Sheet

                                                    2. Gives the financial condition of a business in terms of revenue and expenses over a period of time

- - - - - - - - - - - - - - -

(a) 2; (b) 1

SELF-TEST

The results of this test will indicate whether or not you have mastered the chapter objectives and are ready to go on to the next chapter. Answer each question to the best of your ability. Correct answers and instructions are given at the end of the test.

1. Define bookkeeping: _____

_____

_____

2. How does accounting differ from bookkeeping? _____

_____

_____

_____

3. Which of the following events would probably be recorded as a business transaction by the bookkeeper for Shop-Fair Market?

_____ a. Shop-Fair drops the price of tuna fish from 2 cans for 37¢ to 2 cans for 33¢

_____ b. Shop-Fair closes its doors at 7:30 P. M.

_____ c. Shop-Fair pays its employees their weekly wages

_____ d. John Crack, the floor manager for Shop-Fair, uses $100 of his salary to pay his rent

_____ e. Shop-Fair sells $1100 worth of food

_____ f. Shop-Fair buys a new lock for its front door

4. Classify the following as asset (A), liability (L) or owner's equity (O):

_____ a. land

_____ b. wages payable by business

_____ c. (assets − liabilities)

_____ d. merchandise

_____ e. cash

_____ f. loan payable by business

5. Write the Fundamental Accounting Equation.

_____

6. Green's Taxi service has $5000 in the bank and owns two new cars costing $4000 each. The business owes $7000 to Business Loans Corporation. How much equity does Harvey Green, the owner, have in the business?

_____

7. Fill in the blanks below to show the complete <u>bookkeeping</u> <u>model</u>:

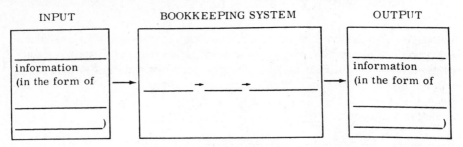

INPUT   BOOKKEEPING SYSTEM   OUTPUT

information
(in the form of

)

information
(in the form of

)

8. Invoices, cash register tapes, and adding machine tapes are all examples

of _____.

9. What information is conveyed by the <u>Balance</u> <u>Sheet</u>? _____

_____

_____

10. What information is conveyed by the <u>Income</u> <u>Statement</u>? _____

_____

_____

Self-Test Answers

Compare your answers to the Self-Test with the correct answers given below. If all of your answers are correct, you are ready to go on to the next chapter. If you missed any questions, study the frames indicated in parentheses following the answer. If you miss many questions, go over the entire chapter carefully.

1. Bookkeeping is the recording, sorting, and summarizing of events (expressed in dollars) that affect the financial condition of a business. (Frames 1-6)

2. Accounting includes bookkeeping and deals with the interpretation and analysis of events that affect the financial condition of a company. Accounting also deals with the establishing of bookkeeping systems. (Frames 7-8)

3. (a); (c); (e); (f). (Frames 9-10)

4. (a) A; (b) L; (c) O; (d) A; (e) A; (f) L. (Frames 11-18)

5. ASSETS = LIABILITIES + OWNER'S EQUITY. (Frames 19-20)

6. $6000 ($5000 + $4000 + $4000 - $7000). (Frames 19-21)

7.

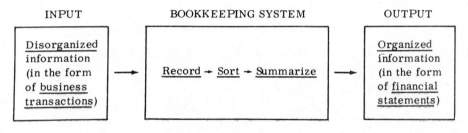

(Frames 26-30)

8. Business documents. (Frames 22-25)

9. The financial condition of a business in terms of assets, liabilities, and owner's equity as of a certain date. (Frames 30-32)

10. The financial condition of a business in terms of expenses and revenue over a certain period of time. (Frames 33-34)

CHAPTER TWO
Business Transactions

OBJECTIVES

When you complete this chapter, you will be able to

- define and recognize a <u>business transaction</u>,

- determine the changes that will occur in assets, liabilities, and owner's equity as a result of a particular business transaction,

- classify assets into <u>current assets</u> and <u>long-term assets</u>,

- classify liabilities into <u>current liabilities</u> and <u>long-term liabilities</u>,

- classify given transactions into <u>accounts receivable</u>, <u>notes receivable</u>, <u>accounts payable</u>, and <u>notes payable</u>.

If you feel that you have already mastered these objectives and might skip all or part of this chapter, turn to the end of this chapter and take the Self-Test. The results will tell you what frames of the chapter you should study. If you answer all questions correctly, you are ready to begin the next chapter.

If this material is new to you, or if you choose not to take the Self-Test now, turn to the Overview and Self-Teaching Sections that follow.

CHAPTER OVERVIEW

TRANSACTIONS AND THEIR EFFECTS

In this chapter we will define the basic terms used to describe business transactions and will teach you to discriminate the major categories into which a
business's assets and liabilities are divided.

In Chapter One we saw that the total value of a business's assets equals its
liabilities (claims on those assets by outside creditors) plus owner's equity
(claims on the remaining assets by the owners of the business). This concept
is the basis of the Fundamental Accounting Equation:

ASSETS = LIABILITIES + OWNER'S EQUITY

A business transaction may be defined as any event expressed in dollars that
is related to a business and affects the assets, liabilities, or owner's equity
of that business.

Common types of business transactions include cash purchases , sales, credit
purchases, borrowing money, paying off loans, new investments in the business, payment
of expenses, and withdrawal of earnings by the owners.   We will consider four basic types
of business transactions:

1. Transactions that have no effect on the total value of the
    assets, but that exchange one asset for another asset.
2. Transactions that increase or decrease total assets and
    also increase or decrease total liabilities.
3. Transactions that increase or decrease total assets and
    also increase or decrease owner's equity.
4. Transactions that have no effect on the total assets but
    increase and decrease liabilities and/or owner's equity
    in equal amounts.

Some business transactions could be analyzed in more than one way, but by
convention and definition, sales are often said to increase assets and owner's
equity, whereas expenses (bills that are paid soon after they are received by
the company) are said to decrease the owner's equity.

THE CLASSIFICATION OF ASSETS AND LIABILITIES

Assets

All assets are classified as either current assets or long-term assets.

Current Assets are assets that are expected to be consumed or converted
to cash in a short period of time, usually in less than one year. Some items
that are usually considered current assets are cash, accounts receivable,
notes receivable, and unused supplies.

Long-Term Assets are assets that are expected to be consumed or disposed of over a fairly long period of time, usually more than one year.   Examples of long-term assets are land, buildings, and heavy equipment.   Except for land, long-term assets depreciate or lose their reported value over a long period of time.   Alternate terms for long-term assets are "fixed" assets or "property, plant, and equipment."

Liabilities

All liabilities are classified as either current liabilities or long-term liabilities.

Current Liabilities are debts that must be paid off in a relatively short period of time, usually in less than one year.   Items usually considered to be current liabilities are accounts payable and notes payable.

Long-Term Liabilities are debts that are due to be paid off more than a year beyond the Balance Sheet date.   One common long-term liability that a business might have is a mortgage on a building which may not be fully paid off for 50 years or more.   Long-term liabilities are often called "fixed" liabilities.

Self-Teaching Section A

TRANSACTIONS AND THEIR EFFECTS

1.   In Chapter One we said that the financial statements (the Balance Sheet and Income Statement) were the output or final products of the accounting system.   Since this is the case, business transactions must be the _____ of the accounting system.

— — — — — — — — — — — — — — — —

inputs

2.   Fill in the following diagram:

Inputs		Outputs (products)
(a) _____ _____	→ ACCOUNTING SYSTEM →	(b) _____ _____

— — — — — — — — — — — — — —

(a) business transactions; (b) financial statements or summaries

3.   A simple definition of a business transaction would be

any event (expressed in dollars) connected with a business that affects the condition of that business.

Since the overall <u>condition of a business</u> is stated on the Balance Sheet in terms of <u>assets</u>, <u>liabilities</u>, and <u>owner's equity</u>, a more complete definition of a business transaction might be:

A business transaction is any event expressed in dollars connected

with a business that affects that business's _____,

_____, or _____.

- - - - - - - - - - - - - - -

assets, liabilities, or owner's equity (in any order)

4. Ace Plumbing borrowed $1000 to purchase some new tools. The assets of Ace Plumbing therefore increased by $1000. (Ace's liabilities also increased by $1000.) Since assets were affected by the event of taking out a loan, we

can say that the loan was a _____.

- - - - - - - - - - - - - - -

business transaction

5. Define <u>business transaction</u>: _____

_____

_____

- - - - - - - - - - - - - - -

any event (expressed in dollars) connected with a business that affects that business's assets, liabilities, or owner's equity

6. Here, once again, is the Fundamental Accounting Equation:

$$ASSETS = LIABILITIES + OWNER'S EQUITY$$

In accounting procedures, <u>this condition of equality must always exist</u>. The sum of total liabilities plus total owner's equity will never be either higher or

lower than the total _____ of the business.

- - - - - - - - - - - - - - -

assets

7. Since it is always true that any business's assets equal its liabilities plus its owner's equity, it follows that any increase or decrease in one side of the equation must result in a similar change on the other side of the equation:

$$ASSETS = LIABILITIES + OWNER'S EQUITY$$

If assets are increased, then to keep the equation in balance, either liabilities or owner's equity must also increase. Consider this example:

When Ace Plumbing borrowed $1000 to purchase tools, the company acquired a liability of $1000 (the loan). At the same time, however, the value of Ace's cash holdings increased by $1000. Therefore, the same transaction that caused an increase in Ace's liabilities also caused an increase in another part of the equation.

In Ace's case, what part of the equation was affected in addition to an increase in liabilities? _____

– – – – – – – – – – – – – – – –

assets (increased)

8. Any business transaction that causes a change in a company's total assets will also cause a similar change in that company's _____

or _____.

– – – – – – – – – – – – – – – –

liabilities or owner's equity (in either order)

9. Business transactions can be subdivided into four basic types:

1. <u>Transactions that</u> have no effect on the total value of the assets, but that <u>exchange one asset for another asset</u>.
2. <u>Transactions that</u> increase or decrease total assets and also <u>increase or decrease total liabilities</u>.
3. <u>Transactions that</u> increase or decrease total assets and also <u>increase or decrease owner's equity</u>.
4. <u>Transactions that</u> have no effect on the total assets but <u>increase or decrease liabilities and/or owner's equity in equal amounts</u>.

   The following chart classifies some of the more common business transactions and shows how each one affects the value of the three elements of the Fundamental Accounting Equation. Examine it carefully.

BUSINESS TRANSACTIONS	ASSETS =	LIABILITIES +	OWNER'S EQUITY
Type A: Exchange one asset for another			
1. cash purchases	no effect	no effect	no effect
Type B: Increase or decrease total liabilities			
2. credit purchases	increase	increase	no effect
3. borrowing money	increase	increase	no effect
4. paying off loans or credit purchases	decrease	decrease	no effect
Type C: Increase or decrease total owner's equity			
5. sales	increase	no effect	increase
6. payment of expenses	decrease	no effect	decrease
7. depreciation of assets	decrease	no effect	decrease
8. new investments in the business	increase	no effect	increase
9. withdrawal of earnings by the owners	decrease	no effect	decrease
Type D: Equal increase or decrease in liabilities and/or owner's equity			
10. renew note at bank	no effect	no effect	no effect
11. issue ownership in the business for a debt	no effect	decrease	increase
12. declare dividend payable in cash	no effect	increase	decrease

10. We said that Type A business transactions had no effect on the value of the business's total assets. Instead, this kind of transaction simply exchanges one type of asset for another.

Cash purchases are the best example. Cash purchases affect the composition of assets without changing their total value. Consider this example:

> Ace Plumbing needs a new truck for making service calls. Bill Hansen, Ace's owner, writes a check drawn on the company's cash account in the amount of $10,000. In exchange for this check, Ace Plumbing is given a truck. Now, instead of having a cash asset of $10,000, Ace Plumbing has an equipment asset worth $10,000 (the truck).

In this example, did the total amount of Ace's assets change? ____ yes ____ no

— — — — — — — — — — — — — — —

no

11. Most transactions are of the B or C types--they <u>do</u> change the total value of the business's assets. And, whenever the total value of the business's assets are altered (increased or decreased), the value of the business's liabilities or owner's equity is also altered. Consider the following example:

> The Fresh Egg (a company that delivers eggs to the doorstep) acquires its inventory (eggs) on credit. That is, Fresh Egg gets its eggs from farmers by promising to pay them for the eggs in the near future. When Fresh Egg gets its eggs the total value of everything the company owns increases. At the same time, the amount that the company owes to outside creditors (the farmers) increases.

Another way of saying this is to say that purchases on credit (borrowing) cause an increase in both _____ and _____.

- - - - - - - - - - - - - - - -

   assets and liabilities (in either order)

12. When a company repays a loan or pays for goods or services it bought on credit, then both assets and liabilities _____.
                                                          (increase/decrease)

- - - - - - - - - - - - - - - -

   decrease

13. When an investor puts money into a business with the hope of getting a return on his investment the business is worth more, so the business's

_____ must have increased. What else must have increased?
_____.

- - - - - - - - - - - - - - - -

   assets; owner's equity (in either order)

14. What is the effect on each of the three parts of the Fundamental Accounting Equation when an investor withdraws money from the business?

   (a) Assets _____

   (b) Liabilities _____

   (c) Owner's Equity _____

- - - - - - - - - - - - - - - -

   (a) assets decrease; (b) liabilities remain the same (no effect); (c) owner's equity decreases

15. Some types of B or C transactions can be analyzed in more than one way. For example, a bill from a printer who prepares business cards could be thought of as a liability. By convention and definition, however, <u>expenses</u> (bills that are paid as they are received by the company) are said to <u>decrease the owner's equity</u>. They are not usually entered in the books as a liability. Thus, the bill from the printer is an expense and its payment causes a decrease in assets and in owner's equity. Likewise, <u>sales</u> are said to increase both assets and owner's equity.

Walden Book Store purchases <u>Principles of Chemistry</u> for $8 per copy and sells them to students for $10 per copy, making a profit of $2 per book sold. The revenue from these sales (in this case $10) causes an increase in both

Walden's _____ and _____.

— — — — — — — — — — — — — — —

assets and owner's equity (in either order)

16. Every month Walden Book Store pays a telephone bill. This bill comes to about $35 and is paid in cash as soon as it is received. This payment decreases the total value of Walden's assets (by about $35 in cash). A decrease

also occurs in Walden's _____.
                        (liabilities/owner's equity)

— — — — — — — — — — — — —

owner's equity

17. A business transaction involving a payment of an expense brings about a

decrease in both _____ and _____.

— — — — — — — — — — — — — —

assets and owner's equity (in either order)

18. Another type of business transaction that can be confusing is when two business transactions appear to occur at the same time. For example:

> Walden Book Store is in big trouble. Unless Caruther's Sign Company gets the $150 for a sign that Walden bought on credit, Caruther's is going to take the sign back. To forestall this event, Walden borrows the money from the Neighborhood Loan Company to pay Caruthers.

The net effect is that Walden has exchanged one liability for another. This is like exchanging one asset for another except that in this case two separate transactions have actually occurred. They are:

Transaction 1: _____

                   Assets _____;

                   Liabilities _____;

                   Owner's Equity _____.

Transaction 2: _____

                   Assets _____;

                   Liabilities _____;

                   Owner's Equity _____.

- - - - - - - - - - - - - - - -

1. Walden borrowed money: assets increased; liabilities increased; owner's equity remained the same.
2. Walden paid Caruthers: assets decreased; liabilities decreased; owner's equity remained the same.

19. Walden Book Store's oldest investor decided to retire (his portion of the owner's equity comes to $4000 and he wants to take this money). A new investor is quickly located who has $4000 to invest. Is there going to be any overall change in the amount of owner's equity as a result of these changes?

_____. How many transactions will occur? _____.
(yes/no)   (1/2/3)

- - - - - - - - - - - - - - - -

no; 2

20. Describe the two transactions that will occur as a result of Walden's changing investors.

Transaction 1: _____

                   Assets _____;

                   Liabilities _____;

                   Owner's Equity _____.

Transaction 2: _____

                   Assets _____;

                   Liabilities _____;

                   Owner's Equity _____.

- - - - - - - - - - - - - - - -

1. Old investor withdraws: assets decrease; liabilities remain the same; owner's equity decreases.
2. New investor joins: assets increase; liabilities remain the same; owner's equity increases.

21. Describe the four main types of transactions:

   1. _____

      _____

   2. _____

      _____

   3. _____

      _____

   4. _____

      _____

- - - - - - - - - - - - - - -

1. One asset is exchanged for another with no effect on the total value of the assets.
2. An increase or decrease occurs in both assets and liabilities.
3. An increase or decrease occurs in both assets and owner's equity.
4. Equal increase and decrease in liabilities and/or owner's equity.

22. The receipt of a bill for electricity <u>might</u> be considered to cause an increase in assets (electrical services received) and an increase in liabilities (money due the electrical company). However, accountants, by convention, do not handle bills that are paid as they are received in this manner. Such

transactions are referred to as (a) _____.

In this case what happens to the elements of the Fundamental Accounting Equation?

   (b) Assets _____

       Liabilities _____

       Owner's Equity _____

- - - - - - - - - - - - - - -

(a) expenses; (b) assets decrease, liabilities remain the same, owner's equity decreases

Self-Teaching Section B

THE CLASSIFICATION OF ASSETS AND LIABILITIES

23. When the financial condition of any company is reported on a <u>Balance Sheet</u>, the major classifications, especially the assets and liabilities, are broken down into separate categories. Examine the simplified Balance Sheet that follows:

WALDEN BOOK STORE

Balance Sheet
July 31, 19--

ASSETS
  Current Assets
      Cash XXXX
      Accounts receivable . XXXX
      Notes receivable . . XXXX
      Inventories . . . . . <u>XXXX</u>
  Total Current Assets . . XXXX

  Long-Term Assets
      Land XXXX
      Building XXXX
      Office equipment . . XXXX
      Less accumulated
        depreciation . . . . <u>XXXX</u>
  Net Long-Term Assets . . XXXX

LIABILITIES
  Current Liabilities
      Accounts payable . . . XXXX
      Notes payable XXXX
      Salary payable XXXX
      Income taxes payable . <u>XXXX</u>
  Total Current Liabilities . XXXX

  Long-Term Liabilities
      Mortgage on building
      5% interest, due 1995 . <u>XXXX</u>
  TOTAL LIABILITIES . . . . <u>XXXX</u>

OWNER'S EQUITY
      Capital XXXX
      Earnings . . . . <u>XXXX</u>

  TOTAL OWNER'S EQUITY . XXXX

  TOTAL LIABILITIES AND
  OWNER'S EQUITY . . . . <u>XXXXX</u>

TOTAL ASSETS . . . . <u>XXXXX</u>

What are the two major subdivisions of assets?

    (a) _____ and _____ .

What are the two major subdivisions of liabilities?

    (b) _____ and _____ .

- - - - - - - - - - - - - - -

    (a) current assets and long-term assets
    (b) current liabilities and long-term liabilities

24. How an asset or liability is classified depends partly on the conventions and definitions of the particular business. As a general rule, assets and liabilities are considered <u>current</u> if they are receivable or payable in a relatively short period of time (usually less than a year).

However, assets and liabilities are usually considered long-term if they are held or paid off over a relatively long period of time (usually more than one year). Fill in the four boxes in the following chart:

	Less than a year	More than a year
Assets:	(a)	(b)
Liabilities:	(c)	(d)

- - - - - - - - - - - - - - - -

(a) current assets; (b) long-term assets; (c) current liabilities; (d) long-term liabilities

25. Which of the following is a current asset?

_____ a. the office building belonging to Continental Clip, Inc.
_____ b. the raw material (steel) of which paper clips are made by Continental Clip, Inc.

- - - - - - - - - - - - - - -

(b)

26. Why is cash on hand or in the bank considered a current asset?

_____

_____

- - - - - - - - - - - - - - -

because cash is expected to be consumed in a relatively short time, usually in less than a year

27. A <u>promise</u> <u>to</u> <u>pay</u> <u>money</u> to a business has a cash value. Therefore, it is considered an asset of the business to which it is owed. Which of the following promises to pay money would be considered a <u>current</u> <u>asset</u>?

_____ a. a promise to repay, in one lump sum, 5 years hence, a $5000 loan
_____ b. a promise to pay from credit customers for monthly purchases

- - - - - - - - - - - - -

(b)

28.   If a current asset is something owned by a business that the business expects to consume or convert to cash in a relatively <u>short</u> time, then a long-term asset is _____

_____

_____

– – – – – – – – – – – – – – – –

something owned by a business that the business expects to consume or convert to cash in a relatively <u>long</u> time

29.   During their investigation of Ace Plumbing, an investment house finds that Ace (a) owns a warehouse that cost $20,000, (b) owns the land occupied by that warehouse, and (c) owns trucks and other equipment that cost $55,000. These items were found on the Balance Sheet under the classification

_____.

– – – – – – – – – – – – – – – –

long-term assets

30.   The way in which business liabilities are classified is similar to the way in which assets are classified. Ace Plumbing has taken out a 50-year mortgage on its warehouse. This means that the full price of the warehouse will probably not be paid for 50 years. You would expect that the part of the mortgage that will be due beyond the current year would be classified on the Balance Sheet of Ace Plumbing as a _____.

– – – – – – – – – – – – – – –

long-term liability

31.   In what period of time do current liabilities come due? _____

_____

– – – – – – – – – – – – – –

in a relatively short period of time, usually less than a year

32.   One of the problems in accounting for long-term assets is that even though they may not be used up for 50 years or more (e.g., as in the case of Ace's warehouse), their value <u>does</u> <u>not</u> remain constant.   Except for land, long-term assets <u>depreciate</u> or lose their reported value over a long period of time -- that is to say, a long-term asset (except land) is expected to lose some of its usefulness as it gets older.   For example, each year that Ace Plumbing owns a truck, it reports that truck to be worth less.   If the truck costs $10,000 and is expected to last for 10 years, the company might depreciate the truck by $1000 each year, so that the time the truck is no longer usable coincides with the time the company reports that the truck is worth nothing. Depreciation is a <u>reporting</u> convention.   It is strictly a method accountants use to apportion the cost of a

long-term asset over its period of expected use.   It is <u>not</u> a way of determining the market value of an asset.

If Ace Plumbing buys a drill press that they expect to use for 5 years and report it as being worth less the second year than it was the first, we say that the press has _____.

- - - - - - - - - - - - - - -

depreciated

33.   There are many different ways to estimate the amount of depreciation for a long-term asset.   Different businesses use different methods.   What kinds of assets depreciate?

_____

_____

- - - - - - - - - - - - - - -

All long-term assets <u>except</u> <u>land</u>.

34.   Some of the subdivisions of current assets and current liabilities are easy to understand.   Some need a little explanation.   Four terms that are sometimes confusing are explained below:

Current <u>Assets</u>
  Accounts <u>Receivable</u>   This means that the business has given someone else goods or services, for which it is owed money by that person or business.

  Notes <u>Receivable</u>   This means that the business has given someone money (or credit) and that someone has given the business a written promise to pay.

Current <u>Liabilities</u>
  Accounts <u>Payable</u>   This means that the business owes someone money for goods or services it has received.

  Notes <u>Payable</u>   This means that the business owes someone money for money (or credit) it received and has given a written promise to pay.

One reason this sometimes seems confusing is because an account payable and an account receivable are reciprocal between two companies.   Study the following example:

```
┌──────────────────────────┐   ┌──────────────────────────┐
│ COMPANY A                │   │ COMPANY B                │
│ Current Liabilities      │   │ Current Assets           │
│                          │   │                          │
│ Account Payable:         │   │ Account Receivable:      │
│   Company A owes company │   │   Company B has given com-│
│   B $300 for goods       │   │   pany A goods for which A│
│   received.              │   │   owes B $300.           │
│                          │   │                          │
│ Note Payable:            │   │ Note Receivable:         │
│   Company A owes company │   │   Company A owes company │
│   B $200 for a loan B    │   │   B $200 to repay loan   │
│   made to A (a short-term│   │   (short-term).          │
│   loan, otherwise this   │   │                          │
│   account could become a │   │                          │
│   long-term liability).  │   │                          │
│                          │   │                          │
│ (right portion of Company│   │ (left portion of Company │
│  A's Balance Sheet)      │   │  B's Balance Sheet)      │
└──────────────────────────┘   └──────────────────────────┘
```

A written promise to repay cash loaned is considered, by the lender, a

_____.

- - - - - - - - - - - - - - - -

   note receivable (it would, of course, have to meet certain legal conditions)

35. Match the following:

_____ a. a firm's written promise to pay   1. note payable
          in the future for money borrowed
          or for credit

_____ b. a firm's promise to pay in the   2. account payable
          future for goods or services re-
          ceived

- - - - - - - - - - - - - - - -

   (a) 1; (b) 2

36. An investment house is trying to decide whether or not to invest capital
in the Ace Plumbing business. In their investigation they read Ace Plumbing's Balance Sheet and find that various people promised to pay Ace Plumbing a total of $1250 for plumbing services performed. The $1250 item on
Ace's Balance Sheet is probably classified as

_____.

- - - - - - - - - - - - - - - -

   an account receivable

37. When will accounts receivable and notes receivable be considered current assets? _____

– – – – – – – – – – – – – – –

when they are due in less than 1 year

38. Since <u>current</u> <u>assets</u> are subdivided into <u>accounts</u> <u>receivable</u> and <u>notes</u> <u>receivable</u>, what subdivisions might you expect in <u>current</u> <u>liabilities</u>?

     (a) _____ payable

     (b) _____ payable

– – – – – – – – – – – – – – –

  (a) accounts payable; (b) notes payable (in either order)

39. When Walden Book Store borrowed $150 in cash from the Neighborhood Loan Company, giving Neighborhood Loan a written promise to repay them in the future, the book store acquired a current liability. This was entered on

Walden's Balance Sheet as _____.

– – – – – – – – – – – – – – –

  a note payable

40. Ace Plumbing decided to mount a massive training program for its employees. Bill Hansen, owner of Ace Plumbing, purchased $200 worth of books and other training materials from the Walden Book Store with a promise to pay for them at the end of the month. What kind of liability has Ace acquired?

A _____ liability.

– – – – – – – – – – – – – – –

  current

41. The entry of this transaction on the Balance Sheet of Ace Plumbing would reflect the fact that the liability was acquired through the purchase of goods rather than through the borrowing of cash. It would, therefore, be entered

under _____ payable.

– – – – – – – – – – – – – – –

  accounts

42. When Ace Plumbing bought the books from Walden Book Store, Ace acquired a current liability in the form of an account payable. On the book store's Balance Sheet, on the other hand, the same transaction was entered

under (a) _____. It was listed as an account
        (current assets/current liabilities)

(b) _____.
    (receivable/payable)

– – – – – – – – – – – – – – – –

   (a) current asset; (b) receivable

43. Study the following sequence of events in the life of a very hypothetical business. This sad tale is taken from the history of James Fingle who borrowed money from his father to buy candy which he then sold door to door. (A technical point: Jimmy himself did not borrow the money; his father loaned the money to Jimmy's business, and Jimmy's business agreed to pay back the loan in three months.)

		Assets	=	Liabilities	+	Owner's Equity
Event 1:	The business borrows $100 in cash.	$100	=	$100	+	0
Comment:	With a loan, the assets and the liabilities of the business increase.					
Event 2:	Owner uses $100 to buy candy.	$100	=	$100	+	0
Comment:	One asset is exchanged for another; liabilities and owner's equity remain the same					
Event 3:	Owner sells $100 worth of candy for $150.	$150	=	$100	+	$50
Comment:	The business's assets increase by $50. The liabilities remain the same, but the $50 in profits increase the owner's equity.					
Event 4:	Owner repays $100 loan.	$50	=	0	+	$50
Comment:	The assets and liabilities each decrease by $100. The assets of the business are now exactly equal to the owner's equity.					
Event 5:	Owner buys $50 worth of candy.	$50	=	0	+	$50
Comment:	One asset is exchanged for another; liabilities and owner's equity remain unchanged.					
Event 6:	The goods are stolen (they were uninsured).	0	=	0	+	0
Comment:	Both assets and owner's equity are decreased. The theft is called an extraordinary loss and leaves our hero back where he began.					

Let's analyze Jimmy Fingle's business history, classifying his assets, liabilities, and changes in owner's equity. (Use the event numbers for your answers.)

Assets
Jimmy had <u>current</u> <u>assets</u> during which events? (a) _____

Jimmy had <u>long-term</u> <u>assets</u> during which events? (b) _____

Liabilities
Jimmy had <u>current</u> <u>liabilities</u> during which events? (c) _____

Jimmy had <u>long-term</u> <u>liabilities</u> during which events? (d) _____

Incidentally, Jimmy's loan was a (e) _____ payable.

Owner's Equity
Jimmy realized a profit during which events? (f) _____

Jimmy realized a loss during which events? (g) _____

— — — — — — — — — — — — — — — —

(a) 1, 2, 3, 4, 5; (b) none; (c) 1, 2, 3; (d) none; (e) note; (f) 3; (g) 6

SELF-TEST

This Self-Test will show you whether or not you have mastered the chapter objectives and are ready to go on to the next chapter. Answer each question to the best of your ability. Correct answers and instructions are on the page following the test.

1. Define business transaction: _____

_____

_____

2. A series of business transactions of Health-Ease Organic Foods is listed below. For each transaction, tell how the total dollar amount of assets, liabilities, and owner's equity is affected. Write an I in the blank if there was an increase, write a D in the blank if there was a decrease, write a 0 in the blank if there was no change.

(a) John Harris, the proprietor of Health-Ease, deposits $5000 in the name of Health-Ease. He will use this money to begin his business.

assets _____, liabilities _____, owner's equity _____

(b) Harris buys a cash register on credit for $500. He agrees to pay the amount in 6 months.

assets _____, liabilities _____, owner's equity _____

(c) At the end of the first month of business, Harris pays himself a cash salary of $600.

assets _____, liabilities _____, owner's equity _____

(d) Harris pays off the $500 debt for the cash register.

assets _____, liabilities _____, owner's equity _____

(e) In the first month of business, Health-Ease brings in $3000 in sales.

assets _____, liabilities _____, owner's equity _____

(f) At the end of the first month of business, John pays the following bills in cash: telephone ($25), rent ($125), utilities ($20), miscellaneous ($40).

assets _____, liabilities _____, owner's equity _____

3. Johnson Hardware has the following assets. (Write a C if it is a current asset, write an L-T if it is a long-term asset.)

(a) $9500 in a checking account _____

(b) Three cash registers costing $300 each _____

(c) A building purchased for $23,000 _____

(d) $350 in accounts receivable that will be paid at the end of the month

_____

(e) Three desks costing $75 each _____

4. The Aquarius Water Bed Company has the following liabilities. (Write a C if it is a <u>current</u> liability, write an L-T if it is a <u>long-term</u> liability.)

(a) That part of a 50-year mortgage of $25,000 that is due after this current year _____

(b) A note in the amount of $3000 payable to Water Bed Supplies, Inc. by Aquarius Water Beds in a 3-month period _____

(c) Accounts payable for the month of July in the amount of $125 _____

5. Aquarius Water Beds purchased bed heaters from Clake Electrical Supplies on credit with a promise to pay at the end of the month. On Aquarius's Balance Sheet this transaction would be shown under _____ liabilities as a(n) _____.

6. The same transaction would be shown on Clake's Balance Sheet under _____ assets and would be classified as a(n) _____.

7. The promise to repay money borrowed is classified by the borrower as a(n) _____.

8. The reported value of the office building owned by Xerox Corporation in Rochester, N.Y., will be less a year from now than it is today. Another way of saying this is that the reported value of the Xerox building will _____.

9. What assets lose reported value over a period of time?

Self-Test Answers

Compare your answers to the Self-Test with the correct answers given below.
If all of your answers are correct, you are ready to go on to the next chapter.
If you missed any questions, study the frames indicated in parentheses following the answer. If you miss many questions, go over the entire chapter carefully.

1. Business transaction: any event (expressed in dollars) that is related to a
business and affects the assets, liabilities, or owner's equity of that business.
(Frames 2-5)

2. (a) I, 0, I
    (b) I, I, 0
    (c) D, 0, D
    (d) D, D, 0
    (e) I, 0, I
    (f) D, 0, D   (Frames 6-22)

3. (a) C
    (b) L-T
    (c) L-T
    (d) C
    (e) L-T   (Frames 24-31)

4. (a) L-T
    (b) C
    (c) C   (Frames 25-31)

5. current; accounts payable (Frames 34-42)

6. current; accounts receivable (Frames 34-42)

7. note payable (Frames 34-42)

8. depreciate (Frames 32 and 33)

9. all plant assets except land (Frames 32 and 33)

CHAPTER THREE

The Accounting Cycle I: From Transaction to Trial Balance

OBJECTIVES

When you complete this chapter, you will be able to

- put in order the six main steps in the <u>accounting</u> <u>cycle</u>,

- classify basic accounts into assets, liabilities, owner's equity, revenue, or expense,

- state whether a particular transaction will increase or decrease a particular account,

- state whether an increase or decrease in a particular account will be entered as a <u>debit</u> or a <u>credit</u>,

- define <u>Journal</u>, and state the advantages and disadvantages of using one,

- define <u>Ledger</u>, and state the advantages and disadvantages of using one,

- make entries in a Journal,

- post Journal entries to a Ledger,

- prepare a Trial Balance.

If you feel that you have already mastered these objectives and might skip all or part of this chapter, turn to the end of this chapter and take the Self-Test. The results will tell you what frames of the chapter you should study. If you answer all questions correctly, you are ready to begin the next chapter.

If this material is new to you, or if you choose not to take the Self-Test now, turn to the Overview and Self-Teaching Sections that follow.

CHAPTER OVERVIEW

THE ACCOUNTING PERIOD

The daily transactions of any business will affect the amount or the composition of its assets, liabilities, or its owner's equity. This chapter will describe the ways in which the effects of business transactions are recorded and summarized. Ultimately, these effects will be reflected in the Balance Sheet and the Income Statement, which we will cover in Chapters 4 and 5.

The accounting procedures, from transaction to financial statement, are repeated by the bookkeeper during each accounting period and thus comprise an accounting cycle. Here is a brief summary of the accounting cycle:

Step 1.   Business transactions of many types are made daily.

Step 2.   The business transactions for each day are entered in the General Journal.

Step 3.   The information in the General Journal is transferred (posted) to a record called a Ledger, which has a separate page for each account.

Step 4.   An 8-column Worksheet is prepared. In order to verify the balances in the Ledger, an interim summary called a Trial Balance is prepared in the first two columns of the Worksheet.

Step 5.   The information obtained in the Trial Balance is adjusted to correct the account balances. The remaining six columns of the Worksheet are used for this purpose.

Step 6.   The adjusted information resulting from the completion of the Worksheet is used to prepare the Balance Sheet and the Income Statement.

The following diagram illustrates the six main steps in the accounting cycle:

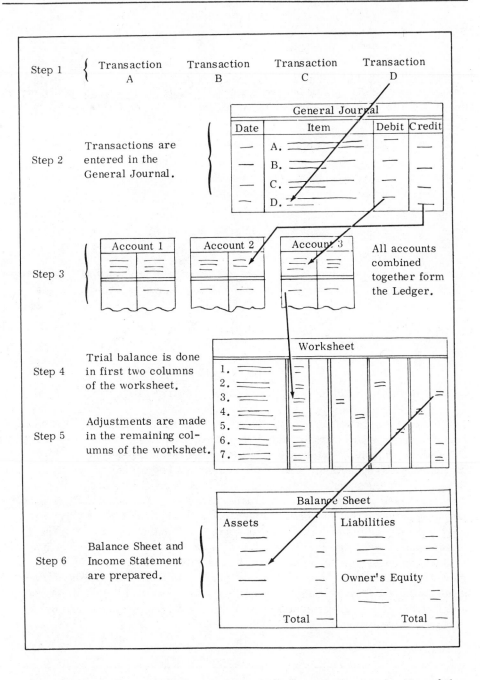

This chapter will cover the accounting cycle through the preparation of the Trial Balance (Step 4).

ACCOUNTS

The basis of accounting systems is the account. An account is a bookkeeping device used to record the increases and decreases of a specific type of asset, liability, or owner's equity brought about by a business transaction. There are five major classes of accounts:

1. Asset Accounts, such as cash and accounts receivable.
2. Liability Accounts, such as accounts payable.
3. Owner's Equity Accounts, such as owner's capital.
4. Revenue Accounts, such as sales.
5. Expense Accounts, such as supplies expense.

A very large business may have thousands of accounts whereas a small business may have only a dozen or so. Part of an account is illustrated here.

Account: *Cash*

Date	Item	p. r.	Debit	Date	Item	p. r.	Credit

DEBITING AND CREDITING ACCOUNTS IN THE GENERAL JOURNAL

Notice that the account form reproduced above is divided into two halves, each containing spaces for entering the date of the transaction, a description of the transaction, a posting reference for tracing the transaction (p. r.), and the amount of the transaction. The amount columns are headed debit (on the left) and credit (on the right). These terms are used throughout bookkeeping to record increases and decreases in accounts or groups of accounts. It is important to remember that in General Journals debit and credit refer only to the position of the columns on the account form (i.e., right or left side); these terms should never be strictly equated with increase and decrease. When a transaction causes an account to increase in value, the column in which this increase is recorded (i.e., whether the account is debited or credited) depends on the class of account involved (i.e., asset account, liability account, etc.). The table below indicates the columns in which increases and decreases are recorded.

Class of Account	Increases are recorded in:	Decreases are recorded in:
Asset Accounts	Debit column	Credit column
Liability Accounts	Credit column	Debit column
Owner's Equity Accounts	Credit column	Debit column
Revenue Accounts	Credit column	Debit column
Expense Accounts	Debit column	Credit column

Whenever a transaction occurs, at least <u>two</u> accounts will be affected. The entry of a debit amount in one account always accompanies a corresponding entry of a credit amount in one or more other accounts. One transaction may affect many accounts, but for any one transaction, total debits and total credits must be equal.

THE GENERAL JOURNAL

The first step in the accounting cycle is a firm's daily transactions. The second step is to record those transactions in a book called the General Journal. Thus, the General Journal always provides a <u>chronological</u> record of business transactions. There are many forms of journals, but all will call for the date of the transaction, the name of the account affected (and the explanation, if necessary), and the amount to be debited or credited. One kind of General Journal form is shown below:

Date	Account Title and Explanation	p.r.	Debit	Credit
Oct. 1	Cash		150.00	
	Sales			150.00
	Daily Cash Receipts			

The transaction entered here is that of cash receipts from sales. You can see that the cash account (an asset account) shows its increase with a debit entry. The other account that is affected is the sales account (revenue account), which shows its increase with a credit entry.

THE LEDGER

A <u>Ledger</u> is <u>a group</u> <u>of</u> <u>accounts</u>. It may be a loose-leaf binder, a card file, or a magnetic tape. When it is a book, its pages will look something like the one shown on page 44. Each page of the Ledger is concerned with one and only one account.

In Step 3, often at the end of the accounting period, the procedure known as <u>posting</u> <u>to the</u> <u>ledger</u> is carried out. This involves <u>copying</u> the information from each Journal entry onto the page of the appropriate account in the Ledger. The balance of each account is found by summing the debits, summing the credits, and subtracting the smaller sum from the larger sum. If the larger total is in the debit column, the account is said to have a debit balance. Likewise, if the larger total is in the credit column, the account is said to have a credit balance.

TRIAL BALANCE

In Step 4, at the end of the accounting period, after the balances of all of the accounts have been determined, a Trial Balance is taken as follows. The balances are transcribed to the Worksheet, the debit balances listed in one column and the credit balances in another. When each of these columns is summed, their totals should be equal. When the totals are not equal, it is probably due to a mistaken entry of some kind. The detection of errors is one of the purposes of the Trial Balance procedure, and it is during this procedure that all errors must be tracked down and corrected.

Self-Teaching Section A

THE ACCOUNTING PERIOD

1. In order to report properly the effect of business transactions on the assets, liabilities, and owner's equity of that business, these transactions must be carefully recorded and summarized. This chapter is concerned with these record-keeping procedures. Through an extended example, we will present all the routine procedures necessary to keep track of the daily transactions in any small or medium-sized enterprise. Beginning with the business transactions themselves, we will take you through the accounting cycle up to the point known as taking a Trial Balance. The following chapters will be devoted to the remainder of the cycle, including the completion of the Balance Sheet and the Income Statement.

Our example will be drawn from the operations of a Mr. Terry Mitty who has decided to go into business as Ter-Mit Exterminators. Since Terry has taken an accounting course very much like this one, he feels he can handle all the bookkeeping himself. Mitty's first task is to decide how often Ter-Mit's Balance Sheet and Income Statement will be prepared. The length of time between the preparation of these financial statements is called the accounting period.

If two consecutive Balance Sheets are prepared, the first on June 30 and the second on September 30, we can say that the company involved has a

three-month _____.

― ― ― ― ― ― ― ― ― ― ― ― ― ― ―

    accounting period

2. Terry Mitty has decided that Ter-Mit's accounting period will be one month. Therefore, each month Ter-Mit must produce reports on the state of the company. To insure that the Balance Sheet is accurate, Ter-Mit will have to make a record every time the company's assets, liabilities, or owner's equity changes or is affected. In other words, a record will have to be made

for each and every _____ that occurs.

― ― ― ― ― ― ― ― ― ― ― ― ― ― ―

business transaction

3. Define <u>accounting period</u>: _____

_____

_____

– – – – – – – – – – – – – – –

    The accounting period is the length of time between the preparation of one Balance Sheet (or Income Statement) and the next.

Self-Teaching Section B

ACCOUNTS

4. The device used to record changes in the value of assets, liabilities, and owner's equity is called an <u>account</u>. The number of separate accounts a firm has will depend on the type of information required by the managers and owners of that business. When the business's <u>cash</u> increases, for example,

that change will be recorded in the cash _____.

– – – – – – – – – – – – – – –

    account

5. Accounts are grouped according to the major classifications of accounts. Thus, asset accounts include such accounts as the cash account, the accounts receivable account, and the supplies account. The owner's capital account and the owner's drawing account (the account in which a business records money taken from the business by the owner) are categorized as owner's equity accounts.

    What class would the accounts payable account, salary payable account,

and notes payable account belong to? _____

– – – – – – – – – – – – – – – –

    liability accounts

6. The number and type of accounts that a business will have depends partially on the kind of information the owner of that business needs. The following chart includes many of the accounts that will be found in this book:

Account Number	Account Title

A first digit of "1" indicates an <u>asset</u> account.

11	Cash
12	Accounts receivable
13	Supplies
14	Prepaid rent
15	Equipment

A first digit of "2" indicates a <u>liability</u> account.

21	Accounts payable
22	Salaries payable

A first digit of "3" indicates an owner's equity account.

31	Owner's capital
32	Owner's drawing

A first digit of "4" indicates a <u>revenue</u> account.

41	Sales

A first digit of "5" indicates an <u>expense</u> account.

51	Salary expense
52	Supplies expense
53	Rent expense
54	Miscellaneous expense

There are many other ways of numbering accounts; the one shown here, however, will be used throughout this book. The kinds of transactions that affect the accounts are usually obvious from the account title. For example,

whenever a business takes in money, the (a) _____ account will be affected. If the account affected has a first digit of "1," the account involved

is a(an) (b) _____ account.

– – – – – – – – – – – – – – – – –

(a) cash; (b) asset

7. Whenever rent is paid in advance (usually more than <u>one</u> month in advance) the <u>prepaid</u> <u>rent</u> <u>account</u> is affected. Referring to the chart of accounts in Frame 6, which two accounts will be affected by a cash payment of just <u>one</u> month's rent in advance?

(a) _____ account

(b) _____ account

– – – – – – – – – – – – – – – –

(a) cash; (b) rent expense (in either order)

8. When the owner of a business invests money, the transaction is recorded in the <u>owner's</u> <u>capital</u> <u>account</u>. Whenever the owner withdraws cash from his business, the transaction is recorded in the

(a) _____ account

(b) _____ account.

_ _ _ _ _ _ _ _ _ _ _ _ _ _

(a) owner's drawing; (b) cash (in either order)

9. The Ter-Mit Balance Sheet reports the position of the business's assets, liabilities, and owner's equity. The Income Statement reports on <u>revenues</u> and <u>expenses</u> for the accounting period. Therefore, in addition to asset, liability, and owner's equity accounts, Ter-Mit will also have groups of accounts

classified as _____ accounts and _____ accounts.

_ _ _ _ _ _ _ _ _ _ _ _ _ _

revenue, expense (in either order)

10. <u>Revenue</u> is the amount a business gains as a result of its operations. If a business sells merchandise to customers, the gross income resulting from those sales is called revenue. Any business transactions that generate revenue are classified as <u>revenue transactions</u>. Which of the following business transactions are revenue transactions?

_____ a. commissions earned
_____ b. daily cash sales
_____ c. receipt of cash borrowed from a bank
_____ d. rent income earned
_____ e. sale of merchandise on account

_ _ _ _ _ _ _ _ _ _ _ _ _ _

(a), (b), (d), and (e)

11. <u>Expense</u> is the amount of resources a business must use in order to operate. Put another way, expense is the cost of generating revenue. Business transactions in which the business uses resources (e.g., money, either in cash or on account) to keep the business operating are classified as <u>expense transactions</u>. Which of the following would be classified as expense transactions?

_____ a. payment to replace a broken store window
_____ b. payment of salesmen's commissions
_____ c. investment in the business by the owner
_____ d. purchase of supplies
_____ e. payment of rent

_ _ _ _ _ _ _ _ _ _ _ _ _ _

(a), (b), (d), and (e)

12.   Ultimately, the <u>revenues</u> of a business go to the owners of the business. Likewise, the <u>expenses</u> of a business, in the final analysis, must be paid by the owners of the business. If we were to give a formula for the value of a business that rightfully belongs to the owners, which one would we write?

_____ a.   owner's equity = investment + expenses - revenue
_____ b.   owner's equity = investment - expenses - revenue
_____ c.   owner's equity = investment + revenue - expenses
_____ d.   owner's equity = revenue + expenses - investment

- - - - - - - - - - - - - - - -

(c)

13.   Rent expense will be an expense of Ter-Mit. This, along with its salary expense, and its utilities expense accounts will be classified as expense accounts. Sales transactions, on the other hand, will affect the sales account which is classified as a _____ account.

- - - - - - - - - - - - - - - -

revenue

14.   Write the names of the five classes of accounts. Indicate the first digit of account numbers that belong in that class.

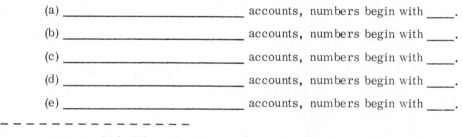

(a) _____ accounts, numbers begin with ____.

(b) _____ accounts, numbers begin with ____.

(c) _____ accounts, numbers begin with ____.

(d) _____ accounts, numbers begin with ____.

(e) _____ accounts, numbers begin with ____.

- - - - - - - - - - - - - - - -

(a) asset, 1; (b) liability, 2; (c) owner's equity, 3; (d) revenue, 4; and (e) expense, 5 (in any order)

15.   In Chapter 2 we said that every transaction has a <u>dual</u> effect. For example, the purchase of a desk for $50 will not only cause the asset of cash to decrease, it will also cause the asset of office equipment to increase. Payment of a debt, on the other hand, brings about both a decrease in assets (cash) and a decrease in liabilities (accounts payable or notes payable). Because of the dual effects of each and every transaction, any transaction will affect, and therefore be recorded in, at least how many accounts? _____

- - - - - - - - - - - - - - - -

two

16. Equipment purchased by a business on account (i.e., on credit, with a promise to pay in the near future) will cause an increase in one asset and one liability account. Identify these two accounts:

____ a. cash   ____ c. salaries payable
____ b. equipment   ____ d. accounts payable

- - - - - - - - - - - - - -

   (b) and (d)

17. When a business makes a credit sale (a sale on account), it means that the customer has agreed to pay in the near future. A sale on account will be recorded in which two accounts?

____ a. sales   ____ c. accounts payable
____ b. owner's equity   ____ d. accounts receivable

- - - - - - - - - - - - - -

   (a) and (d)

18. Terry Mitty establishes Ter-Mit Exterminators as of July 1. The very first business transaction is an investment by the owner (Terry Mitty) of $5000 in cash. This money goes into the owner's capital account (an owner's equity account--31). What other account is also affected?

   _____

- - - - - - - - - - - - - -

   the cash account

Self-Teaching Section C

DEBITING AND CREDITING ACCOUNTS IN THE GENERAL JOURNAL

19. Mitty's $5000 investment must first be entered in a daily record-keeping book called the General Journal. Here is the Journal page showing Ter-Mit's first transaction.

General Journal

Page ____

Date	Description	p. r.	Debit	Credit
19—				
July 1	Cash		5000 00	
	Terry Mitty, capital			5000 00
	Invested in Ter-Mit Exterminators			

On the left-hand side, the date of the transaction is given. Next, the two accounts affected by the transaction (cash, and Terry Mitty, capital) are listed. Usually (as in the example above), some explanation of the transaction is written below the two accounts (i.e., invested in Ter-Mit Exterminators). The amounts by which each of the two accounts is changed are listed in the two columns at the right (ignore the p.r. column for the moment). The two right-hand columns are headed _____ and _____.

----

    debit and credit

20. It is critical that you remember that the words <u>debit</u> and <u>credit</u> refer only to the <u>location of the amount columns on the General Journal page</u>. Debit and credit may appear in different places in special journals (and in more general usage they mean "decrease" and "increase"), but in the General Journal, the debit column is <u>always</u> the (a) _____-hand column and the credit column is always the (b) _____-hand column.

    (a) left; (b) right

21. Look again at the entries shown in Frame 19. Notice that the <u>cash account increased</u> by $5000 and was <u>debited</u> for this amount. The Terry Mitty, capital account also increased by $5000 but it was <u>credited</u> for this amount. Obviously then, depending on the account involved in the transaction, an increase may be noted by:

       ____ a. debit only
       ____ b. credit only
       ____ c. either debit or credit

    (c)

22. The column in which an increase or decrease is entered depends on the class of the account involved. Study the following chart:

Class of Account	Increases are recorded in:	Decreases are recorded in:
Asset Accounts	Debit column	Credit column
Liability Accounts	Credit column	Debit column
Owner's Equity Accounts	Credit column	Debit column
Revenue Accounts	Credit column	Debit column
Expense Accounts	Debit column	Credit column

Notice that increases in an asset account (such as the cash account studied in Frame 19) are recorded as debits. Decreases in asset accounts are entered as credits. The capital account discussed in Frame 19 is an owner's equity account. In the case of owner's equity accounts, increases are recorded as

(a) _____ and decreases are recorded as (b) _____.

- - - - - - - - - - - - - - - -

    (a) credits; (b) debits

23. Asset accounts and owner's equity accounts have their increases recorded:

        ____ a. in the same way
        ____ b. differently

- - - - - - - - - - - - - - -

  (b)

24. Ter-Mit's next transaction was the payment, on July 2, of $300 for three month's rent in advance. Write below the titles of the accounts in which this transaction was recorded, the class of each account, and the way in which the account is changed:

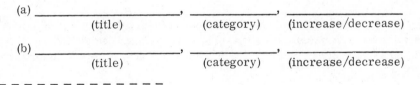

    (a) _____, _____, _____
            (title)   (category)   (increase/decrease)

    (b) _____, _____, _____
            (title)   (category)   (increase/decrease)

- - - - - - - - - - - - - - - -

    (a) cash, asset, decrease; (b) prepaid rent, asset, increase

25. Look once again at the General Journal entry in Frame 19. Notice that:

- The account debited is entered first.

- On the second line, slightly indented, the account credited is entered.

- On the third line, further indented, an explanation of the transaction is often entered.

The date of the entry and the amounts involved are entered in the appropriate columns (keep ignoring p.r. for now). Since you already know that asset increases are debited and that asset decreases are credited, you will be able to journalize the transaction described in Frame 24 on the following form:

General Journal

Page __1__

	Date	Description	p.r.	Debit	Credit
1					
2					
3					
4					

- - - - - - - - - - - - - -

General Journal

Page __1__

	Date	Description	p.r.	Debit	Credit
	19 —				
1	July 2	Prepaid rent		300 00	
2		Cash			300 00
3		Three month's rent in advance			
4					

26. A simpler method for showing a General Journal entry (often used for instructional purposes) is to show only the accounts affected and the amounts debited and credited. Here is the prepaid rent entry in this simpler form:

Prepaid rent $300
    Cash $300
        For three month's rent in advance

As always, the account debited comes first. Using this shorthand style for General Journal entries write out Ter-Mit's next business transaction below--a $200 cash purchase of exterminating supplies on July 2. (Note: supplies are usually recorded as assets until they are used up.)

- - - - - - - - - - - - - -

Supplies $200
    Cash $200
      For purchase of exterminating supplies

27. Terry Mitty purchases $500 worth of equipment on account (on credit) on
July 3. He promises to pay the amount by the end of the following month.
Name the two accounts affected, tell how each is classified, and tell how they
change:

(a) _____, _____, _____
            (title)   (category)   (increase/decrease)

(b) _____, _____, _____
            (title)   (category)   (increase/decrease)

- - - - - - - - - - - - - - - -

(a) equipment, asset, increase (note that the debit should have been listed
first); (b) accounts payable, liability, increase (not notes payable because
it was a purchase of goods, and no written promise was made).

28. In Frame 27 the accounts payable account (a liability account) increased
by $500. Since liability increases and decreases are recorded exactly like
owner's equity increases and decreases, you should be able to show a shorthand General Journal entry for the transaction in the space below:

- - - - - - - - - - - - - - - -

Equipment $500
    Accounts payable $500
        For equipment purchased on account

29. Fill in the blanks with debits and credits to complete the following statements:

(a) asset increases are shown as _____.

(b) asset decreases are shown as _____.

(c) liability increases are shown as _____.

(d) liability decreases are shown as _____.

(e) owner's equity increases are shown as _____.

(f) owner's equity decreases are shown as _____.

- - - - - - - - - - - - - - - -

(a) debits; (b) credits; (c) credits; (d) debits; (e) credits; (f) debits

30. Revenue-generating transactions are recorded in the same way as liability and owner's equity transactions. On July 3, the total cash receipts from Ter-Mit's sales totaled $75. Show the General Journal entry that was made for this transaction at the end of the business day:

– – – – – – – – – – – – – – –

    Cash $75
        Sales $75
        July 3 total cash receipts

31. On July 14, Ter-Mit paid a $25 utilities expense bill. At the end of that business day, the transaction was recorded in the General Journal as follows:

    Utilities expense $25
        Cash $25
        For July gas and electricity

Increases in expense accounts are shown by (a) _____ the
                                              (debiting/crediting)
expense account. Name another class of account for which an increase is

shown in this way. (b) _____

– – – – – – – – – – – – – – –

(a) debiting; (b) asset accounts

32. Fill in the blanks with debits or credits to complete the following statements:

       (a) revenue increases are shown as _____.

       (b) revenue decreases are shown as _____.

       (c) expense increases are shown as _____.

       (d) expense decreases are shown as _____.

– – – – – – – – – – – – – – –

(a) credits; (b) debits; (c) debits; (d) credits

33. You have now learned enough to journalize almost any day-to-day business transaction. For practice and review, here are a few more of Ter-Mit's July transactions. Record them in simplified General Journal form:

(a) On July 15, Ter-Mit pays the owner's assistant a two-week salary of $250 in cash.
(b) On July 20, Ter-Mit pays $300 in cash toward paying off its $500 equipment debt.
(c) On July 31, Mitty, the owner of Ter-Mit, withdraws $800 for his personal use.
(d) On July 31, Ter-Mit purchases supplies on account for $250.

(a)

(b)

(c)

(d)

- - - - - - - - - - - - - - -

(a) Salary expense $250
         Cash $250
              July 15 assistant's salary
(b) Accounts payable. $300
         Cash $300
              Partial payment of equipment debt
(c) Terry Mitty, drawing . . . $800
         Cash $800
              For personal use
(d) Supplies. $250
         Accounts payable. $250
              Supplies purchased

34. A General Journal form follows showing all of Ter-Mit's transactions for July.

General Journal

Page   1

Date	Description	p.r.	Debit	Credit
19 —				
July 1	Cash		5000 00	
	Terry Mitty, capital			5000 00
	Invested in Ter-Mit Exterminators			
2	Prepaid rent		300 00	
	Cash			300 00
	Three month's rent in advance			
2	Supplies		200 00	
	Cash			200 00
	For purchase of exterminating			
	supplies			
3	Equipment		500 00	
	Accounts payable			500 00
	For equipment purchased			
	on account			
14	Utilities expense		25 00	
	Cash			25 00
	For July gas and electricity			
15	Salary expense		250 00	
	Cash			250 00
	For two week's salary (assistant)			
20	Accounts payable		300 00	
	Cash			300 00
	Partial payment of equipment debt			
31	Terry Mitty, drawing		800 00	
	Cash			800 00
	For owner's personal use			
31	Salary expense		250 00	
	Cash			250 00
	For two week's salary (assistant)			
31	Cash		1500 00	
	Sales			1500 00
	July monthly cash receipts			

An actual business would have many more transactions, but for clarity's sake only a few are given here. Another simplification is that the sales transactions are given as a single monthly total. In an actual business there would probably be a sales entry for each day of the month that sales were made.

After examining Ter-Mit's transactions for July, which one or more of the following statements truly reflects the advantage of the General Journal as a record-keeping device?

_____ a. By presenting the dual effects of each transaction, the General Journal gives the immediate impact of each transaction.

_____ b. The General Journal presents a summary of all transactions affecting each individual account.

_____ c. The General Journal gives a chronological report of business transactions.

- - - - - - - - - - - - - - - -

(a) and (c)

Self-Teaching Section D

THE LEDGER

35. One disadvantage of the General Journal is that it is not easy to see the effects of transactions on specific individual accounts. The Ter-Mit cash account, for example, was affected by nine separate transactions during July. Because the nine transactions were spread throughout the General Journal, it would be difficult to isolate and study only those transactions that specifically affected the cash account. This disadvantage is overcome by going through the General Journal and transcribing all transactions that affect one particular account onto one separate page--an account page in the Ledger. This operation may be carried out during or at the end of the accounting period and is referred to as posting to the ledger. Posting to the ledger results in:

_____ a. a chronological record of the transactions for a particular accounting period

_____ b. isolation of all transactions that affect a particular account

- - - - - - - - - - - - - - - -

(b)

36. A Ledger is a group of accounts. A Ledger may be a book, a card file, or, when a computer is used, a magnetic tape. In small businesses, such as Ter-Mit Exterminators, the Ledger is often kept in a loose-leaf binder. In this kind of Ledger, each page is used for a separate account. The information that is posted to the Ledger comes from what other record (book)?

_____

- - - - - - - - - - - - - - -

the General Journal

37. Here, once again, is Ter-Mit's first journalized transaction. Below it is the page from Ter-Mit's Ledger that is used for the <u>cash</u> <u>account</u>. The transaction has been posted to the Ledger from the General Journal. The arrows show how the information was transferred.

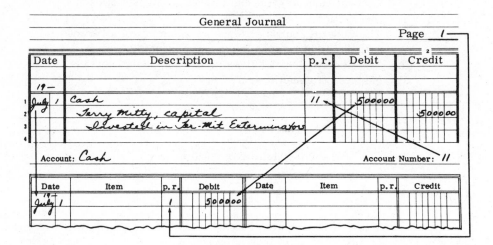

Notice that there is no entry on the account form under the item column. The description on the General Journal form is <u>cash</u>, and since the entry on the account form is only cash transactions there is no need to repeat the description. We will discuss the use of the item column later. For the moment just leave it blank.

Notice also that the account form is divided into two halves: a debit side (on the left) and a credit side (on the right). Since the journalized transaction involved a cash increase (debit), the _____ side of the account form was used to record the $5000 investment.

- - - - - - - - - - - - - - -

left

38. Two other items posted to the Ledger from the General Journal are

(a) _____ and the number 1, which is written in the column

headed (b) _____.

- - - - - - - - - - - - - - -

(a) the date; (b) p.r.

39. The p.r. heading stands for posting reference. (An alternate column heading is "folio, " meaning "page.") The posting reference in the Ledger makes it easier for the bookkeeper or accountant to track down any error that might occur. If you are interrupted when you are posting the Ledger, the p.r. column is a quick way to determine where you were when you later take up the posting again. In the example in Frame 37, you know at a glance that the Ledger entry (investment in Ter-Mit Exterminators) was posted from _____ of the General Journal.

- - - - - - - - - - - - - - - -

    page 1

40. In the posting operation, one piece of information is transferred from the Ledger back to the Journal. This is the account number (in the case of the cash account, 11). If you wanted to know where a particular Journal entry had been posted all you have to do is to look in the General Journal under the column headed _____.

- - - - - - - - - - - - - - - -

    p.r. (or folio)

41. The Ledger isolates all of the changes in a single account for the entire accounting period. Look back to the page of the Ter-Mit General Journal for July (Frame 34) and post the next entry on the cash account form given below:

Account: *Cash*   Account Number: *11*

Date	Item	p.r.	Debit	Date	Item	p.r.	Credit
July 1		1	5 0 0 0 00				

- - - - - - - - - - - - - - - -

                                          Referenced
                                          in journal
                                          ↑

Account: *Cash*   Account Number: *11*

Date	Item	p.r.	Debit	Date	Item	p.r.	Credit
July 1		1	5 0 0 0 00	July 2		1	3 0 0 00

Note that the account number (11) should have been entered in the p.r. column of the General Journal when you posted the entry above.

42. Where should the Terry Mitty, capital, part of the first transaction in the General Journal (Frame 34) be posted?

    _____ a. directly under the last cash debit in the cash account
    _____ b. directly under the last cash credit in the cash account
    _____ c. as a debit on a separate page devoted entirely to the Terry Mitty, capital account
    _____ d. as a credit on a separate page devoted entirely to the Terry Mitty, capital account

- - - - - - - - - - - - - - -

(d)

43. Post the Terry Mitty, capital, entry for July 2:

Account: *Terry Mitty, capital*   Account Number: *31*

Date	Item	p.r.	Debit	Date	Item	p.r.	Credit

In the p.r. column of the General Journal you should write _____ .

- - - - - - - - - - - - - -

Account: *Terry Mitty, capital*   Account Number: *31*

Date	Item	p.r.	Debit	Date	Item	p.r.	Credit
				July 1		1	5000 00

In the p.r. column of the General Journal you should write __31__ .

44. For each journal entry, it's a good idea to post all <u>debits</u> first and then post all credits. This method is more likely to produce accurate results. Following is the entire Ter-Mit Exterminators Ledger. Each account is on a separate page of the Ter-Mit Ledger, but for our purposes we have reproduced only a part of each account page and put them all together to save space. Starting from the very first entry on the General Journal page, post to the Ledger all transactions. Remember to enter all debits from the General Journal first. Also remember to record each Ledger entry in the "p.r" column on the Journal page.

General Journal

Page _1_

Date	Description	p.r.	Debit	Credit
19–				
July 1	Cash		5000 00	
	Terry Mitty, capital			5000 00
	Invested in Ter-Mit Exterminators			
2	Prepaid rent		300 00	
	Cash			300 00
	Three month's rent in advance			
2	Supplies		200 00	
	Cash			200 00
	For purchase of exterminating			
	supplies			
3	Equipment		500 00	
	Accounts payable			500 00
	For equipment purchased			
	on account			
14	Utilities expense		25 00	
	Cash			25 00
	For July gas and electricity			
15	Salary expense		250 00	
	Cash			250 00
	For two week's salary (assistant)			
20	Accounts payable		300 00	
	Cash			300 00
	Partial payment of equipment debt			
31	Terry Mitty, drawing		800 00	
	Cash			800 00
	For owner's personal use			
31	Salary expense		250 00	
	Cash			250 00
	For two week's salary (assistant)			
31	Cash		1500 00	
	Sales			1500 00
	July monthly cash receipts			

Account: *Cash*   Account Number: *11*

Date	Item	p. r.	Debit	Date	Item	p. r.	Credit

Account: *Supplies*   Account Number: *14*

Date	Item	p. r.	Debit	Date	Item	p. r.	Credit

Account: *Prepaid rent*   Account Number: *15*

Date	Item	p. r.	Debit	Date	Item	p. r.	Credit

Account: *Equipment*   Account Number: *18*

Date	Item	p. r.	Debit	Date	Item	p. r.	Credit

Account: *Accounts payable*   Account Number: *21*

Date	Item	p. r.	Debit	Date	Item	p. r.	Credit

Account: *Terry Mitty, capital*   Account Number: *31*

Date	Item	p. r.	Debit	Date	Item	p. r.	Credit

Account: Terry Mitty, drawing   Account Number: 32

Date	Item	p. r.	Debit	Date	Item	p. r.	Credit

Account: Sales   Account Number: 41

Date	Item	p. r.	Debit	Date	Item	p. r.	Credit

Account: Salary expense   Account Number: 51

Date	Item	p. r.	Debit	Date	Item	p. r.	Credit

Account: Utilities expense   Account Number: 54

Date	Item	p. r.	Debit	Date	Item	p. r.	Credit

- - - - - - - - - - - - - - -

Answer:

Account: Cash   Account Number: 11

Date	Item	p. r.	Debit	Date	Item	p. r.	Credit
19 July 1		1	5000 00	19 July 2		1	300 00
31		1	1500 00	2		1	200 00
				14		1	25 00
				15		1	250 00
				20		1	300 00
				31		1	800 00
				31		1	250 00

Account: Supplies — Account Number: 14

Date	Item	p.r.	Debit	Date	Item	p.r.	Credit
19— July 2		1	200 00				

Account: Prepaid rent — Account Number: 15

Date	Item	p.r.	Debit	Date	Item	p.r.	Credit
19— July 2		1	300 00				

Account: Equipment — Account Number: 18

Date	Item	p.r.	Debit	Date	Item	p.r.	Credit
19— July 3		1	500 00				

Account: Accounts payable — Account Number: 21

Date	Item	p.r.	Debit	Date	Item	p.r.	Credit
19— July 20		1	300 00	19— July 3		1	500 00

Account: Terry Mitty, capital — Account Number: 31

Date	Item	p.r.	Debit	Date	Item	p.r.	Credit
				19— July 2		1	5000 00

Account: Terry Mitty, drawing — Account Number: 32

Date	Item	p.r.	Debit	Date	Item	p.r.	Credit
19— July 31		1	800 00				

Account: Sales — Account Number: 41

Date	Item	p.r.	Debit	Date	Item	p.r.	Credit
				19— July 31		1	1500 00

Account: *Salary expense*   Account Number: *51*

Date	Item	p.r.	Debit		Date	Item	p.r.	Credit	
19— July 15		1	250 00						
31		1	250 00						

Account: *Utilities expense*   Account Number: *54*

Date	Item	p.r.	Debit		Date	Item	p.r.	Credit	
19— July 14		1	25 00						

At this point, the "p.r." column of the General Journal should contain all account numbers posted to the Ledger.

Self-Teaching Section E

THE TRIAL BALANCE

45. Since each debit entry in the General Journal or the Ledger is accompanied by an equal credit entry in some other account, barring any errors, you would expect that

_____ a. the total debits and the total credits for any <u>one</u> account will be equal

_____ b. the total debits and the total credits for the entire Ledger will be equal

– – – – – – – – – – – – – – – –

(b)

46. If posting to the Ledger is done accurately, total debits for all accounts taken together should be equal to total credits for all accounts taken together. A good check on the posting procedure is to compare the sum of all of the

_____ for an accounting period to the sum of all of the

_____ for the same period.

– – – – – – – – – – – – – – –

debits, credits (in either order)

47. The procedure for ensuring the equality of the debits and credits is called <u>taking a Trial Balance</u>. It is accomplished in two steps:

    Step 1.   Balance all the accounts.
    Step 2.   Compare the sum of the debit balances with the sum of
                  the credit balances to see if they are equal.

<u>Taking a Trial Balance</u> is a check on the _____ procedure.

– – – – – – – – – – – – – –

posting to the ledger (posting)

48. An account is balanced by

- adding the entries in the debit column to determine the total amount debited,

- adding the entries in the credit column to determine the total amount credited,

- subtracting the smaller total from the larger to determine the difference.

If the total debits are larger, the account is said to have a <u>debit balance</u>. If the total credits are larger, the account is said to have a <u>credit balance</u>.
    Here is Ter-Mit's complete utilities expense account for July:

Account: *Utilities expense*　　　　　　　　　　　　Account Number: *54*

Date	Item	p. r.	Debit	Date	Item	p. r.	Credit
July 14		1	25 00				

The utilities expense account has a _____ balance in the amount of _____ .
                                         (credit/debit)

– – – – – – – – – – – – – –

debit; $25

49. Here is the complete salary expense account for July:

Account: *Salary expense*   Account Number: *51*

Date	Item	p.r.	Debit	Date	Item	p.r.	Credit
July 15		1	250 00				
31		1	250 00				
			500 00				

Notice that <u>when</u> <u>there</u> <u>is</u> <u>more</u> <u>than</u> <u>one</u> <u>entry</u> <u>in</u> <u>a</u> <u>debit</u> <u>or</u> <u>credit</u> <u>column</u>, the column is <u>footed</u> by entering its total in small numbers just under the last entry. In the account above, the footing occurs after the last entry in the

(a) _____ column. The salary expense account has a

(b) _____ of (c) _____.

- - - - - - - - - - - - - - - -

(a) debit; (b) debit balance; (c) $500

50. Here is Ter-Mit's accounts-payable account for July:

Account: *Accounts payable*   Account Number: *21*

Date	Item	p.r.	Debit	Date	Item	p.r.	Credit
July 20		1	300 00	July 3	200.00	1	500 00

Notice that when there are <u>entries</u> <u>in</u> <u>both</u> <u>debit</u> <u>and</u> <u>credit</u> <u>columns</u>, the difference between the two totals is written in small numbers in the <u>item</u> column next to, and slightly beneath, the <u>larger</u> total. When there is more than one entry on each half of the page, each column is footed and then the difference is entered in the appropriate item column. In the account above, the account

has a (a) _____ balance of (b) $_____.

- - - - - - - - - - - - - - -

(a) credit; (b) $200

51. Foot and balance Ter-Mit's cash account:

Account: *Cash*   Account Number: *11*

Date	Item	p.r.	Debit	Date	Item	p.r.	Credit
July 1		1	500 000	July 2		1	30 00
31		1	150 000	2		1	200 00
				14		1	25 00
				15		1	250 00
				20		1	300 00
				31		1	800 00
				31		1	250 00

The cash account has a _____ balance of $_____.

- - - - - - - - - - - - - - -

Account: *Cash*   Account Number: *11*

Date	Item	p.r.	Debit	Date	Item	p.r.	Credit
July 1		1	500 000	July 2		1	30 00
31		1	150 000	2		1	200 00
	4375.00		650 000	14		1	25 00
				15		1	250 00
				20		1	300 00
				31		1	800 00
				31		1	250 00
							2125 00

The cash account has a ____debit____ balance of $ 4375 .

52. On the following page is Ter-Mit's Trial Balance for July. Notice that the accounts are grouped according to their class (assets, liabilities, etc.).

     The balances computed thus far have been entered. Determine the remaining balances from the Ledger in Frame 44, and enter them on the Trial Balance form. Then, add the two columns and draw a double line under the totals to signify that they are equal.

TER-MIT EXTERMINATORS

Trial Balance
July 31, 19--

	Account	Debit	Credit
Assets	Cash	4375.00	
	Supplies		
	Equipment		
	Prepaid rent		
Liabilities	Accounts payable		200.00
Owner's Equity	Terry Mitty, capital		
	Terry Mitty, drawing		
Revenue	Sales		
Expenses	Salary	500.00	
	Utilities	25.00	

- - - - - - - - - - - - - - -

Answer:

TER-MIT EXTERMINATORS

Trial Balance
July 31, 19--

	Account	Debit	Credit
Assets	Cash	4375.00	
	Supplies	200.00	
	Equipment	500.00	
	Prepaid rent	300.00	
Liabilities	Accounts payable		200.00
Owner's Equity	Terry Mitty, capital		5000.00
	Terry Mitty, drawing	800.00	
Revenue	Sales		1500.00
Expenses	Salary	500.00	
	Utilities	25.00	
		6700.00	6700.00

53. The fact that the total credit balances equal the total debit balances proves that the credits posted equal the debits posted. The proof given by the equality in the Trial Balance does not mean that there are no errors. For example, if a supplies debit was recorded as an equipment debit, the total debits would match the total credits, and there would have been an

error in the recording procedure which _____ show up when the
$$\text{(would/would not)}$$
debit and credit balances were compared.

— — — — — — — — — — — — — — —

   would not

54. If a supplies debit of $29 and a cash credit of $29 were mistakenly recorded as a $25 debit and a $25 credit, the total supplies account would show $4 less debit than it should, and the total credit account would show $4 less credit than it should. In this case, the Trial Balance would show an

_____.

(equality/inequality)

— — — — — — — — — — — — — — —

   equality

55. If a transaction is omitted, neither the debit balances nor the credit balances would be affected. In this case the Trial Balance _____
$$\text{(would/would not)}$$
show that a mistake had been made.

— — — — — — — — — — — — — — —

   would not

56. The equal totals of $6700 in Ter-Mit's Trial Balance do not prove which of the following?

_____ a. the total of all debits posted equal all credits posted
_____ b. all transactions were posted to the correct accounts
_____ c. the same amount was posted for both the credit and
         the debit parts of each and every transaction
_____ d. for debit amounts posted, equal credit amounts were
         posted
_____ e. a transaction was omitted

— — — — — — — — — — — —

   (b), (c), and (e)

57. Match the following:

_____ a. a transaction is omitted

_____ b. a debit was correctly recorded, but in the wrong account

_____ c. a debit was omitted from the Ledger

_____ d. both accounts affected by a transaction were debited and credited for the same incorrect amount

_____ e. a credit balance was incorrectly computed

1. an error that will usually give an unequal Trial Balance

2. an error that will not be found by the Trial Balance procedure

----

(a) 2; (b) 2; (c) 1; (d) 2; (e) 1

58. When a Trial Balance yields unequal debit and credit balances, the _differences_ between the balances can often serve as a clue to where the error occurred and how the correction might best be made.

For example, if a debit of $29 has been entered as a credit, the total debit balance will be decreased by $29 and the total credit balance will be increased by $29. Assuming no other errors, the Trial Balance discrepancy will be just twice the amount of the error, or $_____.

$58

59. Frame 58 implies that a discrepancy that is divisible by 2 might be traced to what kind of error? _____

_____

----

one in which a single entry was debited when it should have been credited, or vice versa

60. Discrepancies of less than 10 or divisible by 10 (e.g., 100 or 1000) are often traced to addition errors. Which of the following Trial Balances was probably caused by an addition error?

_____ a. debit, $7294; credit, $8294

_____ b. debit, $5309; credit, $5361

_____ c. debit, $900; credit, $947

_____ d. debit, $425; credit, $426

(a) and (d)

61. Two other kinds of errors that might be suggested by the amount of Trial Balance discrepancy are <u>transpositions</u> and <u>slides</u>. Transposition occurs when digits of an entry are reversed, as when the entry $369 is entered as $639.

Slides occur when a decimal is misplaced. For example, $727.00 may get entered as $72.70 or as $7270.00.

If a Trial Balance discrepancy is divisible by <u>9</u>, it may well have been caused by a transposition or a slide.

Which of the following Trial Balance discrepancies may have been caused by either a transposition or a slide?

____ a. $549.00   ____ c. $14.30
____ b. $2.52   ____ d. $1252.20

- - - - - - - - - - - - - - - -

(a) and (b)

62. When the Trial Balance procedure discloses an error, that error must be corrected. For errors in which an amount has been incorrectly journalized or posted as a debit or a credit, or where the incorrect account title has been entered in the Journal, the technique is simple. Simply draw a line through the incorrect entry, title, or amount; then write the correct entry above it or in the proper column. When an amount has been posted to the wrong account, however, a <u>correcting entry</u> is required.

Suppose, for example, that a $25 payment of utilities expense was mistakenly debited to miscellaneous expense. In other words, the entry was made as

    Miscellaneous expense $25
        Cash. $25

when it should have been made as

    Utilities expense $25
        Cash. $25

If the error is discovered before it is posted, a line may be drawn through "miscellaneous expense" and above it "utilities expense" may be written. If, however, the amount was erroneously posted to the wrong account, another Journal entry is required to document the correction. In that case, the Journal entry would be

    Utilities expense $25
        Miscellaneous expense $25
            To correct erroneous debit to
            miscellaneous expense

A $40 purchase of supplies was mistakenly journalized and posted as

Equipment $40
    Cash $40
         For supplies purchased

How would you correct this error in the Journal?

- - - - - - - - - - - - - -

Supplies $40
    Equipment $40
      To correct erroneous debit to equipment

SELF-TEST

This Self-Test will show you whether or not you have mastered the chapter objectives and are ready to go on to the next chapter. Answer each question to the best of your ability. Correct answers and instructions are given at the end of the test.

1. Here are several steps in the accounting cycle. Number them from 1 to 6 to show their proper order of occurrence:

_____ a. entry into the Journal   _____ d. preparing a Trial Balance

_____ b. business transactions   _____ e. posting to the Ledger

_____ c. determining the account   _____ f. preparing the Balance Sheet
        balance

2. Below is a list of account titles. Classify each as one of the following: Asset (A), Liability (L), Owner's Equity (OE), Revenue (R), Expense (E).

_____ a. owner's drawing   _____ h. equipment

_____ b. supplies   _____ i. cash

_____ c. salaries expense   _____ j. accounts payable

_____ d. accounts receivable   _____ k. prepaid insurance

_____ e. prepaid rent   _____ l. salaries payable

_____ f. sales   _____ m. rent expense

_____ g. owner's capital

3. For each of the transactions given below, select the two accounts (from the list) affected by the transaction and write them in the blanks provided. After each account, write whether the entry will be a <u>debit</u> or a <u>credit</u> entry. The account titles are as follows: cash, sales, owner's drawing, owner's capital, accounts receivable, accounts payable, supplies, prepaid rent, utilities expense, and salaries expense.
   The first one is completed for you.

(a) Total cash receipts collected, $150   <u>cash, debit</u>

                                               <u>sales, credit</u>

(b) The owner invests another $3000   _____

                                               _____

(c) Pay gas and electricity bill of $36   _____

                                               _____

(d) Purchased $700 worth of supplies on account

_____

_____

(e) Owner withdraws $600

_____

_____

(f) Sales on account total $100

_____

_____

(g) Pay $1000 for rent three months in advance

_____

_____

(h) Pay salaries totaling $850

_____

_____

4. Describe an advantage the Ledger has that the Journal does not have:

_____

_____

5. Describe any transaction that would bring about a credit entry to the utilities expense account: _____

6. What is a group of accounts called? _____

7. Which of the following errors would be disclosed by the Trial Balance procedure?

_____ a. incorrect addition in the computation of an account balance
_____ b. posting a debit as a credit
_____ c. posting the debit part of a transaction to the wrong account
_____ d. omission of a transaction
_____ e. a slide
_____ f. posting both the debit and the credit amounts of a transaction correctly but to wrong accounts

8. Adolph's Barber Shop has the following accounts in its Ledger: cash, accounts payable, supplies, equipment, Adolph capital, Adolph drawing, fees earned (sales), prepaid rent, utilities expense, salaries expense, and miscellaneous expense. Adolph hires three barbers. He balances his accounts once a month. Here are Adolph's transactions for January; examine them. Using the Journal page that follows, enter each transaction on the form. After you have journalized each transaction, use the account forms that follow and post all of the General Journal entries to the Ledger. Balance all the accounts and then take a Trial Balance. Work carefully. Be sure that all steps are accomplished and all forms are completed. Note: when describing a transaction (on the third line of the Journal entry) use any phrase you feel

is adequate. However, to avoid confusion do remember to use the same phrase to describe similar transactions.

Adolph's business transactions:

1. On January 1, Adolph paid four month's rent in advance. (Adolph's rent is $200 per month.)

2. Bought $30 worth of barber supplies for cash on January 2.

3. Bought a new barber chair on account for $500 on January 2. Promised to pay by February 28.

4. On January 7, paid his three barbers' salaries: $450.

5. On January 7 bought additional supplies for $85 cash.

6. On January 8 made a partial payment against the debt for the barber chair: $125.

7. Paid $55 for barber chair repair on January 9.

8. Total semi-monthly receipts (barber fees) come to $2700 (January 14).

9. January 14, paid three barbers' salaries: $450.

10. January 14, drew $650 for Adolph's use.

11. January 17, paid for advertising in local paper: $65.

12. January 18, re-invested $200.

13. Paid three barbers' salaries totaling $450 on January 21.

14. January 22, paid another installment on barber chair debt: $125.

15. January 28, paid three barbers' salaries totaling $450.

16. Withdrew $600 for Adolph's use on January 28.

17. January 28, paid month's gas and electric bill of $45.

18. January 28, semi-monthly receipts (barber fees) come to $2000.

General Journal

Page _1_

Date	Description	p.r.	Debit	Credit
1				
2				
3				
4				
5				
6				
7				
8				
9				
10				
11				
12				
13				
14				
15				
16				
17				
18				
19				
20				
21				
22				
23				
24				
25				
26				
27				
28				
29				
30				
31				
32				
33				
34				
35				
36				
37				
38				
39				
40				

General Journal

Page 2

Date	Description	p.r.	Debit	Credit
1				
2				
3				
4				
5				
6				
7				
8				
9				
10				
11				
12				
13				
14				
15				
16				
17				
18				
19				
20				
21				
22				
23				
24				
25				
26				
27				
28				
29				
30				
31				
32				
33				
34				
35				
36				
37				
38				
39				
40				

Account: *Cash*   Account Number: *11*

Date	Item	p. r.	Debit	Date	Item	p. r.	Credit

Account: *Supplies*   Account Number: *13*

Date	Item	p. r.	Debit	Date	Item	p. r.	Credit

Account: *Prepaid rent*   Account Number: *14*

Date	Item	p. r.	Debit	Date	Item	p. r.	Credit

Account: *Equipment*   Account Number: *15*

Date	Item	p. r.	Debit	Date	Item	p. r.	Credit

Account: *Accounts payable*   Account Number: *21*

Date	Item	p. r.	Debit	Date	Item	p. r.	Credit

Account: *Owner's capital*   Account Number: *31*

Date	Item	p. r.	Debit	Date	Item	p. r.	Credit

Account: *Owner's drawing*   Account Number: *32*

Date	Item	p. r.	Debit	Date	Item	p. r.	Credit

Account: *Sales (fees earned)*   Account Number: *41*

Date	Item	p. r.	Debit	Date	Item	p. r.	Credit

Account: *Salary expense*   Account Number: *52*

Date	Item	p. r.	Debit	Date	Item	p. r.	Credit

Account: *Utilities expense*   Account Number: *54*

Date	Item	p. r.	Debit	Date	Item	p. r.	Credit

Account: *Miscellaneous expense*   Account Number: *59*

Date	Item	p. r.	Debit	Date	Item	p. r.	Credit

Prepare Trial Balance:

ADOLPH'S BARBER SHOP Trial Balance January 31, 19--		
Account	Debit	Credit

Self-Test Answers

Compare your answers to the Self-Test with the correct answers given below. If all of your answers are correct, you are ready to go on to the next chapter. If you missed any questions, study the frames indicated in parentheses following the answer. If you miss many questions, go over the entire chapter carefully.

1. (a) 2   (d) 5
    (b) 1   (e) 3
    (c) 4   (f) 6   (Overview, pp. 43-46)

2. (a) OE   (h) A
    (b) A   (i) A
    (c) E   (j) L
    (d) A   (k) A
    (e) A   (l) L
    (f) R   (m) E   (Frames 4-18)
    (g) OE

3. (b) cash, debit; owner's capital, credit
    (c) utilities expense, debit; cash, credit
    (d) supplies, debit; accounts payable, credit
    (e) owner's drawing, debit; cash, credit
    (f) accounts receivable, debit; sales, credit
    (g) prepaid rent, debit; cash, credit
    (h) salaries expense, debit; cash, credit   (Frames 19-24)

4. The Ledger isolates the effects on a single account for study.   (Frames 35 and 36)

5. A refund from the utility company.   (Frames 19-24)

6. A Ledger.   (Frames 35 and 36)

7. You should have checked (a), (b), and (e).   (Frames 53-61)

8. Examine the answer to this question which is given on the following pages, in great detail. You should have filled in the blank forms as shown. If you did not answer this question correctly, be sure you understand what you did wrong before you proceed.

    If you made errors, you may need to examine the entire chapter since this question is so comprehensive. If you had special trouble journalizing, examine Frames 33 and 34. If you had special trouble entering accounts, examine Frames 37 to 44. If you had special trouble doing a Trial Balance, examine Frames 45 to 52.

General Journal

Page 1

Date	Description	p.r.	Debit	Credit
19—				
Jan. 1	Prepaid rent	14	800 00	
	Cash	11		800 00
	Four months in advance			
2	Supplies	13	30 00	
	Cash	11		30 00
	Barber supplies			
2	Equipment	15	500 00	
	Accounts payable	21		500 00
	For barber chair			
7	Salary expense	52	450 00	
	Cash	11		450 00
	For barbers' salaries			
7	Supplies	13	85 00	
	Cash	11		85 00
	Barber supplies			
8	Accounts payable	21	125 00	
	Cash	11		125 00
	Partial payment on barber chair			
9	Miscellaneous expense	59	55 00	
	Cash	11		55 00
	Barber chair repair			
14	Cash	11	2700 00	
	Fees earned	41		2700 00
	Semi-monthly receipts			
14	Salary expense	52	450 00	
	Cash	11		450 00
	For barbers' salaries			
14	Adolph, drawing	32	650 00	
	Cash	11		650 00
	For personal use			

General Journal

Page 2

Date		Description	p.r.	Debit	Credit
19 —					
Jan.	17	Miscellaneous expense	59	6500	
		Cash	11		6500
		For advertising			
	18	Cash	11	20000	
		Adolph, capital	31		20000
		Investment			
	21	Salary expense	52	45000	
		Cash	11		45000
		For barbers' salary			
	22	Accounts payable	21	12500	
		Cash	11		12500
		Partial payment on barber chair			
	28	Salary expense	52	45000	
		Cash	11		45000
		For barbers' salary			
	28	Adolph, drawing	32	60000	
		Cash	11		60000
		For personal use			
	28	Utilities expense	54	4500	
		Cash	11		4500
		For January gas and electricity			
	28	Cash	11	200000	
		Fees earned	41		200000
		Semi-monthly receipts			

Account: *Cash* Account Number: 11

Date	Item	p. r.	Debit	Date	Item	p. r.	Credit
Jan. 19— 14		1	2700 00	Jan. 19— 1		1	80 00
18		2	200 00	2		1	30 00
28		2	2000 00	7		1	450 00
	520.00		4900 00	7		1	85 00
				8		1	125 00
				9		1	55 00
				14		1	450 00
				14		1	650 00
				17		2	65 00
				21		2	450 00
				22		2	125 00
				28		2	450 00
				28		2	600 00
				28		2	45 00
							4380 00

Account: *Supplies* Account Number: 13

Date	Item	p. r.	Debit	Date	Item	p. r.	Credit
Jan. 19— 2		1	30 00				
7		1	85 00				
			115 00				

Account: *Prepaid rent* Account Number: 14

Date	Item	p. r.	Debit	Date	Item	p. r.	Credit
Jan. 19— 1		1	800 00				

Account: *Equipment* Account Number: 15

Date	Item	p. r.	Debit	Date	Item	p. r.	Credit
Jan. 19— 2		1	500 00				

Account: *Accounts payable* Account Number: 21

Date	Item	p. r.	Debit	Date	Item	p. r.	Credit
Jan. 19— 8		1	125 00	Jan. 19— 2		1	500 00
22		2	125 00		250.00		
			250 00				

Account: *Owner's capital*   Account Number: 31

Date	Item	p.r.	Debit	Date	Item	p.r.	Credit
				Jan. 19 — 18		2	2000 00

Account: *Owner's drawing*   Account Number: 32

Date	Item	p.r.	Debit	Date	Item	p.r.	Credit
Jan. 19 — 14		1	650 00				
28		2	600 00				
			1250 00				

Account: *Sales (fees earned)*   Account Number: 41

Date	Item	p.r.	Debit	Date	Item	p.r.	Credit
				Jan. 19 — 14		1	2700 00
				28		2	2000 00
							4700 00

Account: *Salary expense*   Account Number: 52

Date	Item	p.r.	Debit	Date	Item	p.r.	Credit
Jan. 19 — 7		1	450 00				
14		1	450 00				
21		2	450 00				
28		2	450 00				
			1800 00				

Account: *Utilities expense*   Account Number: 54

Date	Item	p.r.	Debit	Date	Item	p.r.	Credit
Jan. 19 — 28		2	45 00				

Account: *Miscellaneous expense*   Account Number: 59

Date	Item	p.r.	Debit	Date	Item	p.r.	Credit
Jan. 19 — 9		1	55 00				
17		2	65 00				
			120 00				

ADOLPH'S BARBER SHOP

Trial Balance
January 31, 19--

Account	Debit	Credit
Cash	520.00	
Supplies	115.00	
Prepaid rent	800.00	
Equipment	500.00	
Accounts payable		250.00
Owner's capital		200.00
Owner's drawing	1250.00	
Sales (fees earned)		4700.00
Salary expense	1800.00	
Utilities expense	45.00	
Miscellaneous expense	130.00	
	5150.00	5150.00

CHAPTER FOUR

The Accounting Cycle II: Adjusting the Ledger and Preparing Financial Statements

OBJECTIVES

When you complete this chapter, you will be able to:

- define and discriminate between accrual and cash basis accounting systems,

- make adjustments to the account balances on the Worksheet,

- prepare a <u>Balance</u> <u>Sheet</u>,

- prepare an <u>Income</u> <u>Statement</u>,

- prepare an <u>Owner's</u> <u>Capital</u> <u>Statement</u>,

- journalize and post adjusting entries.

If you feel that you have already mastered these objectives and might skip all or part of this chapter, turn to the end of this chapter and take the Self-Test. The results will tell you what frames of the chapter you should study. If you answer all questions correctly, you are ready to begin the next chapter.

If this material is new to you, or if you choose not to take the Self-Test now, turn to the Overview and Self-Teaching sections that follow.

CHAPTER OVERVIEW

This chapter will continue to deal with the steps in the accounting cycle. In the last chapter we ended with the Trial Balance. In this chapter we will begin with the Trial Balance and follow the cycle through Steps 5 and 6; we will adjust the Trial Balance to account for unrecorded transactions and to apportion expenses and revenues, prepare financial statements (the Balance Sheet, the Income Statement, and the Capital Statement), and journalize and post the adjusting entries.

In the next chapter we will conclude our study of the accounting cycle by studying those steps that are necessary to prepare the Ledger for the next accounting cycle: we will journalize and post closing entries (entries which bring to zero the balances of all revenue, expense, and drawing accounts in preparation for the next accounting period), rule and balance the accounts, and prepare a Post-Closing Trial Balance.

ADJUSTMENTS TO ACCOUNT BALANCES

Adjustments are made to the balances of certain accounts in the Ledger so that the effects of all transactions occurring within a given accounting period will be reflected on the final statements of that period. There are two common types of accounting systems:

- cash basis accounting systems which show only cash actually received or disbursed during the particular accounting period

- accrual basis accounting systems which show all business transactions that have occurred during a particular accounting period, whether or not cash was actually received or disbursed

Other modified systems may be used, and the procedures for adjusting account balances would differ according to the accounting system used. Adjustments are first made on a Worksheet, and involve adding or subtracting various amounts to balances so that corrected balances may be used on the financial statements.

PREPARING FINANCIAL STATEMENTS

The adjusted account balances are used in the preparation of the Balance Sheet, the Income Statement, and the Owner's Capital Statement. The financial statements are used by anyone concerned with the financial condition of the business, including owners, investors, the government, and the public. Evaluation of these financial statements will be discussed in Chapter 9.

MAKING ADJUSTING ENTRIES

As soon as the Balance Sheet and the Income Statement are prepared, the adjusting entries are journalized from the Worksheet and posted to the Ledger.

Self-Teaching Section A

ADJUSTMENTS TO ACCOUNT BALANCES

1. The last chapter ended with the preparation of the Trial Balance. We will pick up the accounting cycle at that point to show how the Trial Balance is used to prepare the Balance Sheet and the Income Statement.

   The assets, liabilities, and owner's equity accounts are reported on the Balance Sheet. They are derived from the Trial Balance. Likewise, the revenue and expense accounts reported on the Income Statement are taken from the Trial Balance. (If you want to review the entire process, return to page 43, which gives a diagram of the early steps of the accounting cycle.)

   Some account balances simply cannot be transferred to the appropriate statement because they do not report the status of particular accounts with complete accuracy. To be more precise, the Trial Balance often contains certain over- or under-statements that must be adjusted before the financial statements can be prepared.

   One common adjustment involves the expiration of expenses originally recorded as prepaid expenses. For example, on July 2, Ter-Mit Exterminators paid $300 for three month's rent in advance. The prepaid rent account balance, as given on the Trial Balance, correctly shows a $300 debit. On July 31, however, when the financial statements are being prepared, some of that prepaid rent has expired. At the beginning of July, when the debit was made, Ter-Mit had the right to occupy its rented premises for three months.

Is this still the case? ____ yes ____ no

– – – – – – – – – – – – – – – –

   no

2. On July 31 one month has passed since Ter-Mit acquired the $300 prepaid rent asset. Since Ter-Mit's rent is $100 a month, the prepaid rent asset

amounts to $_____ on July 31.

– – – – – – – – – – – – – – –

   $200

3. On July 31 Ter-Mit's prepaid rent asset has been reduced to $200. An adjustment must be made in the prepaid rent account. The $100 that expired must be recorded as:

_____ a. a prepaid asset
_____ b. a liability
_____ c. an expense

- - - - - - - - - - - - - - -

(c)

4. Here is the prepaid rent entry for Ter-Mit's Trial Balance. This diagram shows the first four (of 8) columns of the Worksheet.

Account	Trial Balance		Adjustment	
	Debit	Credit	Debit	Credit
1 *Prepaid rent*	300 00			
2				

Write $100 in the appropriate column under the <u>adjustment</u> <u>heading</u> to show how the prepaid rent account should be adjusted for the $100 decrease.

- - - - - - - - - - - - - - -

Adjustment	
Debit	Credit
	100 00

5. As in all accounting records, a credit entry must be accompanied by a debit entry in some other account, in this case, the rent expense account. Make the appropriate adjusting entry to show how the rent expense account is affected by the expiration of one month of prepaid rent.

Account Title	Trial Balance		Adjustment	
	Debit	Credit	Debit	Credit
1 *Prepaid rent*	300 00			100 00
2 *Rent expense*				

- - - - - - - - - - - - - - -

Account Title	Trial Balance		Adjustment	
	Debit	Credit	Debit	Credit
1 *Prepaid rent*	300 00			100 00
2 *Rent expense*			100 00	

6. These adjustments to the prepaid rent account are necessary because in the Trial Balance the prepaid rent asset is (a) _____ and the rent expense is (b)_____.
(overstated/understated)
(overstated/understated)

— — — — — — — — — — — — — — —

(a) overstated; (b) understated

7. On July 2, Ter-Mit purchased $200 worth of exterminating supplies. Since Ter-Mit had to use some of these supplies in the operation of the business, you would expect that the supplies account balance, as given in the

Trial Balance is _____. Another account that is affected by this information, but not shown in the Trial Balance, is the supplies expense account.

— — — — — — — — — — — — — — —

overstated

8. The adjustments you have just worked with are necessary if the summary statements are to show the changes that took place during a specific accounting period. When all such adjustments are made, the accounting system that we are following is called an accrual basis accounting system. There are actually two main accounting conventions:

- Accrual basis accounting systems, which show all business transactions that have occurred during a particular accounting period, whether or not cash was actually received or disbursed

- Cash basis accounting systems, which show only cash actually received or disbursed during the particular accounting period

An accrual accounting system takes into account:

- unrecorded liabilities, as when a salary liability is incurred for the working days in-between the last pay day of an accounting period and the last day of that same period,

- the apportionment of prepaid expenses, as when part of a prepaid expense must be charged to the accounting period, and

- the apportionment of income earned over more than one accounting period, as when a company receives rent payments in advance.

Most individuals (e.g., on income tax returns) use cash basis accounting, but most businesses use accrual basis accounting (though many, such as farming operations, use a cash basis system). Of course, other modifications may be used.

In a cash basis system, would adjustments be made for the expiration of

prepaid rent? ____ yes ____ no

— — — — — — — — — — — — — —

   no

9. Bob Jones is a farmer who uses the cash basis system of accounting.

When does Bob record income in his books? _____

_____

— — — — — — — — — — — — — —

   when he actually receives money (or equivalent answer)

10. Match the following:

____ a.	adjustments for the use of supplies would not be necessary	1. accrual basis accounting
____ b.	recording for income and expense takes place in the period that cash is actually disbursed or received	2. cash basis accounting
____ c.	income and expense are recorded for the period in which they occur	
____ d.	end-of-period adjustments for the use of supplies would be necessary	

— — — — — — — — — — — — — —

   (a) 2; (b) 2; (c) 1; (d) 1

11. On September 30, Ace Plumbing's Trial Balance shows that the supplies account has a debit balance of $800. Ace's bookkeeper will adjust this figure to account for the supplies that have been consumed. From this, we can

guess that Ace is probably using a(an) _____ basis accounting system.

— — — — — — — — — — — — — —

   accrual

12. On September 1, Ace had $150 worth of supplies on hand. During the month, $800 worth of supplies was purchased. At the end of the month the supplies inventory showed that $550 worth of supplies remained. This means

that the cost of supplies expended was $_____.

— — — — — — — — — — — — — —

   $400

13. Complete the Worksheet below to show how the supplies account and the supplies expense account should be adjusted to reflect accurate balances:

Account	Trial Balance		Adjustment	
	Debit	Credit	Debit	Credit
1 *Supplies*	950 00			
2 *Supplies expense*				
3				

- - - - - - - - - - - - - - - -

Account	Trial Balance		Adjustment	
	Debit	Credit	Debit	Credit
1 *Supplies*	950 00			400 00
2 *Supplies expense*			400 00	
3				

14. Another kind of adjustment that must be made at the end of the accounting period is the adjustment for <u>depreciation</u>. Over a period of time plant assets (such as equipment) depreciate. That is, they are used up or lose their reported value. (We say "reported" because the market value--what the asset can be sold for--may be much higher or much lower than its value after depreciation is taken into account.) Since this loss of value through use over time must be shown on the Balance Sheet and the Income Statement, it must also be reflected in the accounts.

 <u>The Balance Sheet shows both the original cost of a plant asset and the amount of accumulated depreciation taken for that asset. The depreciation amount cannot simply be credited to the asset account.</u> Instead, it is credited to another account called <u>accumulated depreciation</u> (grouped with the asset accounts). The recording takes place in the adjusting process and is accompanied by a debit entry in the <u>depreciation expense</u> account. Ace Plumbing's equipment was depreciated $50 in September. The adjusting entries, therefore, will show a $50 (a) _____ to the depreciation expense account, and

 debit/credit

a similar (b) _____ to the accumulated depreciation account.

 debit/credit

- - - - - - - - - - - - - - -

 (a) debit; (b) credit

15. The procedures covered thus far deal with adjusting the Trial Balance items so that the portion of the prepaid expenses incurred during that period is charged to the appropriate accounts. Another kind of adjustment that may take place is the adjustment for a liability that was incurred during the

accounting period, but not recorded. Here is an example: Ter-Mit pays its assistant a salary of $250 on every second Friday. The last payday in July was the 26th of the month. The end of the accounting period is on the 31st; therefore, there are three full working days (29th, 30th, and 31st) for which the assistant will not be paid until the next period. Since the assistant makes $25 per day, Ter-Mit incurs a $75 liability to the assistant. Which would be the correct way to record this state of affairs on the 31st?

_____ a. a $75 credit to the cash account and a $75 debit to the salary expense account

_____ b. a $75 credit to salary expense and a $75 debit to salary payable

_____ c. a $75 credit to salary payable and a $75 debit to salary expense

- - - - - - - - - - - - - - -

(c)

16. On Thursdays, the Further Book Store pays its cashier $100 for his week's work. The last payday of the period occurred on the 29th, leaving one more working day in the period. On the Worksheet below, show how the adjustments to the Trial Balance items should be made:

Account	Trial Balance		Adjustment	
	Debit	Credit	Debit	Credit
1 *Salary expense*	400 00			
2 *Salary*				
3				

- - - - - - - - - - - - - - -

Account	Trial Balance		Adjustment	
	Debit	Credit	Debit	Credit
1 *Salary expense*	400 00		20 00	
2 *Salary payable*				20 00
3				

17. If, in this situation (Frame 16), the last payday of the month occurred on the last day of the accounting period what kind of adjustment would be made? _____ Why? _____

_____

- - - - - - - - - - - - - - -

none, because all salary expense for the period would be fully paid

18. The Upsy-Daisy Telephone Wake-Up Service does business by the month. It will sell you one or more months of wake-up service for which it receives payment in advance. At the end of its monthly accounting period, Upsy-Daisy will have collected fees which will not actually be earned in that period, but will be applied to future periods.

On October 31, Upsy-Daisy's Trial Balance shows that the account balance for revenue collected (fees) during the month is $1750. An analysis of its customer accounts shows that only $700 of this amount applies to services rendered in the current accounting period. To make the proper adjustment to the Trial Balance item you would show a decrease in the revenue account for the amount that has not yet been actually earned. Which account would you use to show that revenue had been received and will be applied to some future period?

	a.	unearned revenue		c.	cash
	b.	accounts payable		d.	earned revenue

- - - - - - - - - - - - - - - - -

(a)

19. On Upsy-Daisy's Trial Balance, the account balance for revenue collected is $1750, only $700 of which is applied to the current period. On the Worksheet below, show how the adjustments to the Trial Balance items should be made (unearned revenue is classified as a liability account):

Account	Trial Balance		Adjustment	
	Debit	Credit	Debit	Credit
1 _____ revenue				
2 Revenue		1750 00		
3				

- - - - - - - - - - - - - - -

Account	Trial Balance		Adjustment	
	Debit	Credit	Debit	Credit
1 Unearned revenue				1050 00
2 Revenue		1750 00	1050 00	
3				

20. The following Worksheet gives Ter-Mit's Trial Balance for July. Use the adjusting data below to make all the required adjustments (account titles for those accounts not shown on the Trial Balance begin on line 13). Supplies has been done for you.

Adjusting data:
Supplies expended during July $125
Prepaid rent expired during July 100
Depreciation on equipment for July 20
Salary debt incurred 75

TER-MIT EXTERMINATORS

Worksheet
For the month ended July 31, 19--

| | ① | ② | ③ | ④ |
| Account Title | Trial Balance | | Adjustment | |
	Debit	Credit	Debit	Credit
1 Cash	4375 00			
2 Supplies	200 00			125 00
3 Equipment	500 00			
4 Prepaid rent	300 00			
5 Accounts payable		200 00		
6 Terry Mitty, capital		5000 00		
7 Terry Mitty, drawing	800 00			
8 Sales		1500 00		
9 Utilities expense	25 00			
10 Salary expense	500 00			
11	6700 00	6700 00		
12				
13 Supplies expense			125 00	
14 Rent _____				
15 Accumulated depreciation				
16 Depreciation _____				
17 _____ payable				
18				
19				

When all adjusting entries have been made, total the debits and credits in the adjustment column to verify their equality. To show that the debit total is equal to the credit total, a double line is ruled beneath both totals at the bottom of the adjustment column.

_ _ _ _ _ _ _ _ _ _ _ _ _ _ _ _ _

Answer

TER-MIT EXTERMINATORS

Worksheet

For the month ended July 31, 19--

		①	②	③	④
	Account Title	Trial Balance		Adjustment	
		Debit	Credit	Debit	Credit
1	Cash	437500			
2	Supplies	20000			12500
3	Equipment	50000			
4	Prepaid rent	30000			10000
5	Accounts payable		20000		
6	Terry Mitty, capital		500000		
7	Terry Mitty, drawing	80000			
8	Sales		150000		
9	Utilities expense	2500			
10	Salary expense	50000		7500	
11		670000	670000		
12					
13	Supplies expense			12500	
14	Rent expense			10000	
15	Accumulated depreciation				2000
16	Depreciation expense			2000	
17	Salary payable				7500
18				32000	32000
19					

21. The information now on the Worksheet is the basis for the preparation of the Balance Sheet and the Income Statement. The Worksheet that follows is identical to the one in Frame 20 except that four columns have been added: two for the Balance Sheet and two for the Income Statement. To complete these columns, the amounts in the trial balance column are combined with the amounts in the adjustment column (if any) and transferred to one of the four additional columns. Since the Balance Sheet reports on the company's total <u>assets</u>, <u>liabilities</u>, and <u>owner's equity</u> as of a certain date, these accounts are <u>transferred</u> <u>to</u> <u>the</u> <u>balance</u> <u>sheet</u> <u>columns</u> <u>of</u> <u>the</u> <u>Worksheet</u>. Transfer the cash amount to the appropriate column of the Worksheet:

Account	Trial Balance		Adjustment		Income Statement		Balance Sheet	
	Debit	Credit	Debit	Credit	Debit	Credit	Debit	Credit
Cash	4375 00							

- - - - - - - - - - - - - -

Account	Trial Balance		Adjustment		Income Statement		Balance Sheet	
	Debit	Credit	Debit	Credit	Debit	Credit	Debit	Credit
Cash	4375 00						4375 00	

22. Since there was no adjustment to the cash account, it was transferred to the Balance Sheet column without change. The next item to be transferred to the Balance Sheet column is the supplies account. The information given in the Worksheet in Frame 20 suggests that the $200 in the supplies amount

must be (a) _____ for $125 (b) _____ it is transferred.
            (debited/credited)   (before/after)

- - - - - - - - - - - - - -

(a) credited; (b) before

23. Transfer the correct supplies balance to the appropriate column in the Worksheet:

Account	Trial Balance		Adjustment		Income Statement		Balance Sheet	
	Debit	Credit	Debit	Credit	Debit	Credit	Debit	Credit
Cash	4375 00						4375 00	
Supplies	200 00			125 00				

- - - - - - - - - - - - - -

Account	Trial Balance		Adjustment		Income Statement		Balance Sheet	
	Debit	Credit	Debit	Credit	Debit	Credit	Debit	Credit
Cash	4375 00						4375 00	
Supplies	200 00			125 00			75 00	

24. The Balance Sheet gives the company's total assets, liabilities, and owner's equity as of the last day of the period. The Income Statement, on the otherhand, presents, in terms of revenues and expenses, the changes that have taken place as a result of operations during the accounting period.

Therefore revenue and expense accounts on the Worksheet are transferred to the columns headed _____.

– – – – – – – – – – – – – – – –

Income Statement

25. On the next page, the entire Worksheet for Ter-Mit is reproduced with all entries made thus far. Complete the Income Statement columns and the Balance Sheet columns.

When you have done this, add the debits and credits for each set of columns.

TER-MIT EXTERMINATORS
Worksheet
For the month ended July 31, 19--

	Account Title	Trial Balance Debit	Trial Balance Credit	Adjustments Debit	Adjustments Credit	Income Statement Debit	Income Statement Credit	Balance Sheet Debit	Balance Sheet Credit
1	Cash	4375 00						4375 00	
2	Supplies	200 00			125 00			75 00	
3	Equipment	500 00							
4	Prepaid rent	300 00			100 00				
5	Accounts payable		200 00						
6	Jerry Mitty, capital		500 00						
7	Jerry Mitty, drawing	800 00							
8	Sales		1500 00						
9	Utilities expense	25 00		75 00					
10	Salary expense	500 00							
11		6700 00	6700 00						
12									
13	Supplies expense			125 00					
14	Rent expense			100 00					
15	Accumulated depreciation				20 00				
16	Depreciation expense			20 00					
17	Salary payable				75 00				
18				320 00	320 00				
19									

Answer

TER-MIT EXTERMINATORS
Worksheet
For the month ended July 31, 19--

	Trial Balance		Adjustments		Income Statement		Balance Sheet	
Account Title	Debit	Credit	Debit	Credit	Debit	Credit	Debit	Credit
1 Cash	437500						437500	
2 Supplies	20000			12500			7500	
3 Equipment	50000						50000	
4 Prepaid rent	30000			10000			20000	
5 Accounts payable		20000						20000
6 Terry Mitty, capital		500000						500000
7 Terry Mitty, drawing	80000						80000	
8 Sales		150000				150000		
9 Utilities expense	2500				2500			
10 Salary expense	50000		7500		57500			
11	670000	670000						
12								
13 Supplies expense			12500		12500			
14 Rent expense			10000		10000			
15 Accumulated depreciation				2000				2000
16 Depreciation expense			2000		2000			
17 Salary payable				7500				7500
18			32000	32000	84500	150000	595000	529500
19								

26. Once the totals of the Income Statement column and the Balance Sheet column have been determined, the next task is to find the <u>net income</u> or <u>net loss</u>. This amount is the difference between the debit and credit columns of the Income Statement. Here are the four totals obtained in Frame 25:

Income Statement		Balance Sheet	
Debit	Credit	Debit	Credit
845 00	1500 00	5950 00	5295 00

If the debit column is larger, the amount obtained is the net loss. If the credit column is larger, the amount obtained is the net income. The net

(a) _____ of Ter-Mit is $_____ .

- - - - - - - - - - - - - - - -

   (a) income; (b) $655

27. Ter-Mit's net income is $1500 - $845 = $655.

   A final check is given by adding the net income to the total of the Income Statement debits and by adding the same amount to the total of the Balance Sheet credits. Of course, if there is a net <u>loss</u>, it would be added to the Income Statement credits and to the Balance Sheet debits. The totals thus obtained should give equal Income Statement debits and credits and equal Balance Sheet debits and credits. Go back to Frame 25 and perform this operation. When equality is proved, <u>rule double lines beneath the last entries</u> in the Income Statement and Balance Sheet Columns.

- - - - - - - - - - - - - - - -

Income Statement		Balance Sheet	
Debit	Credit	Debit	Credit
845 00	1500 00	5950 00	5295 00
655 00			655 00
1500 00	1500 00	5950 00	5950 00

Self-Teaching Section B

PREPARING FINANCIAL STATEMENTS

28. The Income Statement may now be completed using the adjusted account balances from the Worksheet. Fill in the blanks in the following format to complete the Income Statement:

TER-MIT EXTERMINATORS

Income Statement
Month ending July 31, 19--

Sales . . . . $_____

Expenses:

_____ expense . . . . $ _____

_____ expense . . . . $ _____

_____ expense . . . . $ _____

_____ expense . . . . $ _____

_____ expense . . . . $ _____

   Total expenses . . . . $_____

Net income . . . . $_____

- - - - - - - - - - - - - - - -

TER-MIT EXTERMINATORS

Income Statement
Month ending July 31, 19--

Sales . . . . $*1,500.00*

Expenses:

Utilities _____ expense . . . . $ *25.00*

Salary _____ expense . . . . $ *375.00*

Supplies _____ expense . . . . $ *125.00*

Rent _____ expense . . . . $ *100.00*

Depreciation _____ expense . . . . $ *20.00*

   Total expenses . . . . $ *845.00*

Net income . . . . $ *655.00*

29. The Balance Sheet may now be completed using the adjusted account balances from the Balance Sheet columns of the Worksheet. There is one item, though, that cannot be directly entered--owner's equity. The month of July brought about two changes in Terry Mitty's capital account:

   (1) his company had a net income of $655,
   (2) he withdrew $800 from his personal account.

The <u>withdrawal</u>, of course, represents a <u>decrease</u> <u>in</u> <u>the</u> <u>capital</u> <u>account</u>. The <u>net</u> <u>income</u> <u>of</u> <u>the</u> <u>business</u> <u>represents</u> <u>an</u> <u>increase</u> <u>in</u> <u>capital</u> and belongs to the owner of the business.   The balance of Terry-Mitty's capital account as of July 31 is

$5000 plus (a) $_____ minus (b) $_____ = (c) $_____
(Mitty's original
investment)

– – – – – – – – – – – – – –

$5000 + (a) $655 – (b) $800 = (c) $4855

30.   Since the Terry Mitty drawing account is subtracted from the Terry Mitty capital account, this is now taken into consideration in the owner's-equity entry of the Balance Sheet.   Therefore, the drawing account

_____ be shown on the Balance Sheet.
(should/should not)

– – – – – – – – – – – – – – –

should not

31.   Use the information on the Worksheet in Frame 25 (the balance sheet columns) to complete Ter-Mit's Balance Sheet that follows (take care to use the proper capital-account entry):

TER-MIT EXTERMINATORS

Balance Sheet
July 31, 19--

ASSETS
  Current Assets:

    _____ . . . . $ _____

    _____ . . . . $ _____

    _____ . . . . $ _____

  Total Current Assets . . . . $ _____

  Plant Assets:

    _____ . . . . $ _____

    Less Accumulated _____ . $ _____

  Total Plant Assets . . . . $ _____

Total Assets . . . . $ _____

LIABILITIES
  Current Liabilities

    _____ payable . . . . . $ _____

    _____ payable . . . . . $ _____

  Total Liabilities . . . . $ _____

OWNER'S EQUITY

    _____ . . . . $ _____

Total Liabilities and Owner's Equity . . . . $ _____

Answer

TER-MIT EXTERMINATORS

Balance Sheet
July 31, 19--

ASSETS
  Current Assets:

Cash .... $ 4,375.00

Supplies .... $ 75.00

Prepaid rent .... $ 200.00

Total Current Assets. . . . . $ 4,650.00

Long-Term Assets:

Equipment .... $ 500.00

Less Accumulated Depreciation . $ 20.00

Total Long-Term Assets . . . . $ 480.00

Total Assets . . . . $ 5,130.00

LIABILITIES
  Current Liabilities

Accounts payable . . . . . $ 200.00

Salary payable . . . . . $ 75.00

Total Liabilities . . . . $ 275.00

OWNER'S EQUITY

Terry Mitty, Capital .... $ 4,855.00

Total Liabilities and Owner's Equity. . . . . $ 5,130.00

---

32. In addition to the Balance Sheet and the Income Statement, many other
financial statements may be prepared; these would be described in more advanced accounting books. One, which we will present briefly, is the Owner's
Capital Statement. This statement shows (for a particular accounting period)
the changes that have taken place in the Owner's Equity Account. Use the
information from the Worksheet in Frame 25 to complete Ter-Mit's Owner's
Capital Statement reproduced on the following page:

```
┌─────────────────────────────────────────────────────────┐
│                                                           │
│                 TER-MIT EXTERMINATORS                     │
│                                                           │
│                Owner's Capital Statement                  │
│                  Month of July, 19--                      │
│                                                           │
│  Balance at beginning of period . . . . . . . . . . $ _____    │
│                                                           │
│     Net _____ for period . . . . . . . . . $ _____     │
│                                                           │
│     Sum or difference. . . . . . . . . . . . . . . $ _____     │
│                                                           │
│     _____ for period . . . . . . . . . $  800.00       │
│                                                           │
│  Balance in Capital Account at end of period . . . . . $ _____  │
│                                                           │
└─────────────────────────────────────────────────────────┘
```

– – – – – – – – – – – – – – – – –

```
┌─────────────────────────────────────────────────────────┐
│                                                           │
│                 TER-MIT EXTERMINATORS                     │
│                                                           │
│                Owner's Capital Statement                  │
│                  Month of July, 19--                      │
│                                                           │
│  Balance at beginning of period . . . . . . . . . . $ 5000.00   │
│                                                           │
│     Net  income  for period . . . . . . . . . . $  655.00       │
│                                                           │
│     Sum or difference. . . . . . . . . . . . . . . $ 5655.00    │
│                                                           │
│     Withdrawal for period . . . . . . . . . . $  800.00         │
│                                                           │
│  Balance in Capital Account at end of period . . . . . $ 4855.00 │
│                                                           │
└─────────────────────────────────────────────────────────┘
```

Self-Teaching Section C

MAKING ADJUSTING ENTRIES

33. So far, the entries that record adjustments to the accounts' balances appear only on the Worksheet. The accounts in the Ledger do not yet reflect these adjustments. As always, however, before the entries are made in the Ledger, they must first be recorded in the _____.

– – – – – – – – – – – – – – –

   Journal

34. Here on page two of Ter-Mit's Journal is given the adjusting entry for supplies and supplies expense. This information was taken from the adjustment column of the Worksheet (Frame 25). Journalize the remaining entries:

General Journal

Page 2

	Date	Description	p.r.	Debit	Credit
	19—				
1		*Adjusting Entries*			
2					
3	July 31	Supplies expense		12500	
4		Supplies			12500
5					
6					
7					
8					
9					
10					
11					
12					
13					
14					

- - - - - - - - - - - - - - -

General Journal

Page 2

	Date	Description	p.r.	Debit	Credit
	19—				
1		*Adjusting Entries*			
2					
3	July 31	Supplies expense		12500	
4		Supplies			12500
5					
6	31	Rent expense		10000	
7		Prepaid rent			10000
8					
9	31	Salary expense		7500	
10		Salary payable			7500
11					
12	31	Depreciation expense		2000	
13		Accumulated depreciation			2000
14					

35. Now that the adjusting entries have been journalized, they may be

_____ .

- - - - - - - - - - - - - - -

posted to the Ledger

36. Below is Ter-Mit's <u>supplies expense account</u> showing the properly posted debit portion of the first adjusting entry in the Journal:

Account: Supplies expense   Account Number: 52

Date	Item	p.r.	Debit	Date	Item	p.r.	Credit
July 31	adj.	2	125 00				

Notice that an adjusting entry looks like any other Ledger entry with the exception of the abbreviation (a) _____ in the (b) _____ column.

- - - - - - - - - - - - - - -

(a) adj.; (b) item

37. Using the Journal information in Frame 34, post the adjusting entries to the following accounts (remember, debits first):

Account: Supplies   Account Number: 14

Date	Item	p.r.	Debit	Date	Item	p.r.	Credit
July 2		1	200 00				

Account: Prepaid rent   Account Number: 15

Date	Item	p.r.	Debit	Date	Item	p.r.	Credit
July 2		1	300 00				

Account: Accumulated depreciation   Account Number: 19

Date	Item	p.r.	Debit	Date	Item	p.r.	Credit

Account: Salary payable   Account Number: 22

Date	Item	p.r.	Debit	Date	Item	p.r.	Credit

Account: Rent expense   Account Number: 53

Date	Item	p.r.	Debit	Date	Item	p.r.	Credit

Account: Depreciation expense   Account Number: 54

Date	Item	p.r.	Debit	Date	Item	p.r.	Credit

Account: Salary expense   Account Number: 57

Date	Item	p.r.	Debit	Date	Item	p.r.	Credit
July 12		1	250 00				
26		1	250 00				
			500 00				

- - - - - - - - - - - - - - - -

Answer

Account: Supplies   Account Number: 14

Date	Item	p.r.	Debit	Date	Item	p.r.	Credit
July 2		1	200 00	July 31	Adj.	2	125 00

Account: Prepaid rent   Account Number: 15

Date	Item	p.r.	Debit	Date	Item	p.r.	Credit
July 2		1	300 00	July 31	Adj.	2	100 00

Account: Accumulated depreciation   Account Number: 19

Date	Item	p.r.	Debit	Date	Item	p.r.	Credit
				July 31	Adj.	2	20 00

Account: Salary payable   Account Number: 22

Date	Item	p. r.	Debit	Date	Item	p. r.	Credit
				July 31	Adj.	2	75 00

Account: Rent expense   Account Number: 53

Date	Item	p. r.	Debit	Date	Item	p. r.	Credit
July 31	Adj.	2	1 00 00				

Account: Depreciation expense   Account Number: 54

Date	Item	p. r.	Debit	Date	Item	p. r.	Credit
July 31	Adj.	2	20 00				

Account: Salary expense   Account Number: 57

Date	Item	p. r.	Debit	Date	Item	p. r.	Credit
July 12		1	250 00				
26		1	250 00				
31	Adj.	2	500 00 / 75 00				

SELF-TEST

This Self-Test will show you whether or not you have mastered the chapter objectives and are ready to go on to the next chapter. Answer each question to the best of your ability. Correct answers and instructions are given at the end of the test.

1. Define <u>Accrual</u> <u>Basis</u> <u>Accounting</u>: _____

_____

_____

2. Define <u>Cash</u> <u>Basis</u> <u>Accounting</u>: _____

_____

_____

3. Ace Plumbing's supplies inventory on June 1 was $800. During the month an additional $250 worth of supplies was purchased. The June 30 inventory was $600. Show the necessary adjustments below:

Account Title	Trial Balance		Adjustment	
	Debit	Credit	Debit	Credit
1 *Supplies*	1050 00			
2 *Supplies expense*				
3				

4. Eric Jansen of Jansen Realty pays his secretary a salary of $145 on Friday for a 5-day week ending on that day. Show the Journal entry to record the necessary adjustment assuming that the accounting period (the last day of the month) ends on (a) Wednesday, (b) Thursday:

(a)

(b)

5. Larry's Sanitation Service collected, on April 1, $20 for the collection of 4-months' worth of garbage. The transaction was recorded on April 1 as:

Cash $20
    Unearned fees $20

Show the Journal entry to record the necessary adjustment on April 30:

6. The equipment belonging to Collins Electrical Service is depreciated $65 per month. Show the Journal entry that records the monthly depreciation adjustment:

7. There follows a Worksheet and three financial statements. A Trial Balance for Sidney's Shoe Repair for the month ending May 31 has been entered on the Worksheet. Use the data provided below to adjust the Trial Balance.

Adjustment data:
    Supplies used during May . . . . $ 65
    Prepaid rent expired 200
    One-day salary payable 90
    Equipment depreciation 5

Complete the Worksheet, then prepare each of the financial statements. (Note: When adding account titles to the Worksheet, use any title you think is adequately descriptive and consistent with the other titles given. In practice, the precise title used may vary with the business situation.)

SIDNEY'S SHOE REPAIR

Worksheet
For the month ended May 31, 19--

	Account Title	Trial Balance Debit	Trial Balance Credit	Adjustments Debit	Adjustments Credit	Income Statement Debit	Income Statement Credit	Balance Sheet Debit	Balance Sheet Credit
1	Cash	252000							
2	Supplies	11500							
3	Prepaid rent	80000							
4	Equipment	50000							
5	Accounts payable		25000						
6	Sidney, capital		220000						
7	Sidney, drawing	125000							
8	Fees		470000						
9	Salary expense	180000							
10	Utilities expense	4500							
11	Miscellaneous expense	12000							
12		715000	715000						
13									
14									
15									
16									
17									
18									
19									
20									
21									
22									

SIDNEY'S SHOE REPAIR

Income Statement
Month Ending May 31, 19--

Sales . . . . $ _____

Expenses:

_____ expense . . . $ _____

_____ expense . . . $ _____

_____ expense . . . $ _____

_____ expense . . . $ _____

_____ expense . . . $ _____

_____ expense . . . $ _____

Total expenses . . . . $ _____

Net income . . . . $ _____

SIDNEY'S SHOE REPAIR

Owner's Capital Statement
Month of May, 19--

_____ at beginning of period . . . . . . $ _____

Net _____ for the period . . . . $ _____

Sum or difference . . . . $ _____

_____ for the period . . . . $ _____

Balance in Capital Account at end of period . . . . . $ _____

SIDNEY'S SHOE REPAIR

Balance Sheet
May 31, 19--

ASSETS
  Current Assets:

  _____ . . . . $ _____

  _____ . . . . $ _____

  _____ . . . . $ _____

  Total Current Assets . . . . $ _____

  Long-Term Assets:

  _____ . . . . $ _____

  Less Accumulated _____ . $ _____

  Total Long-Term Assets . . . . $ _____

Total Assets . . . . $ _____

LIABILITIES
  Current Liabilities:

  _____ payable . . . . . $ _____

  _____ payable . . . . . $ _____

Total Liabilities . . . . $ _____

OWNER'S EQUITY

  _____ . . . . $ _____

Total Liabilities and Owner's Equity . . . . $ _____

8. Using the data from the Worksheet provided in Question 7, write out all adjusting entries in simplified Journal form below:

Self-Test Answers

Compare your answers to the Self-Test with the correct answers given below. If all of your answers are correct, you are ready to go on to the next chapter. If you missed any questions, study the frames indicated in parentheses following the answer. If you miss many questions, go over the entire chapter carefully.

1. Accrual Basis Accounting accounts for all transactions that occurred during an accounting period, whether or not cash was actually received or disbursed. (Frames 7-10)

2. Cash Basis Accounting accounts only for cash received or disbursed during the accounting period. (Frames 7-10)

3.

Account Title	Trial Balance		Adjustment	
	Debit	Credit	Debit	Credit
1 Supplies	1050 00			450 00
2 Supplies expense			450 00	
3				

(Frames 1-6; 11-20)

4. (a) Salary expense $87
        Salary payable $87

   (b) Salary expense $116
        Salary payable . . . . $116   (Frames 33-37)

5. Unearned fees $5
        (Fee income) Sales . . . . $5   (Frames 33-37)

6. Depreciation expense $65
       Accumulated depreciation. . . . . $65   (Frames 33-37)

7. Examine the answer to this question which is given on the following pages in great detail. You should have filled in the blank forms exactly as shown on the pages that follow. If you did not answer this question correctly, be sure you understand what you did wrong before you proceed.

    If you made errors, you may need to examine the entire chapter since this question is so comprehensive. If you had special trouble doing adjustments, examine Frames 1-6 and 11-20. If you had difficulty completing the rest of the Worksheet, examine Frames 21-27. If you had difficulty with the financial statements, carefully review Frames 28-32.

8. You should have written the following:

        Rent expense $200
           Prepaid rent $200

        Supplies expense $65
           Supplies. $65

        Depreciation expense $5
           Accumulated depreciation $5

        Salary expense $90
           Salary payable . . . . $90   (Frames 33-37)

SIDNEY'S SHOE REPAIR

Worksheet
May 31, 19--

	Trial Balance		Adjustments		Income Statement		Balance Sheet	
Account Title	Debit	Credit	Debit	Credit	Debit	Credit	Debit	Credit
1 Cash	252000						252000	
2 Supplies	11500			6500			5000	
3 Prepaid rent	80000			20000			60000	
4 Equipment	50000						50000	
5 Accounts payable		25000						25000
6 Sidney, capital		220000						220000
7 Sidney, drawing	125000						125000	
8 Fees		470000				470000		
9 Salary expense	180000		9000		189000			
10 Utilities expense	4500				4500			
11 Miscellaneous expense	12000				12000			
12	715000	715000						
13								
14 Rent expense			20000		20000			
15 Supplies expense			6500		6500			
16 Accumulated depreciation				500				500
17 Depreciation expense			500		500			
18 Salary payable				9000				9000
19			36000	36000	232500	470000	492000	254500
20 Net income					237500			237500
21					470000	470000	492000	492000
22								

SIDNEY'S SHOE REPAIR

Income Statement
Month Ending May 31, 19--

Sales . . . . $ *4,700.00*

Expenses:

Salary _____ expense . . . $ *1,890.00*

Utilities _____ expense . . . $ *45.00*

Miscellaneous expense . . . $ *120.00*

Rent _____ expense . . . $ *200.00*

Supplies _____ expense . . . $ *65.00*

Depreciation expense . . . $ *5.00*

Total expenses. $ *2,325.00*

Net income. . . . . $ *2,375.00*

SIDNEY'S SHOE REPAIR

Owner's Capital Statement
Month of May, 19--

Balance _____ at beginning of period . . . . . . $ *2,200.00*

Net *income* _____ for the period. . . . . $ *2,375.00*

Sum or difference . . . . $ *4,575.00*

Withdrawals for the period. . . . . $ *(1,250.00)*

Balance in Capital Account at end of period . . . . . $ *3,325.00*

SIDNEY'S SHOE REPAIR

Balance Sheet
May 31, 19--

ASSETS
  Current Assets:

    Cash . . . . $ *2,520.00*

    Prepaid rent . . . . $ *600.00*

    Supplies . . . . $ *50.00*

  Total Current Assets . . . . $ *3,170.00*

  Long-Term Assets:

    Equipment . . . . $ *500.00*

    Less Accumulated *Depreciation* . $ *5.00*

  Total Long-Term Assets . . . . $ *495.00*

Total Assets . . . . $ *3,665.00*

LIABILITIES
  Current Liabilities:

    Accounts payable . . . . . $ *250.00*

    Salaries payable . . . . . $ *90.00*

Total Liabilities . . . . $ *340.00*

OWNER'S EQUITY

    Sidney Capital . . . . $ *3,325.00*

Total Liabilities and Owner's Equity . . . . $ *3,665.00*

CHAPTER FIVE

The Accounting Cycle III:
Closing the Books

OBJECTIVES

When you complete this chapter, you will be able to

- journalize closing entries in the standard two-column Journal,

- post all closing entries in the Ledger,

- rule and balance all accounts,

- prepare a Post-Closing Trial Balance.

If you feel that you have already mastered these objectives and might skip all or part of this chapter, turn to the end of this chapter and take the Self-Test. The results will tell you what frames of the chapter you should study. If you answer all questions correctly, you are ready to begin the next chapter.

If this material is new to you, or if you choose not to take the Self-Test now, turn to the Overview and Self-Teaching Sections that follow.

CHAPTER OVERVIEW

This chapter will continue to deal with the steps necessary to prepare the Ledger for the next accounting cycle. After the financial statements have been prepared, but before any transactions occurring in the next accounting period may be recorded, the procedure called <u>closing the books</u> must be undertaken. In closing the books, these steps must be followed:

      (a) Closing entries must be journalized.
      (b) Closing entries must be posted to the Ledger.
      (c) The accounts in the Ledger must be ruled and balanced.
      (d) A Post-Closing Trial Balance must be prepared.

MAKING CLOSING ENTRIES

All revenues resulting from the operations of a business belong to the owner of the business, and so must eventually be credited to the owner's capital account. Likewise, all expenses of the business are ultimately paid for by the owner and so must eventually be debited to the owner's capital account. This is done in an accounting procedure called <u>making closing entries</u>. Generally speaking, in closing entries

      (a) the balances of all of the revenue accounts are credited to (added to) the owner's capital account,
      (b) the balances of all of the expense accounts are debited to (deducted from) the owner's capital account,
      (c) the balance of the owner's drawing account is debited to (deducted from) the owner's capital account.

The overall effect of the closing procedure is to

      (a) bring the balances of all revenue, expense, and drawing accounts to zero (i.e., to <u>close</u> these accounts),
      (b) increase the capital account by the amount of net income (or to decrease it by the amount of net loss).

The closing procedure is often accomplished through the use of an interim summary account called the <u>expense and revenue summary</u>. Closing entries are journalized and posted in the usual way.

BALANCING AND RULING THE ACCOUNTS

When all closing entries have been posted to the Ledger, all accounts have their balances computed. Lines are then ruled beneath the last entries to segregate them from the transactions to be recorded during the next accounting period.

POST-CLOSING TRIAL BALANCE

As a final check on the equality of all debits and credits, add the debit balances and the credit balances from the Ledger; then compare the two totals. This procedure is known as preparing the Post-Closing Trial Balance.

Self-Teaching Section A

MAKING CLOSING ENTRIES

1. All of the revenues received by a company belong to the owners of the company. Likewise, all of the expenses incurred by a company must be borne by those same owners. In fact, the revenue and expense accounts of a company can be thought of as temporary subdivisions of the owner's

_____ account.

– – – – – – – – – – – – – – –

   capital

2. Before the accounting cycle is brought to a close, the records must reflect the fact that the owner has received all the revenues for the period and has absorbed all the expenses for the same period. Another way of putting

this is to say that (a) _____ must be debited to the owner's

capital account and that (b) _____ must be credited to the owner's capital account.

– – – – – – – – – – – – – – –

   (a) expenses; (b) revenues

3. At the end of the accounting cycle, all revenues and expenses are transferred to the owner's capital account in a series of entries called closing entries. At this point, the balance of the owner's drawing account (the amount withdrawn during the accounting period by the owner for his personal use) is also deducted from the owner's capital account.

   The steps in posting all closing entries to the Ledger for a hypothetical company named Pachyderm Ice Cream, Inc., are shown on the following page.

   The diagram uses T-accounts, which are simplified account forms used only for instructional purposes. The account title is put on top of the horizontal line. The vertical line divides the lower area into two areas, a left side for debits and a right side for credits. Closing entries are shown with asterisks (*). The steps in the closing procedure are numbered in boxes. Refer to this diagram when working Frames 4 through 8.

Procedure for Closing Entries:

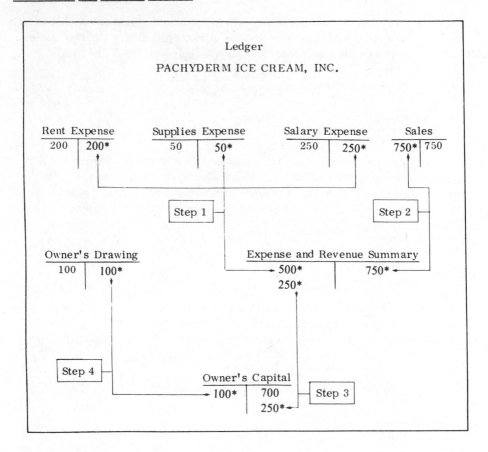

4. Closing Entries: Step 1

(a) Before closing, each expense account has a_____ balance.
(debit/credit)

(b) Step 1 of the closing procedure requires that each expense account be

_____ for the amount of its balance.
(debited/credited)

(c) The sum of all expenses is then _____ to an account
(debited/credited)

called the _____ account.

(d) After Step 1, the balance in each expense account is $_____.

— — — — — — — — — — — — — — —

(a) debit; (b) credited; (c) debited, expense and revenue summary,
(d) 0, or nothing

5. Closing Entries: Step 2

(a) Before closing, the revenue account (sales or fees) has a _____
     (debit/credit)
     balance.

(b) Step 2 of the closing procedure requires that the revenue account be

     _____ for the amount of its balance.
     (debited/credited)

(c) The revenue amount is then _____ to the _____
                                 (debited/credited)
     _____ account.

(d) After Step 2, the balance of the revenue account is $_____.

- - - - - - - - - - - - - - - -

(a) credit; (b) debited; (c) credited, expense and revenue summary;
(d) 0, or nothing

6. Closing Entries: Step 3

(a) The total revenue ($750) exceeds the total expenses ($500), so the

     expense and revenue summary shows a net _____ of $_____.

(b) The expense and revenue summary is _____ for the
                                        (debited/credited)

     amount of net _____ and the _____

     account is _____ for the same amount.

(c) After Step 3, the balance of the expense and revenue account is

     $_____.

- - - - - - - - - - - - - - - -

(a) income, $250; (b) debited, income, owner's capital, credited; (d) 0, or
nothing

7. Closing Entries: Step 4

(a) Before closing, the owner's drawing account has a _____
                                                       (debit/credit)
     balance.

(b) Step 4 of the closing procedure requires that the owner's drawing ac-

     count be _____ for the amount of its balance.
              (debited/credited)

(c) The balance of the drawing account is then _____ to the
                                                (debited/credited)
     _____ account.

(d) After Step 4, the balance of the drawing account is $_____.

― ― ― ― ― ― ― ― ― ― ― ― ― ― ―

(a) debit; (b) credited; (c) debited, owner's capital; (d) 0, or nothing

8. Name the four accounts that are closed (have their balances brought to zero) in the closing process:

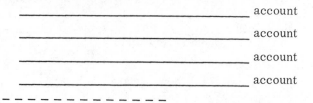

_____ account

_____ account

_____ account

_____ account

― ― ― ― ― ― ― ― ― ― ― ― ― ― ―

expense; revenue; expense and revenue summary; and owner's drawing (in any order)

9. In a business showing a profit, the overall effect of the closing procedure on the owner's capital account is (a) to decrease the capital account by the amount of the _____ account's balance, and (b) to increase the capital account by the amount of net _____.

― ― ― ― ― ― ― ― ― ― ― ― ― ― ―

(a) owner's drawing; (b) income

10. If the company had suffered a <u>net loss</u>, the amount of the loss would have been (a)_____ to the expense and revenue summary account and
(debited/credited)

(b)_____ to the capital account.
(debited/credited)

― ― ― ― ― ― ― ― ― ― ― ― ― ― ―

(a) credited; (b) debited

11. We demonstrated the closing procedure by using the <u>adjusted</u> accounts in the Ledger. In practice, however, closing entries are first journalized and then posted. The information that is journalized may come either from the adjusted Ledger or the Worksheet. In our demonstration we used the information from the Ledger. This time, use it to journalize all the closing entries on the General Journal form that follows. The entry for closing the expense accounts is already entered for you.

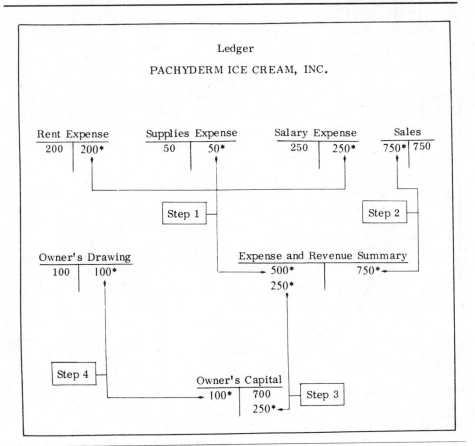

Ledger

PACHYDERM ICE CREAM, INC.

General Journal

Page 3

Date	Description	p.r.	Debit	Credit
19 –				
	Closing Entries			
Dec. 31	Expense and Revenue Summary		500 00	
	Rent expense			200 00
	Supplies expense			50 00
	Salary expense			250 00

Answer

General Journal

Date	Description	p.r.	Debit	Credit
19—				
	Closing Entries			
Dec 31	Expense and Revenue Summary		500 00	
	Rent expense			200 00
	Supplies expense			50 00
	Salary expense			250 00
31	Sales		750 00	
	Expense and Revenue Summary			750 00
31	Expense and Revenue Summary		250 00	
	Owner's capital			250 00
31	Owner's capital		100 00	
	Owner's drawing			100 00

12. In common practice, it is usually easier to obtain the closing information from the company's Worksheet than it is to take it from the Ledger. It
is easier because the Worksheet shows all adjusted account balances on a
single page. For more practice in making closing entries in the General
Journal, we have reproduced part of the Ter-Mit Worksheet. Use the information provided to journalize all Ter-Mit's closing entries on the General
Journal form that follows. If you need help with the journal format, refer
to Frame 11.

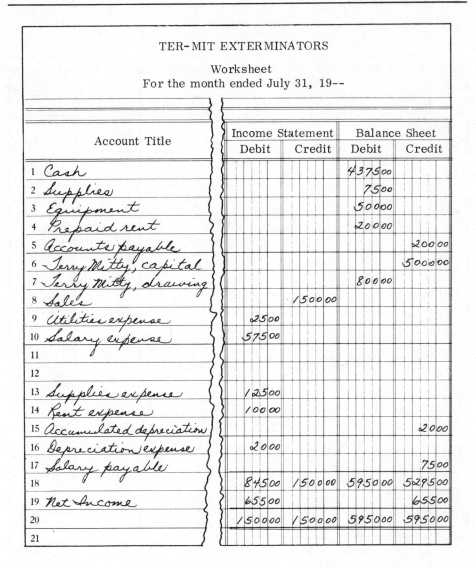

TER-MIT EXTERMINATORS

Worksheet

For the month ended July 31, 19--

Account Title	Income Statement		Balance Sheet	
	Debit	Credit	Debit	Credit
1 Cash			4375 00	
2 Supplies			75 00	
3 Equipment			500 00	
4 Prepaid rent			200 00	
5 Accounts payable				200 00
6 Terry Mitty, capital				5000 00
7 Terry Mitty, drawing			800 00	
8 Sales		1500 00		
9 Utilities expense	25 00			
10 Salary expense	575 00			
11				
12				
13 Supplies expense	125 00			
14 Rent expense	100 00			
15 Accumulated depreciation				20 00
16 Depreciation expense	20 00			
17 Salary payable				75 00
18	845 00	1500 00	5950 00	5295 00
19 Net Income	655 00			655 00
20	1500 00	1500 00	5950 00	5950 00
21				

General Journal

Page 3

Date	Description	p.r.	Debit	Credit

- - - - - - - - - - - - - - - -

General Journal

Page 3

Date	Description	p.r.	Debit	Credit
19—				
	Closing Entries			
July 31	Expense and Revenue Summary		845 00	
	Supplies expense			125 00
	Salary expense			575 00
	Rent expense			100 00
	Depreciation expense			20 00
	Utilities expense			25 00
31	Sales		1500 00	
	Expense and Revenue Summary			1500 00
31	Expense and Revenue Summary		655 00	
	Terry Mitty, capital			655 00
31	Terry Mitty, capital		800 00	
	Terry Mitty, drawing			800 00

13.   After all closing entries are journalized, they are posted to the Ledger. The posting of closing entries is similar to the posting of any other transaction, except that the word "closing" is written in the item column of the entry. Below are all Ter-Mit's accounts that require a closing entry. Use the journalized information in Frame 12 to post the closing entries. The first closing entry—that for the expense and revenue summary (account 33)—is done for you.

Account: J. Mitty, capital   Account Number: 31

Date	Item	p.r.	Debit	Date	Item	p.r.	Credit
				19— July 1		1	5000 00

Account: J. Mitty, drawing   Account Number: 32

Date	Item	p.r.	Debit	Date	Item	p.r.	Credit
19— July 31		1	800 00				

Account: Expense and Revenue Summary   Account Number: 33

Date	Item	p.r.	Debit	Date	Item	p.r.	Credit
19— July 31	Closing	3	845 00				

Account: Sales   Account Number: 41

Date	Item	p.r.	Debit	Date	Item	p.r.	Credit
				19— July 31		1	1500 00

Account: Salary expense   Account Number: 51

Date	Item	p.r.	Debit	Date	Item	p.r.	Credit
19— July 12		1	250 00				
26		1	250 00				
31	adj.	2	500 00 75 00				

Account: Supplies expense   Account Number: 52

Date	Item	p.r.	Debit	Date	Item	p.r.	Credit
19— July 31	adj.	2	12500				

Account: Rent expense   Account Number: 53

Date	Item	p.r.	Debit	Date	Item	p.r.	Credit
19— July 31	adj.	2	10000				

Account: Depreciation expense   Account Number: 54

Date	Item	p.r.	Debit	Date	Item	p.r.	Credit
19— July 31	adj.	2	2000				

Account: Utilities expense   Account Number: 55

Date	Item	p.r.	Debit	Date	Item	p.r.	Credit
19— July 31		2	2500				

– – – – – – – – – – – – – – –

Answer

Account: J. Mitty, capital   Account Number: 31

Date	Item	p.r.	Debit	Date	Item	p.r.	Credit
19— July 31	closing	3	80000	19— July 1		1	500000
				31	Closing	3	65500

Account: J. Mitty, drawing   Account Number: 32

Date	Item	p.r.	Debit	Date	Item	p.r.	Credit
19— July 31		1	80000	19— July 31	Closing	3	80000

Account: Expense and Revenue Summary   Account Number: 33

Date	Item	p. r.	Debit	Date	Item	p. r.	Credit
^{19—} July 31	Closing	3	845 00	^{19—} July 31	Closing	3	1500 00
31	Closing	3	655 00				

Account: Sales   Account Number: 41

Date	Item	p. r.	Debit	Date	Item	p. r.	Credit
^{19—} July 31	Closing	3	1500 00	^{19—} July 31		1	1500 00

Account: Salary expense   Account Number: 51

Date	Item	p. r.	Debit	Date	Item	p. r.	Credit
^{19—} July 12		1	250 00	^{19—} July 31	Closing	3	575 00
26		1	250 00				
31	adj.	2	500 00				
			75 00				

Account: Supplies expense   Account Number: 52

Date	Item	p. r.	Debit	Date	Item	p. r.	Credit
^{19—} July 31	adj.	2	125 00	^{19—} July 31	Closing	3	125 00

Account: Rent expense   Account Number: 53

Date	Item	p. r.	Debit	Date	Item	p. r.	Credit
^{19—} July 31	adj.	2	100 00	^{19—} July 31	Closing	3	100 00

Account: Depreciation expense   Account Number: 54

Date	Item	p. r.	Debit	Date	Item	p. r.	Credit
^{19—} July 31	adj.	2	20 00	^{19—} July 31	Closing	3	20 00

Account: *Utilities expense*   Account Number: 55

Date	Item	p. r.	Debit	Date	Item	p. r.	Credit
19— *July 31*		2	25 00	*19—* *July 31*	*Closing*	3	25 00

Self-Teaching Section B

BALANCING AND RULING OF THE ACCOUNTS

14. The effect of final balancing is to bring the balance of each account forward to be included in the next period's transactions. Certain <u>temporary</u>
accounts have been <u>closed</u> and will, therefore, have no balance (or, rather,
a zero balance) to bring forward.

  For each of the accounts below, write a "0" if the account is closed and
will have no balance to be brought forward. Write "B" if the account has not
been closed and will therefore have a balance to be brought forward.

_____ a. owner's capital account

_____ b. sales account

_____ c. supplies expense account

_____ d. supplies account

_____ e. accumulated depreciation account

_____ f. cash account

_____ g. expense and revenue summary account

_____ h. owner's drawing account

— — — — — — — — — — — — — — — —

  (a) B; (b) 0; (c) 0; (d) B; (e) B; (f) B; (g) 0; (h) 0

15. Generally speaking, closing is done by totaling the debits and credits for
each account and then ruling a double line across all columns on the account
page, except the item columns.

  The procedure of balancing and ruling the accounts is slightly different
for the <u>closed</u> accounts than it is for the <u>unclosed</u> accounts.

  The salary expense account, a <u>closed</u> account, is ruled and balanced as
follows:

Account: *Salary expense*   Account Number: *51*

Date	Item	p.r.	Debit	Date	Item	p.r.	Credit
19— July 12		1	250 00	19— July 31	Closing	3	575 00
26		1	250 00				
31	Adj.	2	75 00				
			575 00				575 00

Notice that the sums of the debit and credit columns are determined and entered below a single line. Then, two lines are drawn beneath the totals and usually all other columns except the item columns.

Here is Ter-Mit's expense and revenue summary. Rule and balance this <u>closed</u> account:

Account: *Expense and Revenue Summary*   Account Number: *33*

Date	Item	p.r.	Debit	Date	Item	p.r.	Credit
19— July 31	Closing	3	845 00	19— July 31	Closing	3	1500 00
31	Closing	3	655 00				

- - - - - - - - - - - - - -

Account: *Expense and Revenue Summary*   Account Number: *33*

Date	Item	p.r.	Debit	Date	Item	p.r.	Credit
19— July 31	Closing	3	845 00	19— July 31	Closing	3	1500 00
31	Closing	3	655 00				
			1500 00				1500 00

16. All the unclosed accounts have <u>nonzero</u> <u>balances</u>, which are recorded as the first amount in the next accounting period. An example of the ruling and balancing of an unclosed account is illustrated on the following page.

In ruling and balancing the Terry Mitty, capital account, notice the following.

    (a) The balance of the account is written <u>on the first available line</u> in the smaller of the two sides so that when they are added, the debits and credits will be equal.

Account: J. Mitty, capital   Account Number: 31

Date	Item	p.r.	Debit	Date	Item	p.r.	Credit
July 31	Closing	3	800 00	July 1		1	5000 00
31	Balance	✓	4855 00	31	Closing	3	655 00
			5655 00				5655 00
				Aug 1	Balance	✓	4855 00

(b) "Balance" is written in the item column and a check mark is made in the "p.r." column to distinguish the entry from a posted entry.

(c) The two sides are then totaled to prove their equality.

(d) Double lines are drawn beneath these totals across all columns except the item columns.

(e) The balance of the account is written beneath the double ruling on the side of the account that was larger to begin with.

(f) The word "balance" is written in the item column next to the last entry. A check mark is placed in the "p.r." column.

(g) This last entry is dated with the first date of the next period.

If an account has only one single entry, it is not balanced and ruled, but is left as it is.

Use this procedure to balance Ter-Mit's cash account:

Account: Cash   Account Number: 11

Date	Item	p.r.	Debit	Date	Item	p.r.	Credit
July 1		1	5000 00	July 2		1	300 00
31		1	1500 00	2		1	200 00
	4,375.00		6500 00	14		1	25 00
				15		1	250 00
				20		1	300 00
				31		1	800 00
				31		1	250 00
							2125 00

Account: *Cash*   Account Number: *11*

Date	Item	p.r.	Debit	Date	Item	p.r.	Credit
July 1		1	5000 00	July 2		1	300 00
31		1	1500 00	2		1	200 00
	4,375.00		6500 00	14		1	25 00
				15		1	250 00
				20		1	300 00
				31		1	800 00
				31		1	250 00
				31	Balance	✓	2125 00 4375 00
			6500 00				6500 00
Aug 1	Balance	✓	4375 00				

17. For practice, here are two more of Ter-Mit's accounts for you to close:

Account: *Supplies*   Account Number: *14*

Date	Item	p.r.	Debit	Date	Item	p.r.	Credit
July 2		1	200 00	July 31	adj.	2	125 00

Account: *Accumulated depreciation*   Account Number: *19*

Date	Item	p.r.	Debit	Date	Item	p.r.	Credit
				July 31	adj.	2	20 00

Account: *Supplies* Account Number: 14

Date	Item	p. r.	Debit	Date	Item	p. r.	Credit
July 2		1	20000	July 31	Adj.	2	12500
				31	Balance	✓	7500
			20000				20000
Aug. 1	Balance	✓	7500				

Account: *Accumulated depreciation* Account Number: 19

Date	Item	p. r.	Debit	Date	Item	p. r.	Credit
				July 31	Adj.	2	2000

Self-Teaching Section C

POST-CLOSING TRIAL BALANCE

18. When all the accounts in the Ledger have been ruled and balanced, only one step remains in the accounting cycle--all of the debit balances must be summed, all of the credit balances must be summed, and the two totals must be compared to test their equality. This procedure is known as taking a Post-Closing Trial Balance. Here is Ter-Mit's Post-Closing Trial Balance:

TER-MIT EXTERMINATORS

Post-Closing Trial Balance
July 31, 19--

Account	Debit	Credit
Cash	4375.00	
Supplies	75.00	
Equipment	500.00	
Prepaid rent	200.00	
Accumulated depreciation		20.00
Accounts payable		200.00
Terry Mitty, capital		4855.00
Salary payable		75.00
	5150.00	5150.00

Not all accounts appear here.   What is the nature of accounts that <u>do</u> <u>not</u> appear on the Post-Closing Trial Balance? _____

_____

— — — — — — — — — — — — — — —

They have been closed, or they have a zero balance, or they were temporary accounts.

SELF-TEST

This Self-Test will show you whether or not you have mastered the chapter objectives and are ready to go on to the next chapter. Answer each question to the best of your ability. Correct answers and instructions are given at the end of the test.

1. The entire Ledger for Sidney's Shoe Repair follows. All adjusting entries have been posted.

    (a) Use the information on the Worksheet that follows to journalize all closing entries in the standard two-column Journal.

    (b) Post all closing entries to the Ledger.

    (c) Rule and balance all accounts.

    (d) Prepare a Post-Closing Trial Balance.

SIDNEY'S SHOE REPAIR
Worksheet
For the month ended May 31, 19--

	Trial Balance		Adjustments		Income Statement		Balance Sheet	
Account Title	Debit	Credit	Debit	Credit	Debit	Credit	Debit	Credit
1 Cash	252000						252000	
2 Supplies	11500			6500			5000	
3 Prepaid rent	80000			20000			60000	
4 Equipment	50000						50000	
5 Accounts payable		25000						25000
6 Sidney, capital		220000						220000
7 Sidney, drawing	125000						125000	
8 Fees		470000				470000		
9 Salary expense	180000		9000		189000			
10 Utilities expense	4500				4500			
11 Miscellaneous expense	12000				12000			
12	715000	715000						
13								
14 Rent expense			20000		20000			
15 Supplies expense			6500		6500			
16 Accumulated depreciation				500				500
17 Depreciation expense			500		500			
18 Salary payable				9000				9000
19			36000	36000	232500	470000	492000	254500
20 Net income					237500			237500
21					470000	470000	492000	492000
22								

(a) Journalize all closing entries.

General Journal

Date	Description	p.r.	Debit	Credit

(b) Post all closing entries to the Ledger.

Account: *Cash*　　　　　　　　　　　　　　　　　　　　Account Number: 11

Date	Item	p.r.	Debit	Date	Item	p.r.	Credit
19— May 1		1	2000 00	19— May 1		1	80 00
14		1	270 00	2		1	30 00
18		2	20 00	7		1	450 00
28		2	2000 00	7		1	85 00
	2,520.00		6900 00	8		1	125 00
				9		1	55 00
				14		1	450 00
				14		1	650 00
				17		2	65 00
				21		2	450 00
				22		2	125 00
				28		2	450 00
				28		2	600 00
				28		2	45 00
							4380 00

Account: *Supplies*   Account Number: *14*

Date	Item	p.r.	Debit	Date	Item	p.r.	Credit
19— May 2		1	30 00	19— May 31	adj.	3	65 00
7		1	85 00				

Account: *Prepaid rent*   Account Number: *15*

Date	Item	p.r.	Debit	Date	Item	p.r.	Credit
19— May 1		1	800 00	19— May 31	adj.	3	200 00

Account: *Equipment*   Account Number: *18*

Date	Item	p.r.	Debit	Date	Item	p.r.	Credit
19— May 2		1	500 00				

Account: *Accumulated depreciation*   Account Number: *19*

Date	Item	p.r.	Debit	Date	Item	p.r.	Credit
				19— May 31	adj.	3	5 00

Account: *Accounts payable*   Account Number: *21*

Date	Item	p.r.	Debit	Date	Item	p.r.	Credit
19— May 8		1	125 00	19— May 2		1	500 00
22		2	125 00		250.00		
			250 00				

Account: *Salary payable*   Account Number: 22

Date	Item	p.r.	Debit	Date	Item	p.r.	Credit
				'9– May 31	Adj.	3	90 00

Account: *Sidney, capital*   Account Number: 31

Date	Item	p.r.	Debit	Date	Item	p.r.	Credit
				'9– May 1		1	2000 00
				18		2	200 00
							2200 00

Account: *Sidney, drawing*   Account Number: 32

Date	Item	p.r.	Debit	Date	Item	p.r.	Credit
'9– May 14		1	650 00				
28		2	600 00				
			1250 00				

Account: *Expense and Revenue Summary*   Account Number: 33

Date	Item	p.r.	Debit	Date	Item	p.r.	Credit

Account: *Fees earned*   Account Number: 41

Date	Item	p.r.	Debit	Date	Item	p.r.	Credit
				'9– May 14		1	2700 00
						2	2000 00

Account: _Salary expense_   Account Number: 51

Date	Item	p. r.	Debit	Date	Item	p. r.	Credit
19— May 7		1	450 00				
14		1	450 00				
21		2	450 00				
28		2	450 00				
31	adj.	3	1 800 00 90 00				

Account: _Supplies expense_   Account Number: 52

Date	Item	p. r.	Debit	Date	Item	p. r.	Credit
19— May 31	Adj.	3	65 00				

Account: _Rent expense_   Account Number: 53

Date	Item	p. r.	Debit	Date	Item	p. r.	Credit
19— May 31	adj.	3	200 00				

Account: _Depreciation expense_   Account Number: 54

Date	Item	p. r.	Debit	Date	Item	p. r.	Credit
19— May 31	adj.	3	5 00				

Account: _Utilities expense_   Account Number: 55

Date	Item	p. r.	Debit	Date	Item	p. r.	Credit
19— May 28		2	45 00				

Account: *Miscellaneous expense*   Account Number: 59

Date	Item	p.r.	Debit	Date	Item	p.r.	Credit
May 9		1	5500				
17		2	6500				

(c) Rule and balance all accounts.

(d) Prepare a Post-Closing Trial Balance.

SIDNEY'S SHOE REPAIR

Post-Closing Trial Balance
May 31, 19--

Account	Debit	Credit

Self-Test Answers

Compare your answers to the Self-Test with the correct answers given below. If all of your answers are correct, you are ready to go on to the next chapter. If you missed any questions, study the frames indicated in parentheses following the answer. If you miss many questions, go over the entire chapter carefully.

Examine the answer to this question which is given on the following pages in great detail. You should have filled in the blank forms exactly as shown on the pages that follow. If you did not answer this question correctly, be sure you understand what you did wrong before you proceed.

If you made errors, you may need to examine the entire chapter since this question is so comprehensive. If you had special trouble use the guidelines below:

(a) Prepare Journal (Frames 1-12)
(b) Post entries to Ledger (Frame 13)
(c) Rule and balance accounts (Frames 14-17)
(d) Prepare Post-Closing Trial Balance (Frame 18)

Answer (a)

General Journal

Page 4

Date	Description	p.r.	Debit	Credit
19 –				
	Closing Entries			
May 31	Expense and Revenue Summary	33	2325 00	
	Salary expense	51		1890 00
	Utilities expense	55		45 00
	Miscellaneous expense	59		120 00
	Rent expense	53		200 00
	Supplies expense	52		65 00
	Depreciation expense	54		5 00
31	Fees	41	4700 00	
	Expense and Revenue Summary	33		4700 00
31	Expense and Revenue Summary	33	2375 00	
	Sidney, capital	31		2375 00
31	Sidney, capital	31	1250 00	
	Sidney, drawing	32		1250 00

Answers (b) and (c)

Account: *Cash* **Account Number:** 11

Date	Item	p.r.	Debit	Date	Item	p.r.	Credit
19– May 1		1	2 000 00	19– May 1		1	8 000 00
14		1	2 700 00	2		1	3 00 00
18		2	2 000 0	7		1	4 500 0
28	2,520.00	2	2 000 00	7		1	8 500
			6 900 00	8		1	1 250 0
				9		1	5 500
				14		1	4 500 0
				14		1	6 500 0
				17		2	6 500
				21		2	4 500 0
				22		2	1 250 0
				28		2	4 500 0
				28		2	6 000 0
				28		2	4 500
				31	Balance	✓	4 380 00 / 2 520 00
			6 900 00				6 900 00
June 1	Balance	✓	2 520 00				

Account: *Supplies* **Account Number:** 14

Date	Item	p.r.	Debit	Date	Item	p.r.	Credit
19– May 2		1	3 0 00	19– May 31	Adj.	3	6 5 00
7		1	8 5 00	31	Balance	✓	5 0 00
			1 1 5 00				1 1 5 00
June 1	Balance	✓	5 0 00				

Account: *Prepaid rent* **Account Number:** 15

Date	Item	p.r.	Debit	Date	Item	p.r.	Credit
19– May 1		1	8 00 00	19– May 31	Adj.	3	2 00 00
				31	Balance	✓	6 00 00
			8 00 00				8 00 00
June 1	Balance	✓	6 00 00				

Account: *Equipment*   Account Number: *18*

Date	Item	p. r.	Debit	Date	Item	p. r.	Credit
19— May 2		1	500 00				

Account: *Accumulated depreciation*   Account Number: *19*

Date	Item	p. r.	Debit	Date	Item	p. r.	Credit
				19— May 31	Adj.	3	5 00

Account: *Accounts payable*   Account Number: *21*

Date	Item	p. r.	Debit	Date	Item	p. r.	Credit
19— May 8		1	125 00	19— May 2	250.00	1	500 00
22		2	125 00				
31	Balance	✓	250 00 250 00				
			500 00				500 00
				June 1	Balance	✓	250 00

Account: *Salary payable*   Account Number: *22*

Date	Item	p. r.	Debit	Date	Item	p. r.	Credit
				19— May 31	Adj.	3	90 00

Account: *Sidney, capital*   Account Number: *31*

Date	Item	p. r.	Debit	Date	Item	p. r.	Credit
19— May 31	Closing	4	1250 00	19— May 1		1	2000 00
31	Balance	✓	3325 00	18		2	200 00
				31	Closing	4	2200 00 2375 00
			4575 00				4575 00
				June 1	Balance	✓	3325 00

Account: Sidney, drawing   Account Number: 32

Date		Item	p.r.	Debit	Date		Item	p.r.	Credit
'19– May	14		1	65000	'19– May	31	Closing	4	125000
	28		2	60000					
				125000					
				125000					125000

Account: Expense and Revenue Summary   Account Number: 33

Date		Item	p.r.	Debit	Date		Item	p.r.	Credit
'19– May	31	Closing	4	232500	'19– May	31	Closing	4	470000
	31	Closing	4	237500					
				470000					
									470000

Account: Fees earned   Account Number: 41

Date		Item	p.r.	Debit	Date		Item	p.r.	Credit
'19– May	31	Closing	4	470000	'19– May	14		1	270000
						28		2	200000
				470000					470000
									470000

Account: Salary expense   Account Number: 51

Date		Item	p.r.	Debit	Date		Item	p.r.	Credit
'19– May	7		1	45000	'19– May	31	Closing	4	189000
	14		1	45000					
	21		2	45000					
	28		2	45000					
	31	Adj.	3	180000					
				9000					
				189000					
									189000

Account: Supplies expense   Account Number: 52

Date		Item	p.r.	Debit	Date		Item	p.r.	Credit
'19– May	31	Adj.	3	6500	'19– May	31	Closing	4	6500

Account: *Rent expense*   Account Number: *53*

Date	Item	p.r.	Debit	Date	Item	p.r.	Credit
19— May 31	adj.	3	200 00	19— May 31	Closing	4	200 00

Account: *Depreciation expense*   Account Number: *54*

Date	Item	p.r.	Debit	Date	Item	p.r.	Credit
19— May 31	adj.	3	5 00	19— May 31	Closing	4	5 00

Account: *Utilities expense*   Account Number: *55*

Date	Item	p.r.	Debit	Date	Item	p.r.	Credit
19— May 28		2	45 00	19— May 31	Closing	4	45 00

Account: *Miscellaneous expense*   Account Number: *59*

Date	Item	p.r.	Debit	Date	Item	p.r.	Credit
19— May 9		1	55 00	19— May 31	Closing	4	120 00
17		2	65 00				
			120 00				120 00

Answer (d)

SIDNEY'S SHOE REPAIR

Post-Closing Trial Balance
May 31, 19--

Account	Debit	Credit
Cash	2520.00	
Supplies	50.00	
Prepaid rent	600.00	
Equipment	500.00	
accumulated depreciation		5.00
account payable		250.00
Salary payable		90.00
Sidney, capital		3325.00
	3670.00	3670.00

CHAPTER SIX

Special Journals
and Subsidiary Ledgers

OBJECTIVES

When you complete this chapter you will be able to

- state the advantages of using special journals and
  subsidiary ledgers,
- record transactions in
    - (a) the Sales Journal
    - (b) the Cash Receipts Journal
    - (c) the Purchases Journal
    - (d) the Cash Disbursements Journal
- post the above journals to
    - (a) the General Ledger
    - (b) the Accounts Payable Subsidiary Ledger
    - (c) the Accounts Receivable Subsidiary Ledger

If you feel that you have already mastered these objectives
and might skip all or part of this chapter, turn to the end of this
chapter and take the Self-Test. The results will tell you what
frames of the chapter you should study. If you answer all questions correctly, you are ready to begin the next chapter.

If this material is new to you, or if you choose not to take
the Self-Test now, turn to the Overview and Self-Teaching Sections that follow.

CHAPTER OVERVIEW

THE NEED FOR SPECIAL JOURNALS AND SUBSIDIARY LEDGERS

The General Journal and General Ledger discussed in the previous chapters are adequate for small businesses or for businesses with relatively few transactions during the accounting period. Larger enterprises, on the other hand, may have hundreds, thousands, or even millions of transactions per month. To rely on the General Journal and General Ledger for the recording of each of these transactions would make the posting labor quite unmanageable.

In general, this difficulty is overcome by recording all transactions of a similar nature (e.g., all sales on account) in a special journal, and at the end of the month posting in the General Ledger (in the sales account and in the accounts payable account) only the total taken from the special journal.

While the special journal certainly saves much periodic posting labor, its exclusive use will result in loss of the detail that is obtained through individual posting. For example, a business that sells goods on account to twenty or thirty different firms each month must know at any given moment which firms still owe money, which are paid up to date, and so forth. This difficulty is avoided through the use of a separate subsidiary ledger in which all accounts of one type are kept. Thus, each customer to whom a firms sells on account will have his own account in the Accounts Receivable Subsidiary Ledger. When a customer makes a purchase on account, the transaction is recorded in the Sales Journal and, at the end of the business day, is also recorded in that customer's account in the Accounts Receivable Subsidiary Ledger. At the end of the month, the effect of this transaction will be recorded in the General Ledger when the Sales Journal total is posted. On the following page is a diagram that shows how the Sales Journal, the Accounts Receivable Subsidiary Ledger, and the General Ledger are affected by sales on account.

The advantages of using special journals and subsidiary ledgers are

    (a) They give a logical grouping of similar accounts making
        summary information readily available.

    (b) They reduce the size of the general books, making for a
        simpler posting operation.

    (c) They provide for a division of labor, allowing more than
        one person to work on the books at the same time.

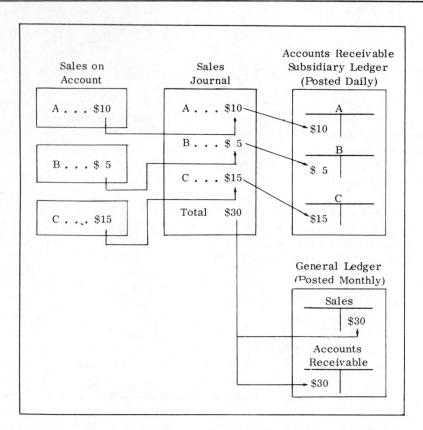

TYPES OF JOURNALS AND SUBSIDIARY LEDGERS

The way in which the basic books of a business will be set up depends, of course, on the kinds of transactions the business is expected to have. For example, a merchandising operation--one in which goods are purchased for resale to customers--is likely to have many of each of the following transactions which will be recorded in the journals indicated:

Transaction	Special Journal Used
sales on account	Sales Journal
cash receipts	Cash Receipts Journal
purchases on account	Purchases Journal
cash disbursements	Cash Disbursements Journal

In addition to these, the merchandising firm will probably make use of both Accounts Receivable and Accounts Payable Subsidiary Ledgers. Moreover, the occurrence of miscellaneous transactions as well as adjusting and closing entries still make it necessary to use the General Journal and the General Ledger.

While there are many other types of special books which streamline the accounting procedures of a business, the above journals and ledgers are the most commonly used. Many firms use preprinted forms, and the headings and items included will vary with the needs of the business. The chapter will emphasize the basic forms of these special journals.

SALES ON ACCOUNT: THE SALES JOURNAL

When there are sufficient transactions to justify the use of a special Sales Journal, the records are kept as follows:

Posted daily to the Accounts Receivable Subsidiary Ledger in the customer's account

	Date		Account Debited	Invoice	p. r.	Amount	
1	June	7	John Doe, Inc.	94		20	00
2		9	XYC Co.	127		10	00
3						30	00
4							

Sales Journal

Posted monthly in the General Ledger (in the accounts receivable and sales account)

The Sales Journal is used only for recording <u>sales</u> <u>on</u> <u>account</u>. All other sales (cash sales, sale of company assets that are no longer needed) are handled in the Cash Receipts Journal. Sales of nonmerchandise on account, such as the sale of unneeded office equipment, are entered into the General Journal and posted in the appropriate accounts in the General Ledger at the end of the month.

CASH RECEIPTS: THE CASH RECEIPTS JOURNAL

Whenever a firm receives cash, for whatever reason, the transaction is recorded in the Cash Receipts Journal. One kind of Cash Receipts Journal is given on the following page:

Money Columns

	Date	Account Credited	p.r.	Sundry Credit	Sales Credit	Accounts Receivable Credit	Cash Debit
		Cash Receipts Journal					
1							
2							

The journalizing and posting procedure for each of the money columns in this journal is given in the following chart:

	Journal Column			
	Sundry Credit	Sales Credit	Accounts Receivable Credit	Cash Debit
Transaction	Nonmerchandise cash receipts*	Cash sales (merchandise)	Receipts from credit customers	All cash receipts
What posted	Amount of transaction	Column total	Amount of transaction and column total	Column total
When posted	Daily	Monthly	Daily and monthly	Monthly
Where posted	General Ledger	General Ledger	Accounts Receivable Subsidiary Ledger and General Ledger	General Ledger

*all cash receipts other than cash
on account from credit customers
or cash for merchandise sold

PURCHASES ON ACCOUNT: THE PURCHASES JOURNAL

In a merchandise operation with sufficient transactions to justify the use of a special Purchases Journal, the records are kept as shown on the following page.

Note that the Purchases Journal is used only for the recording of purchases of merchandise on account. Cash expenditures (cash purchases, cash payment of expenses) are handled in the Cash Disbursements Journal. Purchases of nonmerchandise on account, such as those for equipment or supplies are entered in the General Journal and posted to the General Ledger at the end of the period.

Posted daily to the Accounts
Subsidiary Ledger in the
vendor's account

	Date		Account Credited	p.r.	Amount
			Purchases Journal		
1	Feb	1	John Adams, Inc.		50 00
2		2	ABC, Inc.		25 00
3					75 00
4					

Posted monthly in the General
Ledger (in the accounts payable and purchases accounts)

CASH DISBURSEMENTS: THE CASH DISBURSEMENTS JOURNAL

Whenever a firm makes a cash payment for any reason at all, the transaction
is recorded in the Cash Disbursements Journal. One kind of Cash Disbursements Journal is given below:

Money Columns

	Date	Account Debited	Check	p.r.	Sundry Debit	Accounts Payable Debit	Cash Credit
			Cash Disbursements Journal				
1							

The journalizing and posting procedure for each money column in the journal
is given in the chart on the following page.

THE GENERAL JOURNAL

The General Journal is still used to record all transactions that do not apply
to any of the special journals and all adjusting and closing entries.

	Journal Column		
	Sundry Debit	Accounts Payable Debit	Cash Credit
Transaction	All payments other than on accounts payable	Payment on accounts payable	All cash expenditures
What posted	Amount of transaction	Amount of trans-action and column total	Column total
When posted	Daily	Daily and monthly	Monthly
Where posted	General Ledger	Accounts Payable Subsidiary Ledger and General Ledger	General Ledger (cash account)

Self-Teaching Section A

THE NEED FOR SPECIAL JOURNALS AND SUBSIDIARY LEDGERS

1. The procedures shown thus far for journalizing and posting transactions would be quite inefficient in types of businesses that are involved in many transactions during the accounting period. For example, businesses that purchase goods for resale to customers may purchase goods from 100 differ-ent vendors and re-sell the goods (usually called merchandise) to as many or more customers. When, as is usual, these sales or purchases are made on account, the status of the business's account with each customer or vendor must be known at any given moment. Up to this point we have been taking all transactions for, say, sales on account and lumping them together in the

General Ledger as debits to an account called _____.

- - - - - - - - - - - - - - - -

    accounts receivable

2. Since all sales on account have been lumped together in the accounts of the General Ledger, the only data available on individual customers can be

found in the record called the _____.

- - - - - - - - - - - - - - - -

    General Journal, or journal

3. Remember, however, that the General Journal is a chronological record showing all business transactions, not just those transactions for sales on account. Thus, while details on individual customers are available in the General Journal, they are mixed in with all other transactions of the business and are, therefore, not easily obtainable. A large merchandising enterprise would be at a severe disadvantage if it recorded all its transactions in the General Ledger and the General Journal. What is one disadvantage of using only a General Journal and a General Ledger to record transactions in a mer-

chandising operation? _____

– – – – – – – – – – – – – – – –

    lack of detail on individual accounts, or equivalent answer

4. Another problem with using the General Journal and General Ledger for the many transactions of the merchandising operation is that since all transactions must be posted from the journal at the end of the period, posting will be a time consuming operation and errors will occur often. Here is an example:

> Continental Tribble purchases its tribbles from many distributors and sells them on account to over 100 tribble retail outlets. In March, Continental Tribble made ten sales each to 100 tribble dealers for a total of 1000 sales on account. Each of these transactions was recorded in the General Journal and posted to the General Ledger (sales account and accounts receivable account).

In this example, there were _____ journal entries made, and
                                                (how many?)
_____ ledger entries made.
(how many?)

– – – – – – – – – – – – – – – –

    1000; 2000

5. As shown in the above example, when the General Journal and the General Ledger are used to record many transactions, the posting and journalizing

labor will be _____.
                      (great/small)

– – – – – – – – – – – – – – –

    great

6. What are the two disadvantages in using a General Ledger and a General Journal to record many transactions in a merchandising operation?

(a) _____

(b) _____

— — — — — — — — — — — — — — —

(a) lack of detail on individual accounts; (b) great amount of journalizing and posting labor

7. These problems with using the General Ledger and General Journal for many transactions are compounded by the fact that only one person may work with the books at a time. The result is that

_____ a. there is no opportunity to obtain an independent check on the posting operation

_____ b. the posting operation will take longer

_____ c. errors are more likely to be made

_____ d. all of the above

— — — — — — — — — — — — — — —

(d)

8. The difficulties that come about when many merchandising-type transactions are recorded in a General Journal and a General Ledger are fairly well overcome through the use of special journals and subsidiary ledgers. Even though you may not know precisely how they work at this point, you should be able to state the advantages that special journals and subsidiary ledgers have over the General Ledger and the General Journal. What are they?

(a) _____

(b) _____

(c) _____

— — — — — — — — — — — — — — —

(a) They decrease posting labor and journalizing labor. (b) They provide for details on individual accounts. (c) They make it possible for more than one person at a time to work on the books.

9. We now know that special journals and subsidiary ledgers are most useful when a business is involved in many transactions of the same type. In merchandising operations, which we will use to exemplify these techniques, the transactions that occur most frequently are

(a) sales on account   (c) purchases on account
(b) cash receipts   (d) cash disbursements

In the next self-teaching section we will show how each of these transactions are recorded using special journals and subsidiary ledgers.

Self-Teaching Section B

SALES ON ACCOUNT: THE SALES JOURNAL

10. When a firm sells merchandise to a customer who promises to pay in the near future, a <u>sale</u> <u>on</u> <u>account</u> has taken place. This type of transaction is recognized as soon as the invoice, listing the goods sold and the price, is sent to the customer. The Sales Journal is the book in which sales on account are initially recorded. These are the only transactions recorded in the Sales Journal. Which of the following transactions would you expect to find recorded in the Sales Journal?

    _____ a.   E. K. Masters, Inc., on July 2, reports cash sales of $960.

    _____ b.   Glen Oaks, Co. sells $430 worth of merchandise to Elmo Johnson, who promises to pay by July 31.

- - - - - - - - - - - - - - -

(b)

11. Below is the Sales Journal of Glen Oaks, Inc. The sale on account to Elmo Johnson has been entered.

<table>
<tr><td colspan="6" align="center">Sales Journal</td></tr>
<tr><td></td><td>Date</td><td>Account Debited</td><td>Invoice</td><td>p.r.</td><td>Amount</td></tr>
<tr><td>1</td><td>July 1</td><td>Elmo Johnson</td><td>190</td><td></td><td>430 00</td></tr>
<tr><td>2</td><td></td><td></td><td></td><td></td><td></td></tr>
<tr><td>3</td><td></td><td></td><td></td><td></td><td></td></tr>
<tr><td>4</td><td></td><td></td><td></td><td></td><td></td></tr>
</table>

Notice that the Sales Journal has only one money column in which the amount of the sale is written. There are also columns provided for the entry of the date, the number of the invoice sent, and the title of the account debited with the amount. The title of the account debited is usually the name of the firm or individual to whom the merchandise was sold. Select those transactions from the following list that should be added to the Sale Journal and enter them in the one shown above.

    July 2 – Glen Oaks issues invoice number 194 for merchandise sold on account to F. Sloan, Inc. ($40).

July 3 - Glen Oaks receives invoice number 386 in the amount
of $125 for merchandise purchased from Argyle supplies.
July 3 - Glen Oaks bills Vase, Inc. (invoice number 195) for
merchandise purchased on account for $90.
July 5 - Glen Oaks sells $85 worth of merchandise for cash to
Harvey Larson.

- - - - - - - - - - - - - - - -

	Date		Account Debited	Invoice	p. r.	Amount	
1	July	1	Elmo Johnson	190		430	00
2		2	F. Sloan, Inc.	194		40	00
3		3	Vase, Inc.	195		90	00
4							

Sales Journal

12. Since special journals save posting labor and reduce the bulk of the General Ledger, you would expect the General Ledger's sales and accounts receivable accounts not to be posted with

_____ a. each individual amount in the Sales Journal's money
column
_____ b. the total of the Sales Journal's money column

- - - - - - - - - - - - - - - -

(a)

13. Remember that merchandising operations need information of the status of each individual customer's transactions with the business. Match the following:

_____ a. General Ledger   1. details on individual customers
available but not easily obtainable
_____ b. Sales Journal   2. details on individual customers
not available

- - - - - - - - - - - - - - - -

(a) 2; (b) 1

14. Since the General Ledger is posted only with the total sales on account at the end of the month, it contains no details on individual customers. The Sales Journal records individual sales, but a business sometimes sells to the same customer at different times during the month; therefore, the total amount a customer owes the company may be spread over several pages in the Sales Journal, and not be readily available. The details on individual

customers that do business with Glen Oaks, Inc. are found in a separate book called the Accounts Receivable Subsidiary Ledger. At the end of each business day, Glen Oaks's accountant posts all of the sales on account for that day to the Accounts Receivable Subsidiary Ledger. You would expect this ledger to include:

_____ a. the sales account and the accounts receivable account
_____ b. a separate accounts receivable account for each of Glen Oaks' customers

- - - - - - - - - - - - - - -

(b)

15. Here is the Glen Oaks Accounts Receivable Subsidiary Ledger:

Elmo Johnson			
Date	Debit	Credit	Balance
July 1	Balance		100.00
1	430		530.00

F. Sloan, Inc.			
Date	Debit	Credit	Balance
July 1	Balance		50.00

Vase, Inc.			
Date	Debit	Credit	Balance
July 1	Balance		60.00

The accounts shown here are called balance column accounts because they include a column headed "balance." These accounts report a new balance each time an entry is made. If the account has a credit balance, and the new entry is a debit, the amount of the entry is deducted from the old balance to give a new balance, which is then entered beneath the old balance. If the account has a credit balance and the new entry is also a credit, the entry is added to the old balance and the new balance is entered beneath the old balance. The sale on account to Elmo Johnson has been entered in his account. The increase is noted by a debit because accounts receivable is a(n)

_____ account.
(what classification?)

- - - - - - - - - - - - - - -

asset

16. Since a sale on account is always posted to an individual customer's accounts receivable account, the entry will always be on the _____

(debit/credit)

side of the account, and the account will have either a _____ balance

(debit/credit)

or a zero balance.

- - - - - - - - - - - - - - - -

debit; debit (unless the customer has returned merchandise or overpaid on his account)

17. Notice that the accounts in the Accounts Receivable Subsidiary Ledger are not given account numbers. These accounts are usually arranged alphabetically. Posting these accounts is noted by placing a check-mark in the "p. r." column of the Sales Journal.

Post the remaining entries in the Sales Journal (Frame 11) to the Accounts Receivable Subsidiary Ledger (Frame 15).

- - - - - - - - - - - - - - - -

F. Sloan, Inc.

Date	Debit	Credit	Balance
July 1	Balance		50.00
2	40.00		90.00

Vase, Inc.

Date	Debit	Credit	Balance
July 1	Balance		60.00
3	90.00		150.00

p.r.
✓
✓
✓

18. Since the transactions entered in the Sales Journal record the amounts Glen Oaks expects to receive in the future, you would expect the amounts posted in the money column to eventually affect which two accounts in the General Ledger?

_____ a. sales and cash
_____ b. cash and accounts receivable
_____ c. accounts receivable and accounts payable
_____ d. sales and accounts receivable
_____ e. sales and accounts payable

- - - - - - - - - - - - - - - -

(d)

19. As we have said, special journals save posting labor and reduce the bulk of the General Ledger, but you would expect the General Ledger's sales account and accounts receivable account will be posted with

     _____ a. each individual amount in the Sales Journal's money
            column
     _____ b. the total of the Sales Journal money column

- - - - - - - - - - - - - - -

  (b)

20. An increase in the sales account is recorded as a _____. An in-
                                                (debit/credit)

crease in the accounts receivable account is recorded as a_____.
                                                 (debit/credit)

- - - - - - - - - - - - - - -

  credit; debit

21. Since the accounts receivable account in the General Ledger is posted with the column total of the sales credit column, the accounts receivable account is a summary of the _____ Ledger.

- - - - - - - - - - - - - - -

  Accounts Receivable Subsidiary

22. An account which summarizes a subsidiary ledger is called a (General Ledger) <u>controlling</u> account. If at the end of the accounting period, you added up all the credits posted to the accounts in the Accounts Receivable Subsidiary Ledger, you would find that they equaled the amount credited to

the accounts receivable _____ account (assuming no errors).

- - - - - - - - - - - - - - -

  controlling

23. At the end of the accounting period (monthly, in the case of Glen Oaks, Inc.) the amount column in the Sales Journal is totaled and then is posted to the General Ledger. Assuming Glen Oaks recorded only the three transactions shown in Frame 12 for the month of July, post the Sales Journal to the General Ledger, given on the following page. (To show that the posting has occurred, write the numbers of the accounts to which they were posted beneath the total in the amount column of the Sales Journal.)

Sales			No. 41
Date	Debit	Credit	Balance
			O

Accounts Receivable			No. 12
Date	Debit	Credit	Balance
July 1	Balance		300.00

- - - - - - - - - - - - - - - -

Sales			No. 41
Date	Debit	Credit	Balance
			O
July 31		560.00	560.00

Accounts Receivable			No. 12
Date	Debit	Credit	Balance
July 1	Balance		300.00
31	560.00		860.00

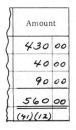

Amount	
430	00
40	00
90	00
560	00
(41)(12)	

24. You should now know how to post and journalize sales-on-account transactions using the special Sales Journal and the Accounts Receivable Subsidiary Ledger. The transactions for Masters Plumbing Supplies are given below for the month of December. Journalize the appropriate transactions in the Sales Journal provided on the following page. Then post the Sales Journal to the Accounts Receivable Subsidiary Ledger and to the General Ledger. (Remember: the Sales Journal records only the <u>sale</u> of <u>merchandise</u> <u>on</u> <u>account.</u>)

December 2 - Masters issues invoice number 46 for merchandise sold on account to Ace Plumbing ($60).

3 - Sales in cash total $450.

4 - Carter Supplies purchases $75 worth of merchandise on account from Masters. Invoice number 47 issued.

4 - Masters sells unneeded office equipment on account to Arnold Jones for $30.

5 - Masters issues invoice number 48 to Harold Crown, Inc. for supplies sold on account ($130).

9 - Masters receives $60 cash from Ace Plumbing in payment for merchandise purchased on account.

15 - Masters sells $500 worth of merchandise on account to Mark Wilson (invoice number 49).

16 - Masters sells $440 worth of merchandise on account to Harold Crown, Inc. (invoice number 50).

December 21 - Masters receives $30 cash from Arnold Jones for office
equipment purchased on account.
27 - Masters issues invoice number 51 to Ace Plumbing for
$210 worth of merchandise sold on account.

Sales Journal

	Date		Account Debited	Invoice	p.r.	Amount
1						
2						
3						
4						
5						
6						
7						
8						
9						

Accounts Receivable Subsidiary Ledger

Ace Plumbing

Date	Debit	Credit	Balance

Harold Crown, Inc.

Date	Debit	Credit	Balance

Carter Supplies

Date	Debit	Credit	Balance

Mark Wilson

Date	Debit	Credit	Balance
Dec. 1	Balance		350.00

General Ledger

Accounts Receivable   No. 12

Date	Debit	Credit	Balance
Dec. 1	Balance		350.00

Sales   No. 41

Date	Debit	Credit	Balance
			0

Answer

Sales Journal

	Date		Account Debited	Invoice	p.r.	Amount	
1	Dec.	2	Ace Plumbing	46	✓	60	00
2		4	Carter Supplies	47	✓	75	00
3		5	Harold Crown, Inc.	48	✓	130	00
4		15	Mark Wilson	49	✓	500	00
5		16	Harold Crown, Inc.	50	✓	440	00
6		27	Ace Plumbing	51	✓	210	00
7						1415	00
8						(12) (41)	
9							

Accounts Receivable Subsidiary Ledger

Ace Plumbing

Date	Debit	Credit	Balance
Dec 2	60.00		60.00
27	210.00		270.00

Harold Crown, Inc.

Date	Debit	Credit	Balance
Dec. 5	130.00		130.00
16	440.00		570.00

Carter Supplies

Date	Debit	Credit	Balance
Dec. 4	75.00		75.00

Mark Wilson

Date	Debit	Credit	Balance
Dec. 1	Balance		350.00
Dec. 15	500.00		850.00

General Ledger

Accounts Receivable No. 12

Date	Debit	Credit	Balance
Dec. 1	Balance		350.00
31	1,415.00		1,765.00

Sales No. 41

Date	Debit	Credit	Balance
			0
Dec. 31		1,415.00	1,415.00

Note that since the invoices are issued in serial order and the numbers are recorded in the Sales Journal, it is easy to tell when a sale has been missed because a break in the serial numbers would occur.

Self-Teaching Section C

CASH RECEIPTS: THE CASH RECEIPTS JOURNAL

25. When a merchandising operation has many transactions that involve the receipt of cash, either in the form of currency or checks the transactions are entered initially in the Cash Receipts Journal. Into which journal would you enter each of the transactions below? Write "S" for Sales Journal, "CR" for Cash Receipts Journal, or "O" for some other journal.

_____ a. payment received for over-the-counter cash sale

_____ b. check received for previous sale on account

_____ c. purchase of office supplies

_____ d. receipt of payment for sale on account of unneeded office furniture

_____ e. payment of salaries

_____ f. sale of merchandise on account

- - - - - - - - - - - - - - - -

(a) CR; (b) CR; (c) O; (d) CR; (e) O; (f) S

26. The column headings for the Cash Receipts Journal are given below:

Money Columns

	Date	Account Credited	p.r.	Sundry Credit	Sales Credit	Accounts Receivable Credit	Cash Debit
		Cash Receipts Journal					
1							
2							

Notice that the journal includes four money columns: a cash _____ column and three _____ columns.

- - - - - - - - - - - - - - -

debit; credit

27. The use of the Cash Receipts Journal is largely a matter of knowing which types of cash receipts transactions are entered in which money columns in the journal. Since an increase in cash will eventually result in a debit to the cash account in the General Ledger, you would expect an entry to be made in the cash debit column for which of the following?

_____ a. for all transactions that are recorded in the Cash Receipts Journal

_____ b. only for some transactions that are recorded in the Cash Receipts Journal

- - - - - - - - - - - - - - - -

(a)

28. All cash receipts transactions result in an entry to the cash debit column of the Cash Receipts Journal. All cash receipts transactions may be divided into three types:

(a) cash receipts resulting from the sale of merchandise for cash,

(b) cash receipts resulting from customers paying on their accounts,

(c) cash receipts resulting from other transactions; for example, from the sale of nonmerchandise such as unneeded company assets. (More advanced books discuss handling of other transactions, such as borrowing.)

Look at the first three money columns in the Cash Receipts Journal in Frame 26. Write the name of the money column used to record the amounts of the types of transactions given here:

Type of Transaction	Money Column Used
(a) sale of merchandise for cash	_____
(b) cash receipts for payments by customers on account	_____
(c) cash receipts for sale of nonmerchandise	_____

- - - - - - - - - - - - - - - -

(a) sales credit; (b) accounts receivable credit; (c) sundry credit

29. All cash transactions, regardless of type, will be entered in the money column headed _____ .

- - - - - - - - - - - - - - - -

cash debit

30. On the following page are three cash-receipts transactions of the types described in Frame 28:

August 3 - $100 cash received from Elmo Johnson in payment on his
  account (for merchandise)
  4 - $85 cash received from daily cash sales
  5 - $40 cash received for unneeded equipment

These three transactions have been properly journalized in the Cash Receipts
Journal below:

	Date		Account Credited	p.r.	Sundry Credit	Sales Credit	Accounts Receivable Credit	Cash Debit
			Cash Receipts Journal					
1	Aug	3	Elmo Johnson				100 00	100 00
2		4	Sales			85 00		85 00
3		5	Equipment		40 00			40 00
4								
5								
6								
7								
8								
9								
10								

Here are six more transactions involving cash receipts. Journalize them in
the Cash Receipts Journal above.

August 6 - $110 received from daily cash sales
  7 - $150 received from Vase, Inc., on account (for merchandise)
  8 - $10 received for cash sale of unneeded supplies
  9 - $15 cash received for sale of unneeded equipment
  10 - $430 received from Elmo Johnson on account (for merchandise)
  11 - $65 received from daily cash sales

	Date		Account Credited	p.r.	Sundry Credit	Sales Credit	Accounts Receivable Credit	Cash Debit
			Cash Receipts Journal					
1	Aug	3	Elmo Johnson				100 00	100 00
2		4	Sales			85 00		85 00
3		5	Equipment		40 00			40 00
4		6	Sales			110 00		110 00
5		7	Vase, Inc.				150 00	150 00
6		8	Supplies		10 00			10 00
7		9	Equipment		15 00			15 00
8		10	Elmo Johnson				430 00	430 00
9		11	Sales			65 00		65 00
10								

31. Each money column of the Cash Receipts Journal is posted separately. To post this journal you must know, for each money column:

- • WHERE it is posted (in the Accounts Receivable Subsidiary Ledger, or in the General Ledger),
- • WHAT is posted (the total of the column or the amount of the individual transaction),
- • WHEN it is posted (monthly or daily).

Here are three rules that will help you remember how to handle each column (study them carefully):

- • WHERE: The only thing posted from the Cash Receipts Journal to the Accounts Receivable Subsidiary Ledger are credits to customer accounts. All other credits are posted to the General Ledger.
- • WHAT: If there is one account in the ledger that summarizes the transactions in the column, the column total is posted. If not, the individual transaction must be posted.
- • WHEN: The only thing posted at the end of the month is a column total. If the individual transaction amount is posted, it will be done daily.

Notice that these rules must be applied in the order given. (In practice, especially with large firms, the column total may be posted more often, sometimes daily. However, for illustration, we will assume a small firm with few transactions.)

32. Let's figure out the posting procedure for the sundry credit column of the Cash Receipts Journal by applying the three rules above. Refer to them if necessary in answering the questions in the next few frames.

Does the sundry credit column record credits to customer accounts? _____

— — — — — — — — — — — — — — —

    no

33. The sundry credits column must, then, be posted where?

    _____

— — — — — — — — — — — — — — —

    to the General Ledger

34. From what you have learned about the General Ledger, is there one account in the General Ledger that summarizes the transactions of the sundry credits column (i.e., an account that combines things like supplies and

equipment)? _____

— — — — — — — — — — — — — — —

no

35. The item(s) to be posted from the sundry credits column to the General
Ledger is(are) what?

          ____ a. the column total
          ____ b. the individual transaction amounts

\- \- \- \- \- \- \- \- \- \- \- \- \- \- \-

  (b)

36. Since the individual transaction amounts are posted from the sundry
credits column to the General Ledger, the posting whould take place when?

     _____
     (daily/monthly)

\- \- \- \- \- \- \- \- \- \- \- \- \- \- \-

  daily

37. Regarding the sundry credit column of the Cash Receipts Journal:

    (a) Where is it posted? _____

    (b) What is posted? _____

    (c) When is it posted? _____

\- \- \- \- \- \- \- \- \- \- \- \- \- \- \-

  (a) General Ledger; (b) the individual transaction amounts; (c) daily

38. Identify the ledger below, and post the sundry credit column from the
Cash Receipts Journal in Frame 30:

               _____ Ledger

Supplies			No. 14
Date	Debit	Credit	Balance
Aug. 1	Balance		150.00

Equipment			No. 18
Date	Debit	Credit	Balance
Aug. 1	Balance		700.00

\- \- \- \- \- \- \- \- \- \- \- \- \- \- \-

General Ledger

Supplies			No. 14
Date	Debit	Credit	Balance
Aug. 1	Balance		150.00
8		10.00	140.00

Equipment			No. 18
Date	Debit	Credit	Balance
Aug. 1	Balance		700.00
5		40.00	660.00
8		15.00	645.00

The account numbers (supplies-14 and equipment-18) should now appear in the "p.r." column of the journal.

39. We will now apply the Where, What, and When rules from Frame 31 to determine the posting procedure for the sales credit column of the Cash Receipts Journal.

Does the sales credit column record credits to customer accounts? _____

— — — — — — — — — — — — — — —

no

40. The sales credit column must, then, be posted where?

_____

— — — — — — — — — — — — — — —

to the General Ledger

41. From what you have learned about accounts, is there an account in the General Ledger that summarizes the transactions of the sales credit column?

_____

— — — — — — — — — — — — — — —

yes

42. The item(s) to be posted from the sales credit column to the General Ledger must be _____.

— — — — — — — — — — — — — — —

the column total

43. How often is the sales credit column total posted? _____

(daily/monthly)

— — — — — — — — — — — — — —

monthly

44. Identify the ledger below and then post the sales credit column in the Cash Receipts Journal (Frame 30).

_____ Ledger

Sales			No. 41
Date	Debit	Credit	Balance

Note: be sure to place the proper posting reference in the sales credit column.

_ _ _ _ _ _ _ _ _ _ _ _ _ _ _

____ General ____ Ledger

Sales			No. 41
Date	Debit	Credit	Balance
Aug. 31		260.00	260.00

Sales Credit
65 00
260 00
(41)

45. Use the rules in Frame 31 to determine the posting procedure for the cash debit column of the Cash Receipts Journal and answer the following questions.

With reference to the cash debit column:

(a) Where is it posted? _____

(b) What is posted? _____

(c) When is it posted? _____

_ _ _ _ _ _ _ _ _ _ _ _ _ _ _

(a) the General Ledger; (b) the column total; (c) monthly

46. Identify the ledger below and then post the cash debit column from the Cash Receipts Journal in Frame 30:

_____ Ledger

Cash			No. 11
Date	Debit	Credit	Balance
Aug. 1	Balance		100.00

Note: be sure to place the proper posting reference in the cash credit column.

- - - - - - - - - - - - - - -

_____General_____ Ledger

Cash			No. 11
Date	Debit	Credit	Balance
Aug. 1	Balance		100.00
31	1,005.00		1,105.00

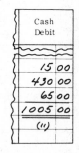

Cash Debit	
15	00
430	00
65	00
1005	00
(11)	

47. The accounts receivable credit column of the Cash Receipts Journal shows cash received from customers paying on their accounts.

   (a) The individual transactions in this column are posted daily

   to the _____ Ledger.

   (b) The column total of this column is posted monthly to the

   account in the General Ledger called the _____

   _____ account.

- - - - - - - - - - - - - - -

   (a) Accounts Receivable Subsidiary; (b) accounts receivable

48. The amounts from which column in the Cash Receipts Journal are posted to both the Accounts Receivable Subsidiary Ledger as well as to the General

Ledger? _____

- - - - - - - - - - - - - - -

   accounts receivable credit column

49. Identify the ledgers below and then post the accounts receivable credit column from the Cash Receipts Journal in Frame 30.

_____ Ledger

Accounts Receivable			No. 12
Date	Debit	Credit	Balance
July 1	Balance		300.00
31	560.00		860.00

_____ Ledger

Elmo Johnson			
Date	Debit	Credit	Balance
July 1	Balance		100.00
1	430.00		530.00

Vase, Inc.			
Date	Debit	Credit	Balance
July 1	Balance		60.00
4	90.00		150.00

_ _ _ _ _ _ _ _ _ _ _ _ _ _ _

_____ General _____ Ledger

Accounts Receivable		No. 12	
Date	Debit	Credit	Balance
July 1	Balance		300.00
31	560.00		860.00
Aug. 31		680.00	180.00

Accounts
Receivable
Credit

430 00
680 00
(12)

Accounts Receivable Subsidiary Ledger

Elmo Johnson			
Date	Debit	Credit	Balance
July 1	Balance		100.00
1	430.00		530.00
Aug. 3		100.00	430.00
10		430.00	0

Vase, Inc.			
Date	Debit	Credit	Balance
July 1	Balance		60.00
4	90.00		150.00
Aug. 7		150.00	0

There should be a check-mark in the "p. r." column of the Cash Receipts
Journal for each entry in the Subsidiary Ledger.

50. You should now know how to post and journalize transactions involving
cash receipts. Here are the transactions for Masters Plumbing Supplies for
the month of January. Journalize the appropriate transactions in the Cash
Receipts Journal on the following page. Then post the Cash Receipts Journal
to the Accounts Receivable Subsidiary Ledger and to the General Ledger.
(Remember: the Cash Receipts Journal records only the receipt of cash.)

January 2 - Check received from Carter supplies in the amount of $50 for
            payment of goods sold to him on account.
        3 - Invoice number 69 issued to Harold Crown, Inc., for merchan-
            dise purchased on account ($40).
        4 - Daily cash sales are $50.

January 5 - $500 check received from Mark Wilson in payment for merchandise sold to him on account.

11 - $270 check received from Ace Plumbing in payment for merchandise sold on account

13 - Daily cash sales are $75.

13 - Check received from Carter Supplies for $25 in payment for merchandise purchased on account.

14 - Check number 345 issued for purchase of supplies.

17 - Cash received for sale of unneeded supplies ($25).

21 - Check in the amount of $570 received from Harold Crown, Inc., for merchandise sold on account.

23 - Cash sale of unneeded equipment ($40).

23 - Daily cash sales are $90.

It is usual to "crossfoot" the figures in the Cash Receipts Journal. To do this, total the sundry credit column. (The others will already be totaled for your posting.) Then add the column totals, add the row totals, and compare the two sums. If they are equal, draw a double line under the sundry credit column and put a checkmark in parentheses below it.

	Date	Account Credited	p.r.	Sundry Credit	Sales Credit	Accounts Receivable Credit	Cash Debit
Cash Receipts Journal							
1							
2							
3							
4							
5							
6							
7							
8							
9							
10							
11							
12							
13							

Accounts Receivable Subsidiary Ledger

Ace Plumbing

Date	Debit	Credit	Balance
Jan. 1	Balance		270.00

Carter Supplies

Date	Debit	Credit	Balance
Jan. 1	Balance		75.00

Harold Crown, Inc.

Date	Debit	Credit	Balance
Jan. 1	Balance		570.00

Mark Wilson

Date	Debit	Credit	Balance
Jan 1	Balance		500.00

General Ledger

Cash   No. 11

Date	Debit	Credit	Balance
Jan. 1	Balance		1,000.00

Accounts Receivable No. 12

Date	Debit	Credit	Balance
Jan. 1	Balance		1,765.00

Supplies   No. 14

Date	Debit	Credit	Balance
Jan. 1	Balance		75.00

Equipment   No. 18

Date	Debit	Credit	Balance
Jan. 1	Balance		375.00

Sales   No. 41

Date	Debit	Credit	Balance

Answer

Cash Receipts Journal

	Date		Account Credited	p.r.	Sundry Credit		Sales Credit		Accounts Receivable Credit		Cash Debit	
1	Jan	2	Carter Supplies	✓					50	00	50	00
2		4	Sales				50	00			50	00
3		5	Mark Wilson	✓					500	00	500	00
4		11	Ace Plumbing	✓					270	00	270	00
5		13	Sales				75	00			75	00
6		13	Carter Supplies	✓					25	00	25	00
7		17	Supplies	14	25	00					25	00
8		21	Harold Crown, Inc.	✓					570	00	570	00
9		23	Equipment	18	40	00					40	00
10		23	Sales				90	00			90	00
11					65	00	215	00	1415	00	1695	00
12					(✓)		(41)		(12)		(11)	
13												

Accounts Receivable Subsidiary Ledger

Ace Plumbing

Date	Debit	Credit	Balance
Jan. 1 Balance			270.00
11		270.00	0

Carter Supplies

Date	Debit	Credit	Balance
Jan. 1 Balance			75.00
2		50.00	25.00
13		25.00	0

Harold Crown, Inc.

Date	Debit	Credit	Balance
Jan. 1 Balance			570.00
21		570.00	0

Mark Wilson

Date	Debit	Credit	Balance
Jan. 1 Balance			500.00
5		500.00	0

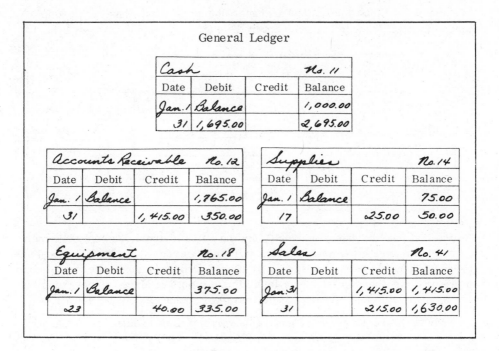

General Ledger

Cash   No. 11

Date	Debit	Credit	Balance
Jan. 1	Balance		1,000.00
31	1,695.00		2,695.00

Accounts Receivable   No. 12

Date	Debit	Credit	Balance
Jan. 1	Balance		1,765.00
31		1,415.00	350.00

Supplies   No. 14

Date	Debit	Credit	Balance
Jan. 1	Balance		75.00
17		25.00	50.00

Equipment   No. 18

Date	Debit	Credit	Balance
Jan. 1	Balance		375.00
23		40.00	335.00

Sales   No. 41

Date	Debit	Credit	Balance
Jan. 31		1,415.00	1,415.00
31		215.00	1,630.00

Self-Teaching Section D

PURCHASES ON ACCOUNT: THE PURCHASES JOURNAL

51. A firm makes a purchase on account when it buys goods from a vendor
and promises to pay that vendor in the near future. When a purchase on ac-
count is made, the transaction is entered into a Purchases Journal. The
Purchases Journal is used strictly for merchandise purchased on account.
Which of the following transactions would you expect to find recorded in the
Purchases Journal?

    ____ a. Marvin Corp., which sells elevator buttons, purchases
          $75 worth of office supplies on account.

    ____ b. Elmo Johnson, a plumbing supplies dealer, purchases
          $430 worth of plumbing supplies on account.

    ____ c. Elmo Johnson issues check number 46 for payment of
          merchandise purchased on account.

- - - - - - - - - - - - - - - -

(b)

52. Below is Elmo Johnson's Purchases Journal. A purchase on account made by Elmo Johnson has been entered.

	Purchases Journal			
	Date	Account Credited	p.r.	Amount
1	May 1	Crank Supplies		35 00
2				
3				
4				
5				

Notice that the Purchases Journal, like the Sales Journal, has only one money column in which the amount of the purchase is recorded. In fact, the Purchases Journal is used almost exactly like the Sales Journal. Here are some more of Elmo Johnson's transactions for the month of May. Select those that are appropriate and journalize them into the Purchases Journal above.

May 3 - Purchases on account: $45 worth of merchandise from Masters Plumbing Supplies.
     4 - Total cash sales for the day are $60.
     5 - Purchases $20 worth of office supplies with cash.
     6 - Purchases $85 worth of merchandise from International Fencing Corp. on account.
     9 - Purchases $70 worth of merchandise with cash.
     10 - Purchases $190 worth of merchandise on account from Masters Plumbing Supplies.

— — — — — — — — — — — — — — —

	Purchases Journal			
	Date	Account Credited	p.r.	Amount
1	May 1	Crank Supplies		35 00
2	3	Masters Plumbing Supplies		45 00
3	6	International Fencing Corp.		85 00
4	10	Masters Plumbing Supplies		190 00
5				

53. Posting the Purchases Journal is almost like posting the Sales Journal. Since the Sales Journal's individual transactions are posted to an Accounts Receivable Subsidiary Ledger, you would expect the Purchases Journal to be

posted to a ledger called the _____

Ledger.

— — — — — — — — — — — — — — — —

Accounts Payable Subsidiary Ledger

54. The Accounts Payable Subsidiary Ledger includes an account for all of those businesses from which purchases on account are made. Below are three simplified accounts. Referring to Elmo Johnson's Purchases Journal (Frame 52), write in the account titles for the accounts in Elmo Johnson's Accounts Payable Subsidiary Ledger:

Accounts Payable Subsidiary Ledger

Date	Debit	Credit	Balance

Date	Debit	Credit	Balance

Date	Debit	Credit	Balance

— — — — — — — — — — — — — — —

International Fencing Corp.

Date	Debit	Credit	Balance

Crank Supplies

Date	Debit	Credit	Balance

Masters Plumbing Supplies

Date	Debit	Credit	Balance

55. Post the Purchases Journal of Elmo Johnson to the Accounts Payable Subsidiary Ledger in Frame 54.

— — — — — — — — — — — — — —

Crank Supplies			
Date	Debit	Credit	Balance
May 1		35.00	35.00

International Fencing Corp.			
Date	Debit	Credit	Balance
May 6		85.00	85.00

Masters Plumbing Supplies			
Date	Debit	Credit	Balance
May 3		45.00	45.00
10		190.00	235.00

There should be a check-mark in the "p. r." column next to each entry in the journal.

56. As you will recall, the total in the Sales Journal at the end of the period is posted to both the sales account and the accounts receivable account. The total in the Purchases Journal is also posted to the General Ledger at the end of the period. One of the accounts to which the column total of the Purchases Journal is posted is called the purchases account. The purchases account is treated like an asset or an expense account. Therefore, an increase in the amount of purchases would be recorded in the General Ledger as a

_____.

(debit/credit)

— — — — — — — — — — — — — — —

    debit

57. The column total of the Sales Journal is posted as a debit to the accounts receivable account in the General Ledger. You would expect, therefore, that

the Purchases Journal would be posted as a _____ to the

                           (debit/credit)

_____ account in the General Ledger.

— — — — — — — — — — — — — — —

    credit; accounts payable

58. Here are the June transactions of The Tape Measure, a fabric distributor. Journalize the appropriate transactions in the Purchases Journal on the next page. Then, post the Purchases Journal to the Accounts Payable Subsidiary Ledger and to the General Ledger. (Remember: only purchases on account are journalized in the Purchases Journal.)

    June 1 - Purchased $70 worth of merchandise on account from Town Fabrics.
          1 - Purchased $100 worth of merchandise on account from Marshall, Inc.

June 2 – Sold $125 worth of merchandise on account to Harkins, Inc.

    2 – Purchased merchandise on account from Knitting Supplies, Inc., in the amount of $20.

    5 – Purchased merchandise on account from the Fabric Co. in the amount of $15.

    6 – Purchased merchandise for cash $40.

  11 – Purchased $225 worth of merchandise on account from Marshall, Inc.

  17 – Sold $170 worth of merchandise on account to Inverness Dress Co.

  23 – Purchased $25 worth of merchandise on account from the Fabric Co.

	Date		Account Credited	p.r.	Amount
1					
2					
3					
4					
5					
6					
7					
8					
9					

Purchases Journal

Accounts Payable Subsidiary Ledger

Fabric Company

Date	Debit	Credit	Balance

Marshall, Inc.

Date	Debit	Credit	Balance

Knitting Supplies

Date	Debit	Credit	Balance

Town Fabrics

Date	Debit	Credit	Balance

General Ledger

Accounts Payable   No. 21

Date	Debit	Credit	Balance

Purchases   No. 55

Date	Debit	Credit	Balance

- - - - - - - - - - - - - - -

Purchases Journal

	Date		Account Credited	p.r.	Amount
1	June	1	Town Fabrics	✓	70 00
2		1	Marshall, Inc.	✓	100 00
3		2	Knitting Supplies, Inc.	✓	20 00
4		5	The Fabric Co.	✓	15 00
5		11	Marshall, Inc.	✓	225 00
6		23	The Fabric Co.	✓	25 00
7					455 00
8					(21)(55)
9					

Accounts Payable Subsidiary Ledger

Fabric Company

Date	Debit	Credit	Balance
June 5		15.00	15.00
23		25.00	40.00

Marshall, Inc.

Date	Debit	Credit	Balance
June 1		100.00	100.00
11		225.00	325.00

Knitting Supplies

Date	Debit	Credit	Balance
June 2		20.00	20.00

Town Fabrics

Date	Debit	Credit	Balance
June 1		70.00	70.00

General Ledger

Accounts Payable   No. 21

Date	Debit	Credit	Balance
June 31		455.00	455 00

Purchases   No. 55

Date	Debit	Credit	Balance
June 31	455.00		455.00

Self-Teaching Section E

CASH DISBURSEMENTS: THE CASH DISBURSEMENTS JOURNAL

59. When a business makes many payments in the form of currency or checks, the transactions can be recorded in a <u>Cash Disbursements Journal.</u>   Which of the following transactions would be journalized in the Cash Disbursements Journal?

_____ a. purchase of merchandise on account
_____ b. purchase of supplies on account
_____ c. purchase of supplies for cash
_____ d. issuance of a check as payment for merchandise
            previously purchased on account
_____ e. payment of employees' salaries
_____ f. payment of the telephone bill
_____ g. payment of an advertising expense

- - - - - - - - - - - - - - -

(c); (d); (e); (f); (g)

60. The headings of the Cash Disbursements Journal are presented below:

Money Columns

	Date	Account Debited	Check	p.r.	Sundry Debit	Accounts Payable Debit	Cash Credit
		Cash Disbursements Journal					
1							

Notice that, like the Cash Receipts Journal, the Cash Disbursements Journal has more than one money column. It also has a column headed "check." This column is used to record the number of the check that is used (if any) to make the cash payment recorded.

61. The Cash Disbursements Journal is recorded and posted very much like the Cash Receipts Journal. Therefore, since every cash disbursement will cause a decrease in the amount of cash a company has, you would expect that <u>every</u> entry in the Cash Disbursement Journal to be recorded in the money

column headed _____.

- - - - - - - - - - - - - - -

cash credit

62. Apply what you have already learned to the posting of the cash credit column:

    (a) Where is it posted? _____

    (b) What is posted? _____

    (c) When is it posted? _____

– – – – – – – – – – – – – – –

    (a) General Ledger; (b) column total; (c) monthly

63. What kind of transaction would you expect to be entered in the accounts payable debit column?

    ____ a. transactions involving cash disbursements for cash purchases
    ____ b. transactions involving cash disbursements to creditors for merchandise purchased on account
    ____ c. transactions involving cash disbursements for expenses such as salaries and supplies
    ____ d. all of the above

– – – – – – – – – – – – – – –

    (b)

64. The accounts payable debit column will be posted to

    ____ a. the General Ledger
    ____ b. the Accounts Payable Subsidiary Ledger
    ____ c. both of the above

– – – – – – – – – – – – – – –

    (c)

65. The individual transactions in the accounts <u>receivable</u> credit column of the Cash Receipts Journal are posted to the Accounts Receivable Subsidiary Ledger on a daily basis. The individual transactions in the accounts payable debit column of the Cash Disbursements Journal will be posted to the

_____ Ledger on a

_____ basis.

– – – – – – – – – – – – – –

    Accounts Payable Subsidiary; daily

66. The <u>column</u> total of the accounts payable debit column of the Cash Disbusements Journal will be posted:

    Where? _____ Ledger

    When? _____

– – – – – – – – – – – – – –

in the General Ledger; monthly

67. All transactions for disbursements of cash <u>except</u> those for payment of merchandise purchased on account will be recorded in the

_____ column.

– – – – – – – – – – – – – –

sundry debit

68. Which of the following transactions would be recorded in the sundry debit column of the Cash Disbursements Journal?

_____ a. payment of salaries
_____ b. purchase of supplies for cash
_____ c. payment for merchandise purchased on account
_____ d. payment of an advertising expense
_____ e. a sale on account
_____ f. receipt of payment for merchandise sold on account

– – – – – – – – – – – – – – – –

(a); (b); (d)

69. With respect to the sundry debit column:

(a) Where is it posted? _____ Ledger

(b) What is posted? _____

(c) When is it posted? _____

– – – – – – – – – – – – – –

(a) General; (b) the individual transaction amount; (c) daily

70. Below are the transactions for July of Tape Measure Fabric Distributors. Journalize the appropriate transactions in the Cash Disbursements Journal on the following page. To check equality, crossfoot the totals. Then post the Cash Disbursements Journal to the Accounts Payable Subsidiary Ledger and the General Ledger. (Remember: the Cash Disbursements Journal is used <u>only</u> to record transactions involving a payment of cash.)

July 1 – Paid part-time clerk last month's salary of $100 (check no. 801).
   2 – Issued check no. 802 in payment to Marshall, Inc., for merchandise purchased on account ($200).
   3 – Issued check no. 803 paying the Fabric Company $40 for merchandise purchased on account.
   3 – Issued check no. 804 to Knitting Supplies for purchase of merchandise on account ($20).

July 8 - Paid last month's rent ($150) with check no. 805 (debit rent expense).

9 - Received check from Nolan's Housewear ($60) for merchandise purchased on account.

9 - Issued check 806 to Town Fabrics in payment for merchandise purchased on account ($35).

10 - Sold $90 worth of merchandise to Kapp's, Inc., on account.

15 - Purchased supplies for cash (check no. 807, $10).

17 - Daily cash sales are $35.

17 - Issued check 808 to Town Fabrics in payment for merchandise purchased on account ($35).

22 - Issued check no. 809 to Marshall, Inc., in payment for merchandise purchased on account ($125).

26 - Purchased supplies for cash (check no. 810, $15).

Cash Disbursements Journal

	Date	Account Debited	Check	p.r.	Sundry Debit	Accounts Payable Debit	Cash Credit
1							
2							
3							
4							
5							
6							
7							
8							
9							
10							
11							
12							
13							

Accounts Payable Subsidiary Ledger

Fabric Company

Date	Debit	Credit	Balance
July 1		Balance	40.00

Knitting Supplies

Date	Debit	Credit	Balance
July 1		Balance	20.00

Marshall, Inc.

Date	Debit	Credit	Balance
July 1		Balance	325.00

Town Fabrics

Date	Debit	Credit	Balance
July 1		Balance	70.00

General Ledger

Cash   No. 11

Date	Debit	Credit	Balance
July 1	Balance		1,500.00

Supplies   No. 14

Date	Debit	Credit	Balance
July 1	Balance		200.00

Accounts Payable   No. 21

Date	Debit	Credit	Balance
July 1		Balance	455.00

Salary Expense   No. 51

Date	Debit	Credit	Balance

Rent Expense   No. 53

Date	Debit	Credit	Balance

- - - - - - - - - - - - - - -

Cash Disbursements Journal

	Date		Account Debited	Check	p.r.	Sundry Debit	Accounts Payable Debit	Cash Credit
1	July	1	Salaries expense	801	51	100 00		100 00
2		2	Marshall, Inc.	802	✓		200 00	200 00
3		3	Fabric Co.	803	✓		40 00	40 00
4		3	Knitting Supplies	804	✓		20 00	20 00
5		8	Rent expense	805	53	150 00		150 00
6		9	Town Fabrics	806	✓		35 00	35 00
7		15	Supplies	807	14	10 00		10 00
8		17	Town Fabrics	808	✓		35 00	35 00
9		22	Marshall, Inc.	809	✓		125 00	125 00
10		26	Supplies	810	14	15 00		15 00
11						275 00	455 00	730 00
12						(✓)	(21)	(11)
13								

Accounts Payable Subsidiary Ledger

Fabric Company

Date	Debit	Credit	Balance
July 1		Balance	40.00
3	40.00		0

Knitting Supplies

Date	Debit	Credit	Balance
July 1		Balance	20.00
3	20.00		0

Marshall, Inc.

Date	Debit	Credit	Balance
July 1		Balance	325.00
2	200.00		125.00
22	125.00		0

Town Fabrics

Date	Debit	Credit	Balance
July 1		Balance	70.00
9	35.00		35.00
17	35.00		0

General Ledger

Cash   No. 11

Date	Debit	Credit	Balance
July 1	Balance		1,500.00
31		730.00	770.00

Supplies   No. 14

Date	Debit	Credit	Balance
July 1	Balance		200.00
15	10.00		210.00
26	15.00		225.00

Accounts Payable   No. 21

Date	Debit	Credit	Balance
July 1		Balance	455.00
31	455.00		0

Salary Expense   No. 51

Date	Debit	Credit	Balance
July 1	100.00		100.00

Rent Expense   No. 53

Date	Debit	Credit	Balance
July 8	150.00		150.00

Note that since checks are issued in serial number order and the numbers are recorded in the Cash Disbursements Journal, it is easy to tell when a check has been missed because a break in serial numbers would occur.

Self-Teaching Section F

THE GENERAL JOURNAL

71. Since we have been doing so much work on the special journals, you might be wondering what ever became of the General Journal. Even when special journals are used, the General Journal is a very important record-keeping device. It is used to record all transactions that do not apply to any of the special journals. If the special journals discussed in this chapter were used by a business, which of the following transactions would be recorded in the General Journal?

_____ a. sale of merchandise on account
_____ b. purchase of office supplies (nonmerchandise) on account
_____ c. receipt of cash for equipment (nonmerchandise) sold on account
_____ d. payment of a loan installment (in cash)
_____ e. sale of nonmerchandise on account

- - - - - - - - - - - - - - - -

   (b); (e)

72. In addition to its use for recording sales and purchases of nonmerchandise items on account, the General Journal is used at the end of the period to record _____ entries and _____ entries.

- - - - - - - - - - - - - - -

   closing; adjusting

SELF-TEST

This Self-Test will show you whether or not you have mastered the chapter objectives and are ready to go on to the next chapter. Answer each question to the best of your ability. Correct answers and instructions are given at the end of the test.

1. What are three advantages of using special journals and subsidiary ledgers?

(a) _____

_____

(b) _____

_____

(c) _____

_____

2. Clearview Optical Supplies, Inc., purchased optical goods on account from a number of suppliers. Clearview stocks these goods for over-the-counter cash sales to optical labs as well as for sales on account. Below are several of Clearview's transactions for the month of October. Each transaction is dated. For each transaction, write the date on which the entry would affect the book specified (either by itself, or included in a column total). If the transaction would not affect a given book, write a "0" (assume that final posting is as of the last day of the month).

(a) October 7 - Clearview sends a check for $300 in payment for merchandise purchased on account.

date of entry in Cash Disbursements Journal _____

date of entry in General Ledger
(accounts payable controlling account) _____

date of entry in Purchases Journal _____

date of entry in Accounts Payable Subsidiary Ledger _____

(b) October 9 - Clearview's total daily cash sales of merchandise is $125.

date of entry in Cash Receipts Journal _____

date of entry in General Journal _____

date of entry in Sales Journal _____

date of entry in General Ledger (cash and sales accounts) _____

date of entry in Accounts Receivable Subsidiary Ledger _____

(c) October 11 – Clearview sells unneeded office equipment for $70 cash.

    date of entry in General Journal _____

    date of entry in Cash Receipts Journal _____

    date of entry in Sales Journal _____

    date of entry in General Ledger
    (cash and equipment accounts) _____

(d) October 20 – Clearview sends a $300 check for merchandise purchased on account.

    date of entry in Accounts Payable Subsidiary Ledger _____

    date of entry in General Ledger (purchases account) _____

    date of entry in Purchases Journal _____

    date of entry in Cash Disbursements Journal _____

    date of entry in General Ledger
    (accounts payable controlling and cash accounts) _____

(e) October 21 – Clearview sells $250 worth of merchandise on account to Del-Mer Optical Laboratory.

    date of entry in General Ledger
    (account receivable controlling and sales accounts) _____

    date of entry in Sales Journal _____

    date of entry in Accounts Receivable Subsidiary Ledger _____

    date of entry in Cash Receipts Journal _____

(f) October 27 – Clearview receives a $250 check from Del-Mer for merchandise purchased on account.

    date of entry in Cash Receipts Journal _____

    date of entry in Accounts Receivable Subsidiary Ledger _____

    date of entry in General Ledger (sales account) _____

    date of entry in General Ledger
    (accounts receivable controlling and cash accounts) _____

3. Orville's Auto Supplies, Inc., sells parts and tools on account to steady customers as well as to cash customers. Orville's stocks its retail outlet and warehouse with merchandise purchased on account from a number of suppliers. Daily transactions are recorded in any of the following:

    (a) a General Journal   (d) a Sales Journal
    (b) a Purchases Journal   (e) a Cash Disbursements Journal
    (c) a Cash Receipts Journal

Each of these journals is given on the following pages. For each of the transactions below enter the information correctly on the appropriate journal.

January 2 - Purchased merchandise on account from Mack, Inc. ($480).

3 - Purchased merchandise on account from Clamouth Parts Company ($120).

3 - Sold merchandise on account to Mark's Garage, invoice no. 67 ($350).

6 - Daily cash sales ($90).

9 - Sold merchandise on account to Olaf Auto Suppliers, invoice no. 68 ($110).

10 - Issued check no. 901 to Mack, Inc., for January 2 purchase ($480).

11 - Sold unneeded warehouse equipment for cash ($100).

13 - Purchased merchandise on account from Clamouth Parts Co. ($75).

13 - Daily cash sales ($70).

14 - Purchased office supplies on account from Rex Stationers ($20).

15 - Sold merchandise on account to Olaf Auto Suppliers, invoice no. 69 ($500).

15 - Sold merchandise on account to Barnes Auto Parts, invoice no. 70 ($325).

16 - Issued check no. 902 to Clamouth Parts Co., for January 3 purchase ($120).

17 - Received check from Mark's Garage ($350).

18 - Received check from Olaf Auto Suppliers ($110).

19 - Issued check no. 903 to Rex Stationers for supplies purchased on account ($20).

21 - Daily cash sales ($95).

22 - Issued check no. 904 for next month's rent ($300).

25 - Received check from Olaf Auto Suppliers ($500).

31 - Paid salaries for month with check nos. 905 ($400) and 906 ($450).

General Journal

Page /

Date	Description	p. r.	Debit	Credit
1				
2				
3				
4				

Purchases Journal

	Date	Account Credited	p. r.	Amount
1				
2				
3				
4				
5				
6				

Sales Journal

	Date	Account Debited	Invoice	p. r.	Amount
1					
2					
3					
4					
5					
6					
7					

Cash Receipts Journal

	Date	Account Credited	p. r.	Sundry Credit	Sales Credit	Accounts Receivable Credit	Cash Debit
1							
2							
3							
4							
5							
6							
7							
8							
9							
10							

Cash Disbursements Journal

	Date	Account Debited	Check	p. r.	Sundry Debit	Accounts Payable Debit	Cash Credit
1							
2							
3							
4							
5							
6							
7							
8							
9							

4. On the following pages are all the ledgers used by Orville's Auto Supplies:

    (a) the General Ledger
    (b) the Accounts Payable Subsidiary Ledger
    (c) the Accounts Receivable Subsidiary Ledger

Using the journal entries in Question 3, do the following:

    (a) Post the appropriate entries to the General Ledger.
    (b) Post the appropriate entries to the Accounts Payable Subsidiary Ledger
    (c) Post the appropriate entries to the Accounts Receivable Subsidiary Ledger
    (d) Prove the equality of the debits and credits in the General Ledger by taking a Trial Balance.

General Ledger

Cash			No. 11
Date	Debit	Credit	Balance
Jan. 1	Balance		1,100.00

Accounts Receivable			No. 12
Date	Debit	Credit	Balance
Jan. 1	Balance		100.00

Supplies			No. 14
Date	Debit	Credit	Balance

Prepaid Rent			No. 15
Date	Debit	Credit	Balance

Equipment			No. 18
Date	Debit	Credit	Balance
Jan. 1	Balance		200.00

Accounts Payable			No. 21
Date	Debit	Credit	Balance
Jan. 1		Balance	100.00

Orville's Capital			No. 31
Date	Debit	Credit	Balance
Jan. 1		Balance	1,300.00

Sales			No. 41
Date	Debit	Credit	Balance

Salary Expense			No. 51
Date	Debit	Credit	Balance

Purchases			No. 55
Date	Debit	Credit	Balance

Accounts Receivable Subsidiary Ledger

Mark's Garage			
Date	Debit	Credit	Balance
Jan. 1	Balance		100.00

Olaf's Auto Suppliers			
Date	Debit	Credit	Balance

Barnes Auto Parts			
Date	Debit	Credit	Balance

Accounts Payable Subsidiary Ledger

Mack, Inc.

Date	Debit	Credit	Balance
Jan. 1		Balance	100.00

Clamouth Parts Co.

Date	Debit	Credit	Balance

ORVILLE'S AUTO SUPPLIES

Trial Balance
January 31, 19--

Account	Debit	Credit

Self-Test Answers

Compare your answers to the Self-Test with the correct answers given below. If all of your answers are correct, you are ready to go on to the next chapter. If you missed any questions, study the frames indicated in parentheses following the answer. If you miss many questions, go over the entire chapter carefully.

1. (a) They allow more than one person to work on the books at a time.
   (b) They give a logical grouping of similar accounts making summary information readily obtainable.
   (c) They reduce the size of the general books, making for a simpler posting operation. (Frames 1-9)

2. (a) Cash Disbursements Journal - October 7
       General Ledger (accounts payable controlling account) - October 31
       Purchases Journal - 0
       Accounts Payable Subsidiary Ledger - October 7
   (b) Cash Receipts Journal - October 9
       General Journal - 0
       Sales Journal - 0
       General Ledger (cash and sales accounts) - October 31
       Accounts Receivable Subsidiary Ledger - 0
   (c) General Journal - 0
       Cash Receipts Journal - October 11
       Sales Journal - 0
       General Ledger (cash and equipment accounts) - October 31
   (d) Accounts Payable Subsidiary Ledger - October 20
       General Ledger (purchases account) - 0
       Purchases Journal - 0
       Cash Disbursements Journal - October 20
       General Ledger (accounts payable controlling and cash accounts) -
           October 31
   (e) General Ledger (accounts receivable controlling and sales accounts) -
           October 31
       Sales Journal - October 21
       Accounts Receivable Subsidiary Ledger - October 21
       Cash Receipts Journal - 0
   (f) Cash Receipts Journal - October 27
       Accounts Receivable Subsidiary Ledger - October 27
       General Ledger (sales account) - 0
       General Ledger (accounts receivable controlling and cash accounts) -
           October 31

Note to Questions 2, 3, and 4

The tasks presented by Questions 2, 3, and 4 are quite comprehensive. If
you made any errors, be sure that you understand how and why they occurred
before going on. Use the table below to refer back to the appropriate frames
for review.

Journal	Frames for Journalizing	Frames for Posting
Sales	10-11	12-24
Cash Receipts	25-30	31-50
Purchases	51-52	53-58
Cash Disbursements	59-60	61-70
General	71-72	71-72

3. Answer

General Journal

Page 1

	Date	Description	p. r.	Debit	Credit
	19—				
1	Jan. 14	Supplies	14	2000	
2		Accounts payable	21		2000
3		For store supplies			
4					

Purchases Journal

	Date	Account Credited	p.r.	Amount
1	Jan. 2	Mack, Inc.	✓	4800
2	3	Clamouth Parts Co.	✓	1200
3	13	Clamouth Parts Co.	✓	7500
4				6750 0
5				(21)(55)
6				

Sales Journal

	Date		Account Debited	Invoice	p.r.	Amount
1	Jan	3	Mark's Garage	67	✓	350 00
2		9	Olaf Auto Suppliers	68	✓	110 00
3		15	Olaf Auto Suppliers	69	✓	500 00
4		15	Barnes Auto Parts	70	✓	325 00
5						1285 00
6						(41) (12)
7						

Cash Receipts Journal

	Date		Account Credited	p.r.	Sundry Credit	Sales Credit	Accounts Receivable Credit	Cash Debit
1	Jan.	6	Sales			90 00		90 00
2		11	Warehouse equipment	18	100 00			100 00
3		13	Sales			70 00		70 00
4		17	Mark's Garage	✓			350 00	350 00
5		18	Olaf Auto Suppliers	✓			110 00	110 00
6		21	Sales			95 00		95 00
7		25	Olaf Auto Suppliers	✓			500 00	500 00
8					100 00	255 00	960 00	1315 00
9					(✓)	(41)	(12)	(11)
10								

Cash Disbursements Journal

	Date		Account Debited	Check	p.r.	Sundry Debit	Accounts Payable Debit	Cash Credit
1	Jan	10	Mack, Inc.	901	✓		480 00	480 00
2		16	Clamouth Parts	902	✓		120 00	120 00
3		19	Accounts payable - stationary	903	21	20 00		20 00
4		22	Prepaid rent	904	15	300 00		300 00
5		31	Salaries expense	905	51	400 00		400 00
6		31	Salaries expense	906	51	450 00		450 00
7						1170 00	600 00	1770 00
8						(✓)	(21)	(11)
9								

4. Answer

General Ledger

Cash — No. 11

Date	Debit	Credit	Balance
Jan. 1	Balance		1,100.00
31	1,315.00		2,415.00
31		1,770.00	645.00

Accounts Receivable — No. 12

Date	Debit	Credit	Balance
Jan. 1	Balance		100.00
31	1,285.00		1,385.00
31		960.00	425.00

Supplies — No. 14

Date	Debit	Credit	Balance
Jan. 14	20.00		20.00

Prepaid Rent — No. 15

Date	Debit	Credit	Balance
Jan. 22	300.00		300.00

Equipment — No. 18

Date	Debit	Credit	Balance
Jan. 1	Balance		200.00
11		100.00	100.00

Accounts Payable — No. 21

Date	Debit	Credit	Balance
Jan. 1		Balance	100.00
14		20.00	120.00
19	20.00		100.00
31		675.00	775.00
31	600.00		175.00

Orville's Capital — No. 31

Date	Debit	Credit	Balance
Jan. 1		Balance	1,300.00

Sales — No. 41

Date	Debit	Credit	Balance
Jan. 31		1,285.00	1,285.00
31		255.00	1,540.00

Salary Expense — No. 51

Date	Debit	Credit	Balance
Jan. 31	400.00		400.00
31	450.00		850.00

Purchases — No. 55

Date	Debit	Credit	Balance
Jan. 31	675.00		675.00

Accounts Receivable Subsidiary Ledger

Mark's Garage

Date	Debit	Credit	Balance
Jan. 1	Balance		100.00
3	350.00		450.00
17		350.00	100.00

Olaf's Auto Suppliers

Date	Debit	Credit	Balance
Jan. 9	110.00		110.00
15	500.00		610.00
18		110.00	500.00
25		500.00	0

Barnes Auto Parts

Date	Debit	Credit	Balance
Jan. 15	325.00		325.00

Accounts Payable Subsidiary Ledger

Mack, Inc.

Date	Debit	Credit	Balance
Jan. 1		Balance	100.00
2		480.00	580.00
10	480.00		100.00

Clamouth Parts Co.

Date	Debit	Credit	Balance
Jan. 3		120.00	120.00
3		75.00	195.00
16	120.00		75.00

ORVILLE'S AUTO SUPPLIES

Trial Balance
January 31, 19--

Account	Debit	Credit
Cash	645.00	
Accounts receivable	425.00	
Supplies	20.00	
Prepaid rent	300.00	
Equipment	100.00	
Accounts payable		175.00
Orville's capital		1300.00
Sales		1540.00
Salary expense	850.00	
Purchases	675.00	
	3015.00	3015.00

CHAPTER SEVEN

Inventory

OBJECTIVES

When you complete this chapter you will be able to

- recognize and apply the terms "inventory," "physical inventory," "periodic inventory system," and "perpetual inventory system,"
- cost an inventory using either the fifo, lifo, or weighted average method,
- value an inventory using either cost or lower of cost or market methods,
- use the retail inventory method and the gross profit method to determine inventory,
- locate the merchandise inventory entry on a Balance Sheet and determine if that entry is adequate.

If you feel that you have already mastered these objectives and might skip all or part of this chapter, turn to the end of the chapter and take the Self-Test. The results will tell you what frames of the chapter you should study. If you answer all questions correctly, you are ready to begin the next chapter.

If this material is new to you, or if you choose not to take the Self-Test now, turn to the Overview and Self-Teaching Sections that follow.

CHAPTER OVERVIEW

INVENTORY SYSTEMS

There are two general types of inventory: (a) merchandise held for sale in the normal course of business, and (b) materials in the process of production, or held for such use in a manufacturing enterprise. Our discussion will be general, but we will be primarily concerned with inventory as merchandise held for sale.

In a typical merchandising operation, the movement of salable items is the essence of the business. In determination of net income, the largest deduction from sales is the original cost of the merchandise sold. A large portion of any merchandising firm's resources are invested in inventory, which is commonly the largest item in current assets. Thus, the accurate determination of inventory quantities and costs is very important to any merchandise or manufacturing operation. Inventory data and techniques are also of great interest to a company's stockholders, creditors, and the government.

The actual act of counting items in stock is referred to as taking a physical inventory, and there are two basic systems of inventory accounting.

The Periodic Inventory System

Only the costs of sales are recorded in this system; no entries are made that charge profit or loss with the cost of merchandise sold. A physical inventory is required at the end of each accounting period. This system is generally used by stores selling lots of small items (e.g., groceries, hardware, drugs).

The Perpetual Inventory System

This system uses accounting records that continually disclose the amount of inventory that remains. Increases in inventory are recorded as debits, and decreases in inventory are recorded as credits to appropriate accounts. When using the perpetual inventory method a physical inventory must be taken at least once a year to check the accuracy of the records, but it may occur at any convenient time. This system is generally used by stores selling fewer, more expensive items (e.g., furniture, autos).

Determining Inventory Quantities

The actual determination of inventory quantities is done by a physical inventory. All the merchandise in the possession of the company is physically counted, weighed, or measured, as appropriate. The physical count is often conducted at night or during a special period when all other business operations are suspended. As a general rule, a physical inventory is conducted once a year, usually at the end of the accounting period.

Various conventions determine whether merchandise in the process of being shipped from one point to another is considered the property of the seller or buyer. It is necessary to examine both sales and purchase invoices for several days surrounding the day of the physical inventory to locate any purchases in transit and to add or delete them from the inventory.

DETERMINING INVENTORY COSTS

The cost of merchandise inventory is the purchase price and all expenditures incurred in acquiring such merchandise, including purchasing costs, transportation, customs duties, and insurance. The purchase price is easy to determine. General costs, such as transportation, add to the amounts determined as used or sold. The most common way of treating purchase discounts is to reduce the cost of inventory used or sold.

The biggest problem in costing inventory is that identical items may have been purchased at various prices. At the end of the accounting period, however, a cost must be assigned to the items remaining in the inventory. If some way of identifying specific items with actual costs (called specific identification) is available, it is used. Otherwise, a method or convention for determining the flow of costs must be used. The three major conventions are:

- First In, First Out (fifo): Costs are charged against revenue in the order in which they were incurred. Using this method, the cost of inventory will be calculated based on the most recent purchases.
- Last In, First Out (lifo): The most recent costs are charged against revenue first. Using this method, the cost of inventory will be calculated based on the earliest purchases.
- Weighted Average Method (Average Cost): Costs are based on a computed average.

An individual company should be consistent in its use of a costing method. The method of costing should always be indicated on the Balance Sheet and any change in method should be fully disclosed.

DETERMINING INVENTORY VALUE

One way to determine the value of inventory is to simply use cost as described above; an alternative method is to compare cost with market price and use the lower of the two. This procedure is referred to as the lower of cost or market. "Market" refers to the cost of replacing the merchandise on the inventory date. Thus, in determining the cost of inventory, each item would be costed and its market price (replacement cost) would also be determined. The lower of the two costs would be used for inventory purposes.

A special method of inventory costing is widely used in retail business (especially department stores) and is called the retail inventory method. To use this method, the inventory is taken using the retail prices and then converted to cost by applying the ratio prevailing between costs and retail prices during that period. This method is popular because it does not require a physical inventory for the preparation of interim financial statements, and the individual cost of items need not be determined, thus saving considerable clerical time and effort.

When perpetual inventories are maintained or when the retail inventory method is employed--and especially when monthly financial statements are required by management--a gross profit method of estimating inventory is commonly used. This method takes the net sales for a period and subtracts the historically or empirically determined gross profit to arrive at the gross cost of merchandise sold. The gross cost of merchandise sold is subtracted from the cost of merchandise available for sale to yield an inventory of merchandise still on hand.

BALANCE SHEET PRESENTATION

Merchandise inventory is normally presented on a Balance Sheet as an asset and entered just below receivables. The balance sheet entry for merchandise inventory should always indicate both the method of costing the inventory (lifo, fifo, or average) and the method of valuing the inventory (cost, or lower of cost or market). This information is shown on the Balance Sheet in either a parenthetical notation or a footnote.

Self-Teaching Section A

INVENTORY SYSTEMS

1. There are two general types of inventory. Materials used in the process of production or held for such a use in a manufacturing enterprise are called

inventory. Inventory can also refer to _____

_____

– – – – – – – – – – – – – – – –

merchandise held for sale in the normal cost of business

2. In this chapter we shall be mainly concerned with merchandise held for sale. Inventory is very important in merchandise enterprises because it usually constitutes a large portion of a firm's resources.

Bud's Ford Dealership has the following resources. Which items are considered inventory?

        _____ a. a building and lot valued at $60,000
        _____ b. good will valued at $10,000
        _____ c. cars to be sold valued at $125,000
        _____ d. cash in the bank totaling $30,000

214 ACCOUNTING ESSENTIALS

– – – – – – – – – – – – – – –

(c)

3. Since inventory data and techniques are so important in the determination of profit
and therefore, also income taxes, the _____ is very interested in a company's
inventory (and inventory procedures).

– – – – – – – – – – – – – – –

the government, or the internal revenue service

4. The actual act of counting items in stock is referred to as taking a <u>physi-
cal</u> <u>inventory</u>. Once a year Mr. Jones goes through his stamp and coin shop
and counts all of the stamps and coins he has in the store. Thus, we can say

that once a year Mr. Jones takes a _____.

– – – – – – – – – – – – – – –

physical inventory

5. There are two basic systems of inventory accounting: (a) <u>the</u> <u>periodic</u>
<u>inventory</u> <u>system</u> in which only the costs of sales are recorded; no entries
are made that charge profit or loss with the cost of merchandise sold; and
(b) <u>the</u> <u>perpetual</u> <u>inventory</u> <u>system</u> in which the accounting records used continually disclose the amount of inventory that remains. Increases in inven-
tory are recorded as debits and decreases in inventory are recorded as credits to appropriate accounts.
    Using a rough analogy, consider the money in a checking account as in-
ventory. Each time Bill writes a check, he enters the amount of the check
but doesn't balance his checkbook except when he gets a monthly statement.
Sally, on the other hand, continually makes adjustments in her checkbook
for checks written, so she always knows exactly how much money she has
in her account. By analogy, we could say that Bill is using the

(a) _____ system to account for

his inventory (money). Sally is using the (b) _____
system to account for hers.

– – – – – – – – – – – – – – –

(a) periodic inventory; (b) perpetual inventory

6. The <u>periodic</u> <u>inventory</u> <u>system</u> is usually used by stores selling lots of
small items, such as groceries, hardware, and drug stores. The <u>perpetual</u>
<u>inventory</u> <u>system</u> is generally used by stores selling fewer, more expensive
items, such as furniture or autos. This makes sense, because the perpetual
inventory system is much more elaborate and time consuming than the periodic inventory system. As you can imagine, it would be much more difficult to keep
an up-to-the-minute account for breakfast cereal stock boxes than it would for

your stock of 2½ ton trucks. When there are more things to count, count them periodically.

Mr. Smith sells 342 items a day and the average sale is $.95. His accountant will probably urge him to use the (a) _____ system. Mrs. Weigel sells 1 item every three days and the average sale is $84.50. Her accountant will probably suggest she use the

(b) _____ system.

– – – – – – – – – – – – – – –

(a) periodic inventory; (b) perpetual inventory

7. No matter which inventory system is used, a physical inventory is necessary. In the case of the periodic inventory system, the physical inventory is taken at the end of the accounting period (usually once a year) to determine the actual quantity of items in stock. In the case of the perpetual inventory system, the physical inventory merely serves as a check on the accuracy of the inventory accounting procedures. The physical inventory is conducted at least once a year, but usually at a convenient time, not necessarily at the end of the accounting period.

We might say that a physical inventory serves to provide the actual inventory, in the case of the (a) _____ system. In the case of the (b) _____ system, the physical inventory is only a check on what is already known.

– – – – – – – – – – – – – – –

(a) periodic inventory; (b) perpetual inventory

8. In the case of the perpetual inventory system, we don't have to conduct a physical inventory every year. _____
(true/false)

– – – – – – – – – – – – – – –

false (in both systems, a yearly physical inventory is necessary)

9. The actual determination of inventory quantities is done by the physical inventory. All merchandise in the possession of the company is physically counted, weighed, or measured, as most appropriate. This physical counting is often conducted at night, or during a special period when all other business operations are suspended.

Once a year Mr. Schwartz closes his Food Market for three days and counts all his stock. Mr. Schwartz is taking his _____.

– – – – – – – – – – – – – – –

(annual) physical inventory

10. When Mr. Schwartz is taking his physical inventory, he faces one problem. He ordered some new items, and he knows they have already left the warehouse for his store. Does he count them as his or leave them for the warehouse's inventory? This decision is faced by many businessmen, especially manufacturers who are constantly shipping products to retailers. Conventions in different fields solve this problem. Some businesses "pass title to merchandise <u>FOB</u> (free on board) <u>shipping point</u>." This means that the title to goods passes to the purchaser when the goods are delivered to the common carrier and that the goods belong to the purchaser during transit. Other trades sell merchandise by the <u>FOB destination</u> convention, which means that the manufacturer maintains title to the goods until they reach their destination.

If a businessman buys or ships goods on FOB shipping point, he must examine sales or purchases invoices several days before and after the last day of the accounting period to be sure he includes all the goods he owns that are in transit. These must be added to his inventory.

Mr. Schwartz sells food goods for cash, and buys all his stock FOB destination. Does he need to worry about the goods that are in a truck coming to his store from the warehouse? Explain:

_____

_____

– – – – – – – – – – – –

No; FOB destination means the goods are not the property of Mr. Schwartz (and hence not part of his inventory) until they actually arrive at his store.

Self-Teaching Section B

DETERMINING INVENTORY COSTS

11. The cost of merchandise inventory is the purchase price <u>and all</u> <u>expenditures incurred in acquiring such merchandise</u>, including purchasing costs, transportation costs, customs duties, and insurance. The purchase price is easy to determine. General costs, such as transportation, are added to the amounts determined as used or sold. This is usually done by dividing the general costs by the number of items, and then assigning an equal portion of the cost to each item.

Similarly, the most common way of treating purchase discounts is to reduce the cost of inventory used or sold by an equal portion of the purchase discount.

Mr. Schwartz bought 60 large cans of peaches at $.15 per can. The shipping bill for the peaches came to $3.00. Mr. Schwartz figured that his time in ordering, checking the shipment, etc., came to $12.00. What cost for a

can of peaches should Mr. Schwartz enter on his inventory books? _____

– – – – – – – – – – – – – – –

$.40 $\begin{cases} \$3.00 + \$12.00 = \$15.00 \ . \ . \ \text{Total general costs} \\ \$15.00 \div 60 = \$.25 \ . \ . \ . \ . \ . \ \text{Additional costs assigned each item} \\ \$.15 + \$.25 = \$.40 \ . \ . \ . \ . \ . \ \text{Total inventory cost per item} \end{cases}$

12. The largest problem in costing inventory is that identical items, over the course of time, may have been purchased at different prices. For example, Mr. Schwartz bought peaches during 1971 at the following prices:

January 30	100 cans @ 28¢/can
March 30	100 cans @ 29¢/can
June 31	100 cans @ 31¢/can
August 1	100 cans @ 31¢/can
October 30	100 cans @ 30¢/can
December 15	100 cans @ 31¢/can

At the end of the accounting period, however, a cost must be assigned to the items remaining. In Mr. Schwartz's case, he had 150 cans left. Should he list those cans as costing 28¢, 29¢, 30¢, or 31¢ per can?

If some way of identifying specific items with actual costs is available, it is used. Such a process is called <u>specific identification</u>. For example, Mr. Brodski, the Dodge truck dealer, has an identification number on each truck on his lot. He may pay different prices for the same model trucks in the course of a year, but by recording each truck's identification number and price, he can always tell exactly what each truck on his inventory originally cost him. Mr. Brodski can determine inventory cost by

(a) _____. Mr. Schwartz can not do that, however, since peach cans don't have numbers, and besides there are too many of them to make specific identification reasonable. Mr. Schwartz must adopt some convention to determine the <u>flow of costs</u>. Thus, there are two general procedures for determining costs:

(b) _____ or some convention

that determines (c) _____.

- - - - - - - - - - - - - - - -

(a) specific identification; (b) specific identification; (c) flow of costs

13. There are three common conventions or procedures for determining <u>flow of costs</u>.

- <u>First In, First Out (fifo)</u>: Costs are charged against revenue in the order in which they were incurred. Using this method, the cost of inventory will be calculated based on the <u>most recent</u> purchases.
- <u>Last In, First Out (lifo)</u>: The most recent costs are charged against revenue first. Using this method, the cost of inventory will be calculated based on the <u>earliest purchases</u>.
- <u>Weighted Average Method (ave. cost)</u>: Costs are based on a computed average.

Miss Diamond purchased 50 balls of yarn on February 30 for $3.00 per ball. In September she purchased 50 balls at $3.10 per ball. At the end of the accounting period she had 50 balls left. If she figured her inventory as

50 balls at $3.00 per ball she would be using the (a)_____ method.
(abbreviate)

If she figured her inventory costs as 50 balls at $3.05 per ball she would be

using the (b)_____ method. If she figured her inventory costs as 50
(abbreviate)

balls at $3.10 per ball she would be using the (c)_____ method.
(abbreviate)

- - - - - - - - - - - - - - - -

(a) lifo; (b) ave. cost; (c) fifo

14. Different flow of cost conventions have different effects, as you can see from the following chart.

Effects in Times of Rising Costs

Cost Method	On Stated Value of Inventory	On Net Income of Firm
First in, first out (fifo)	Highest value of inventory	Highest possible amount of net income
Last in, first out (lifo)	Lowest value of inventory	Lowest possible amount of net income
Weighted average (ave. cost)	Average value of inventory	Average net income

In a period of _falling_ prices, which method of costing would make a business

look more profitable? (a) _____. Over a period of several years, which method would make the inventory of a business look most consistent?

(b) _____.

- - - - - - - - - - - - - - - -

(a) lifo; (b) ave. cost

15. An individual company should be consistent in its use of a costing method, and the method should always be indicated on the Balance Sheet; any change in method should be fully disclosed.

During a period when prices had been consistently rising for several years, Mr. Olvel switched from the average cost method to the lifo method without warning or disclosure (a clearly unacceptable practice!). Mr. Olvel always had a large inventory, and upon reading the new Balance Sheet, several of Mr. Olvel's investors and creditors were shocked to see how the

inventory had _____.

— — — — — — — — — — — — — —

    dropped during the last year (or equivalent answer)

16. Examine the following data:

PURCHASES (1985)		
January 1	100 units @ $5 each	$ 500
February 1	50 units @ $6 each	300
July 1	100 units @ $7 each	700
October 1	100 units @ $8 each	800
		$2300
SALES (1985)		
April 1	50 units @ $8 each	$400
December 30	25 units @ $9 each	225
		$625

To calculate the inventory on the first of the next year (1986), we total the units sold and subtract it from the units purchased. The inventory, as of January 1, 1986, is

_____.

— — — — — — — — — — — — — —

    275 units (350 − 75)

17. If we were using the <u>fifo</u> method, in Frame 16 we would start at the most recent purchases and work <u>backward</u> until we had costed enough units to equal the number in the inventory. Thus,

<u>Inventory = 275 units</u>

October 1	100 units @ $8 each	= $800
July 1	100 units @ $7 each	= $700
February 1	50 units @ $6 each	= $300
January 1	25 units @ $5 each	= $125
	275 units	$1925--inventory cost using fifo method

If we were using the <u>lifo</u> method, we would start at the oldest purchase and work <u>forward</u> until we had costed enough units to equal the inventory. Thus,

Inventory = 275 units

January 1	100 units @ $5 each	= $500
February 1	50 units @ $6 each	= $300
July 1	100 units @ $7 each	= $700
October 1	25 units @ $8 each	= $200
	275 units	$1700--inventory cost using lifo method

Using the average cost method, we divide the total purchase price by the total number of units purchased ($2300 ÷ 350). This yields an average cost per unit of $6.57 (carried out to three decimal places and rounded off to two). To determine inventory cost using the average cost method, the same number of units (275) is multiplied by the average cost per unit ($6.57) to yield $1806.75.

Fill in the three blank boxes in the following chart (using the information from Frames 16 and 17):

Cost Method	In a period of rising costs, on a stated value of inventory	Fill in figures from example above
fifo	Highest value of inventory	(a)
ave. cost	Average value of inventory	(b)
lifo	Lowest value of inventory	(c)

- - - - - - - - - - - - - - - - -

(a) $1925; (b) $1806; (c) $1700

18. Examine the following data:

PURCHASES			
January 1	100 units @ $30 each	$ 3,000
February 1	100 units @ $30 each	3,000
July 1	100 units @ $25 each	2,500
October 1	100 units @ $28 each	2,800
		$11,300
SALES		
March 30	25 units @ $52 each	$1,300
September 30	75 units @ $52 each	3,900
December 30	30 units @ $50 each	1,500
		$6,700

At the end of the accounting period represented, the inventory consists of

(a) _____ units. The ending inventory, computed on the fifo method, is

(b) $_____. The ending inventory, computed by the lifo method, is

(c) $_____. The weighted average cost per unit is (d) $_____,

thus the average cost inventory is (e) $_____.

- - - - - - - - - - - - - - - -

    (a) 270; (b) $7400; (c) $7750; (d) $28.25; (e) $7627.50 (If you had any
trouble with these answers, re-examine Frames 16 and 17 carefully,
and calculate the answers again.)

Self-Teaching Section C

DETERMINING INVENTORY VALUE

19. After costing inventory, it is still necessary to place a value on the inventory. The simplest method is to assume that the value of the inventory is
exactly equal to its cost. This method of valuing inventory is simply called
cost. An alternative method is to compare the cost with the market price and
use the lower of the two. This method of valuing inventory is referred to as
lower of cost or market (market refers to the cost of replacing the merchandise on the inventory date.)
    In applying the lower of cost or market method, each individual type of
item is costed (by the unit). Then the market price for that unit, or the date
of inventory, is determined. The lower of the two costs is used in subsequent
calculations. For income tax purposes, one can determine the value of inventory using either cost or lower of cost or market. One cannot, however,
apply lower of cost or market valuation to an inventory costed by the lifo
method.
    Mr. Alexander wants to use the lower of cost or market method to value
his inventory. Thus, for tax purposes, he must cost his inventory by one of

what two methods? (a) _____ (b) _____

- - - - - - - - - - - - - - - -

    (a) fifo; (b) ave. cost

20. Examine the following data:

PURCHASE	QUANTITY	UNIT COST PRICE (Average Cost Method)	UNIT MARKET PRICE
Item A	100	$10.00	$12.00
Item B	200	5.00	7.00
Item C	300	3.00	2.00
Item D	200	7.00	7.00

If the figures above were from a company that valued its inventory by the cost method, we would simply multiply unit costs times quantity and then add to determine the total value of the inventory. Thus,

$$100 \times \$10 = \$1000$$
$$200 \times 5 = 1000$$
$$300 \times 3 = 900$$
$$200 \times 7 = \underline{1400}$$
$$\underline{\$4300} \quad \text{total value of inventory, valued on the } \underline{\text{cost}} \text{ method}$$

If these figures were from a company that valued its inventory by the lower of cost or market method, the calculations would be more complex. Thus,

	Unit Cost Price	Unit Market Price	Multiply Lower of Two Unit Costs	Total Cost of Item
Item A 100	$10	$12	(100 x 10)	$1000
Item B 200	5	7	(200 x 5)	1000
Item C 300	3	2	(300 x 2)	600
Item D 200	7	7	(200 x 7)	1400

Total value of inventory, valued at the lower of cost
or market method $4000

When using the lower of cost or market method you can never get a total higher than the total cost, but you can get a lower total.

21. Examine the following data:

PURCHASE	QUANTITY	UNIT COST PRICE	UNIT MARKET PRICE
Item A	20	$2500	$2300
Item B	100	6500	6550
Item C	300	3780	3780
Item D	1000	175	180
Item E	10	7200	7100

(a) What is the inventory's total value at <u>cost</u>? $_____

(b) What is the inventory's total value at <u>lower of cost or market</u>?

$_____

– – – – – – – – – – – – – – – –

   (a) $2,081,000; (b) $2,076,000. If you had any trouble with these answers, re-examine Frame 20, then recalculate your answers.

22. There are two special inventory methods used to both <u>cost</u> and <u>value</u> inventory in special circumstances. One, which is widely used in the retail business (especially department stores), is called the <u>retail inventory method</u>. To use this method, the inventory is taken using market retail prices. It is then converted to cost by applying the business's average ratio between costs and retail prices prevailing for that inventory period. This method is necessarily somewhat inaccurate, but works well enough if the business has a large number of reasonably cheap items. This method is popular because it does not require a physical inventory for the preparation of interim financial statements, and because the individual costs of items need not be determined.

   Consider the following data:

	COST	RETAIL
Merchandise inventory, beginning of period	$20,000	$30,000
Purchases (net)	30,000	38,000
Merchandise available for sale	$50,000	$68,000
Less sales for period		42,000
Merchandise inventory, end of period (at retail prices)		$26,000
Ratio between cost and retail of merchandise available for sale ($50,000 ÷ $68,000)		74%

To determine the inventory for the store whose data is displayed above, we multiply the merchandise inventory (calculated at retail prices of $26,000) by the ratio (74%). Using the <u>retail inventory method</u>, we can say that this store has an inventory of $19,240.

Now examine this data:

	COST	RETAIL
Merchandise inventory, beginning of period	$100,000	$163,000
Purchases (net)	10,000	12,000
Merchandise available for sale	$110,000	$175,000
Less sales for period		$159,000
Merchandise inventory, end of period (at retail price)		$16,000
Ratio between cost and retail of merchandise available for sale ($110,000 ÷ $175,000)		62%

Using the retail inventory method, what is the merchandise inventory for the period summarized above? $_____

- - - - - - - - - - - - - - - -

$9920

23. A second special method of obtaining an inventory is called the gross profit method. This method is commonly used when perpetual inventories are maintained, and when a company's management wants monthly financial statements. This method takes the gross sales for a period and subtracts the historically or empirically derived gross profit to arrive at the gross cost of merchandise sold. The gross cost of merchandise sold is subtracted from the cost of merchandise available for sale to yield the cost of the merchandise on hand (i.e., inventory).

The FARB Company has a beginning inventory of $50,000. Its net purchases come to $10,000, so the total merchandise available for sale is $60,000. Net sales come to $50,000. We are told that gross profit amounts to 36% of net sales. By subtracting 36% from 100% we determine that 64% of the net sales were from merchandise available for sale. We multiply 64% times the net sales ($50,000) to get $32,000. We then subtract this amount from the total inventory available for sale ($60,000) to arrive at the remaining inventory--$28,000.

Try this yourself in this example. Company XYZ has a beginning inventory of $80,000. Net purchases for the period come to $30,000. Net sales come to $82,000. The company's estimated profit is 21%. Using the gross profit method, estimate the inventory for the period described. $_____

- - - - - - - - - - - - - - - -

$45,220

Self-Teaching Section D

BALANCE SHEET PREPARATION

24. Merchandise inventory is normally presented on a Balance Sheet as an asset and entered below receivables. The Balance Sheet merchandise inventory entry should always indicate both the method of costing the inventory (lifo, fifo, or ave. cost) and the method of valuing the inventory (cost, or lower of cost or market), or some special method if used (retail or gross profit). This information should be entered in parenthetical notation or a footnote.

Is the following portion of a Balance Sheet correct? _____

```
                                        COMPANY XYZ
                                        Balance Sheet
                                        January 1, 19--

        ASSETS

          Current Cash

            Cash . . . . . . . . . . . . . . . . . . $ 51,001.25

            Accounts Receivable . . . . . . . . . . $121,035.01

            Inventory (fifo, cost)  . . . . . . . . . $321,000.31
```

– – – – – – – – – – – – – – – –

yes

25. Where on the Balance Sheet is the merchandise inventory normally located? (a) _____

What information should be provided besides the cost of the inventory?

(b) _____

_____

– – – – – – – – – – – – – – –

(a) an asset entered just below receivables; (b) the method of costing and the method of valuing used (usually in parentheses or as a footnote)

SELF-TEST

This Self-Test will show you whether or not you have mastered the chapter objectives and are ready to go on to the next chapter. Answer each question to the best of your ability. Correct answers and instructions are given at the end of the test.

1. Match the following items (one item can match more than one definition).

   (a) fifo
   (b) lifo
   (c) weighted average
   (d) lower of cost or market
   (e) market (price)
   (f) retail inventory method

   (g) gross profit method
   (h) taking a physical inventory
   (i) inventory
   (j) periodic inventory system
   (k) perpetual inventory system

   _____ (1) The actual act of counting items in stock.

   _____ (2) Merchandise held for sale in the normal course of business.

   _____ (3) Uses accounting records that continually disclose the amount of inventory that remains.

   _____ (4) Costs are charged against revenue in the order in which they were incurred.

   _____ (5) Cost of replacing the merchandise on the inventory date.

   _____ (6) Materials in the process of production, or held for such use in a manufacturing enterprise.

   _____ (7) The most recent costs are charged against revenue first.

   _____ (8) Costs are compared with market price and the lower of the two is used to value the inventory.

   _____ (9) Costs are charged against revenues on the basis of a computed average.

   _____ (10) Only the sales are recorded; no entries are made that charge profit or loss with the cost of merchandise sold.

   _____ (11) Inventory is taken using the retail prices and then converted to cost by applying the ratio prevailing between costs and retail prices during that period.

   _____ (12) Gross profit is subtracted from gross sales to determine gross cost of merchandise sold. This is then subtracted from the total cost of merchandise available for sale to yield an inventory of merchandise still on hand.

2. Using this data, fill in the blanks below:

PURCHASES		
January 30	10 units @ $6 each	$ 60
February 30	20 units @ $7 each	140
April 1	50 units @ $8 each	400
July 1	50 units @ $8 each	400
		$1000
SALES		
March 30	15 units @ $10 each	$150
August 30	25 units @ $12 each	300
		$450

(a) A September 1 ending inventory consists of _____ units.

(b) The ending inventory, computed on the fifo method, is $_____.

(c) The ending inventory, computed on the lifo method, is $_____.

(d) The weighted average cost per unit is $_____; thus, the weighted
     average cost inventory is $_____.

(e) From the data we can see that unit prices are gradually rising; which
     costing method will yield the lowest value of inventory during such a
     period?   ____ fifo, ____ lifo, ____ weighted average

3. Examine the following data:

PURCHASE	QUANTITY	UNIT COST PRICE	UNIT MARKET PRICE
Item A	100	$10.00	$12.50
Item B	300	5.00	7.50
Item C	100	4.00	3.00
Item D	500	6.00	6.00

Assume the data to be from a company that values its inventory on the
lower of cost or market rule.

(a) What is the inventory's total value at cost? $_____

(b) What is the inventory's total value at lower of cost or market? $_____

4. Examine the following data:

	COST	RETAIL
Merchandise inventory, beginning of period	$ 5,000	$ 6,000
Purchases (net)	20,000	25,000
Merchandise available for sale	$25,000	$31,000
Less sales for period		21,000
Merchandise inventory, end of period (at retail price)		$10,000
Ratio between cost and retail of merchandise available for sale ($25,000 ÷ $31,000)		83%

Using the retail inventory method, what is the value of the merchandise inventory for the period summarized above? $_____

5. Consider these facts: The beginning inventory is $30,000; net purchases for the period come to $10,000; net sales come to $25,000; the estimated gross profit is 30%. Using the gross profit method, estimate the inventory for this period. $_____

6. Where on the Balance Sheet is the merchandise inventory normally located? (a) _____
What information should be provided besides the cost of the inventory?

(b) _____

Self-Test Answers

Compare your answers to the Self-Test with the correct answers given below. If all of your answers are correct, you are ready to go on to the next chapter. If you missed any questions, study the frames indicated in parentheses following the answer. If you miss many questions, go over the entire chapter carefully.

1. (1) h (Frames 4, 7-9)   (7) b (Frames 13-18)
    (2) i (Frames 1-2)   (8) d (Frames 19-21)
    (3) k (Frames 5-6)   (9) c (Frames 13-18)
    (4) a (Frames 13-18)   (10) j (Frames 5-6)
    (5) e (Frame 19)   (11) f (Frame 22)
    (6) i (Frames 1-2)   (12) g (Frame 23)

2. (a) 90 units; (b) $720; (c) $680; (d) $7.69, $692.10; (e) lifo (Frames 11-18)

3. (a) $5900; (b) $5800 (Frames 19-21)

4. $8300 (Frame 22)

5. $22,500 (Frame 23)

6. (a) As an asset entered just below receivables.
    (b) The method of costing and the method of valuing used.
                                            (Frames 24-25)

CHAPTER EIGHT

Internal Control

OBJECTIVES

When you complete this chapter, you will be able to

- explain the guidelines for internal control,
- evaluate the adequacy of an internal control system,
- place in order the steps in the voucher system,
- determine items that would be included in the petty cash system,
- reconcile a bank statement.

If you feel that you have already mastered these objectives and might skip all or part of this chapter, turn to the end of the chapter and take the Self-Test. The results will tell you what frames of the chapter you should study. If you answer all questions correctly, you are ready to begin the next chapter.

If this material is new to you, or if you choose not to take the Self-Test now, turn to the Overview and Self-Teaching Sections that follow.

CHAPTER OVERVIEW

THE CONCEPT OF INTERNAL CONTROL

In any accounting system, the internal controls are all those procedures that insure

(a) the protection of business assets, and
(b) the accuracy of record keeping.

As a business gets larger and larger, the steps that must be taken to insure adequate control get more and more complex. The chances of error increase with size and the risks of error involving company assets become greater with increased complexity and decentralization. The possibility of error, however, exists even in the business where the owner is the only employee. Thus, the need for some sort of internal control applies to all companies, small as well as large. The general guidelines for internal control are as follows.

(a) The responsibility of taking care of any asset and the job of keeping the records for that asset should be assigned to two different individuals.
(b) Where possible, any job involving record keeping should involve two or more people.
(c) Mechanical devices, such as adding machines and cash registers, should be used whenever possible.

CONTROL OF RECEIPTS

All businesses should have some set procedure for handling incoming cash (currency, checks, etc.). The following diagram shows a simple cash receipt system which involves three people: a clerk, a cashier, and an accountant. Notice that all of the guidelines for control are included in this system.

A SIMPLE CASH RECEIPTS SYSTEM

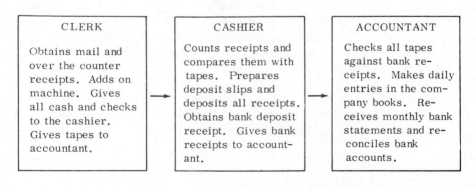

CLERK	CASHIER	ACCOUNTANT
Obtains mail and over the counter receipts. Adds on machine. Gives all cash and checks to the cashier. Gives tapes to accountant.	Counts receipts and compares them with tapes. Prepares deposit slips and deposits all receipts. Obtains bank deposit receipt. Gives bank receipts to accountant.	Checks all tapes against bank receipts. Makes daily entries in the company books. Receives monthly bank statements and reconciles bank accounts.

CONTROL OF DISBURSEMENTS

The foremost concern of the control of disbursements (payments) is to maximize accuracy and to protect the company's assets from improper disbursements. So it is customary for payments to be made only when authorized by a single individual who is given that responsibility. Such control is further strengthened when all payments are made by check.

Even in moderate-sized organizations, a voucher system is used. A simple voucher system involving a clerk and a financial officer is illustrated below:

A SIMPLE VOUCHER SYSTEM

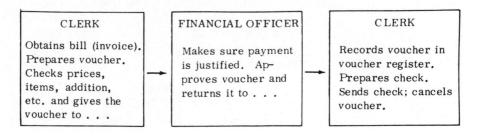

CLERK	FINANCIAL OFFICER	CLERK
Obtains bill (invoice). Prepares voucher. Checks prices, items, addition, etc. and gives the voucher to . . .	Makes sure payment is justified. Approves voucher and returns it to . . .	Records voucher in voucher register. Prepares check. Sends check; cancels voucher.

In larger organizations, payment of the voucher is a separate step: When the voucher is to be paid, the clerk delivers it to the disbursements clerk, who prepares the check and makes the journal entries. The check is then forwarded to the treasurer for signature and approval; the voucher, marked "Paid," is returned to the voucher clerk.

Notice that, like the cash receipts system, the voucher system follows the guidelines for internal control:

    (a) a separation of custody of an asset from records for that asset,

    (b) a division of responsibility, and

    (c) the use of mechanical devices whenever possible.

The voucher system is not practical for the small day-to-day expenditures that are necessary in a business of any size. For this reason, cash for such things as postage, carfare, and the like is disbursed through a petty cash fund. In this procedure, a check is drawn to a petty cashier who cashes it. Any employee who needs a small amount of cash fills out a petty cash voucher, gets it approved, and presents it to the petty cashier who then gives him the cash he needs. The employee returns receipts or other records to the cashier that prove how the cash was used. When the money in the petty cash fund drops below a certain level, the cashier requests that a check be drawn in the total amount of all of the paid vouchers, thus replenishing the money in the fund. The amount of the paid vouchers, plus the cash remaining in the fund, should be equal to the total amount of the fund.

THE BANK ACCOUNT

Most businesses use a bank for holding and protecting cash. Cash transactions involving checks and money orders go through the bank and are thus subjected to an external check. Banks also extend many useful business services such as credit, automatic deductions, and safe deposit boxes.

Each month at a specified time, a bank sends the depositor a record of his monthly transactions and all the cancelled checks paid by the bank. This record is called a <u>bank</u> <u>statement</u>. On receipt of the statement, a bookkeeper or accountant checks the company's books against the statement to be sure that they agree. This checking procedure is called <u>reconciling</u> <u>the</u> <u>account</u>. The reconciliation procedure can be summarized as follows:

- To the balance given in the bank statement,
    - (a) add deposits not yet recorded by the bank, and
    - (b) subtract outstanding checks
- To the balance given in the company checkbook,
    - (a) add amounts that have been collected automatically by the bank (notes, etc.), but not recorded in the checkbook, and
    - (b) subtract bank charges not yet recorded by the company (service charges, non-sufficient funds charges, etc.)
- When these operations have been carried out the two totals obtained should agree. In this case, the account is said to be reconciled.

Self-Teaching Section A

THE CONCEPT OF INTERNAL CONTROL

1. <u>Internal</u> <u>controls</u> <u>are</u> <u>those</u> <u>procedures</u> <u>that</u> <u>insure</u> <u>the</u> <u>protection</u> <u>of</u> <u>the</u> <u>company's</u> <u>assets</u> <u>and</u> <u>the</u> <u>accuracy</u> <u>of</u> <u>its</u> <u>records</u>. Which of the following procedures are likely to be the direct concern of an internal control system?

        _____ a. the hiring of a night watchman
        _____ b. the purchase of a water cooler
        _____ c. making sure that a check is drawn in the proper amount
        _____ d. locking the safe at night
        _____ e. ringing up the correct amount on the cash register

- - - - - - - - - - - - - - - -

   (a), (c), (d), and (e)

2. Internal controls are all procedures that insure _____

_____ and _____.

- - - - - - - - - - - - - - - -

    protection of assets <u>and</u> accuracy of records (in either order)

3. The Donald Duck Company employs over 400 people in such diverse departments as accounts payable, accounts receivable, sales, purchasing, maintenance, and so forth. The Mickey Mouse Company, on the other hand, employs only two people, the owner and an assistant. Which of these two companies is likely to have more errors in record keeping?

    ____ a. The Donald Duck Company
    ____ b. The Mickey Mouse Company

— — — — — — — — — — — — — — —

   (a)

4. As companies get more complex, their total assets are usually greater and therefore justify more complex protection procedures. Also, as companies get more complex there is a greater likelihood that record-keeping errors will occur. Therefore, as companies get more complex, they require

_____ formal control procedures.
(more/less)

— — — — — — — — — — — — — — —

   more

5. Small companies also need control procedures, but they can employ

_____ formal procedures than large companies.
(more/less)

— — — — — — — — — — — — — — —

   less

6. One problem with any organization is that individuals who handle cash may be tempted to steal. They are not as tempted, however, if at the end of the day there is an accurate and independent recording of the sales that they made and the amount of cash that they turn in. If you were assigning jobs to employees, you would probably want to make sure that the job of taking in cash (called <u>maintaining custody</u>) and the job of checking sales against end-

of-day totals (<u>record keeping</u>) were done by _____ individual(s).
                                   (different/the same)

— — — — — — — — — — — — — — —

   different

7. Using the information in the last frame, write a <u>general</u> guideline to be followed in order to protect a company's assets:

In protecting any asset, it is important to _____

_____

- - - - - - - - - - - - - - -

separate the responsibility for custody of an asset from the responsibility for record keeping for that asset (or equivalent)

8. Mr. Schneider, the bookkeeper for Markle's Appliance Distributors, always has his assistant total the credit balances in the Accounts Payable Subsidiary Ledger as he himself posts the Purchases Journal to the General Ledger. They have caught many errors in this way. From this we can generalize that in order to assure accurate arithmetic and accurate record keeping, it is a good idea to make sure that a record-keeping task is designed so that it involves

_____ a. the accountant of the firm
_____ b. the company's best mathematician
_____ c. at least two persons

- - - - - - - - - - - - - - -

(c)

9. The main reason that record-keeping tasks should involve two people is so that

_____ a. one can post the General Ledger
_____ b. each can act as a check on the other's work

- - - - - - - - - - - - - - -

(b)

10. Results are usually more accurate if people use mechanical devices, such as cash registers and adding machines. Use of these devices usually decreases the number of _____ in the record-keeping process.

- - - - - - - - - - - - - - -

errors or mistakes

11. Three general guidelines for protecting assets and insuring accurate accounting records are:

(a) To protect an asset _____

_____

(b) For any record-keeping job _____

_____ and

(c) _____

- - - - - - - - - - - - - - -

(a) separate the custody of the asset from the record keeping for that same asset; (b) involve at least two people in any task; and (c) use mechanical devices whenever possible

12. It stands to reason that assets which are small and easily disposed of need more careful protection than assets which are large and difficult to dispose of. Most established control procedures concentrate on keeping track of which asset? _____

— — — — — — — — — — — — — —

cash

Self-Teaching Section B

CONTROL OF RECEIPTS

13. Cash comes into a business in the form of currency or check payments by customers. Cash goes out of a business in the form of currency or checks for purchases by the business. Internal control of cash, therefore, is divided into two parts:

    (a) the control of cash receipts, and
    (b) the control of cash disbursements.

Larson Television is a T. V. sales and service company in downtown Minneapolis. Larson's income comes from cash sales to its retail customers as well as checks in payment of sales on account. The currency and checks taken in on any day represent Larson's total daily _____ receipts.

— — — — — — — — — — — — — —

cash

14. Larson's system for processing incoming cash receipts involves the following three activities:

    (a) Receipts are obtained and added together.
    (b) Bank deposit tickets are prepared and the receipts are deposited in the bank.
    (c) The amount of the receipts is entered on the company books.

In accordance with the principles of internal control, the individual who is given the responsibility for activity _____ should not also be given the
            (a), (b), or (c)
responsibility for either activity _____ or _____.

— — — — — — — — — — — — — —

(c); (a) and (b)

15.   Bob Smith is a counter salesman for Larson Television. It is his job to take cash from the retail customers and to ring up the sales on the cash register while the customer looks on. Locked within the cash register is an automatic adding machine that totals the amounts rung up and prepares a tape record of each transaction and its total. At the end of the day, the cashier unlocks the register and removes the tape. What internal control principles

help to insure that Bob rings up the right amount? _____

_____

_____

— — — — — = — — — — — — — — — —

   There are two people involved in the initial record keeping, Bob and the customer; Bob uses a machine to do the addition; and Bob knows the the tape will later be checked against receipts.

16.   What mechanical device helps Bob produce accurate records of his

transactions? _____

— — — — — — — — — — — — — — — —

   the cash register

17.   In addition to ringing up cash sales, Bob Smith has been given another responsibility--to open the mail each day, to gather mailed receipts, and to add them together on an adding machine which produces a tape showing the addition.
   The cashier, whose job it is to check Bob's work and to deposit the receipts in the bank, has to obtain <u>four</u> different items from Bob at the end of each day:

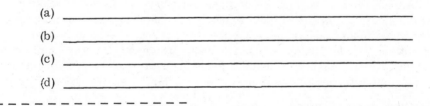

(a) _____

(b) _____

(c) _____

(d) _____

— — — — — — — — — — — — — — — —

   (a) cash receipts, (b) cash register total, (c) mailed receipts, and (d) adding machine total (Bob's tapes are given to the company accountant or bookkeeper.)

18.   When the cashier obtains these things from Bob, he counts the currency (cash receipts) and compares his total with Bob's total. He then totals the mailed receipts (mostly checks) by machine and compares his total with Bob's total. When he is satisfied that all is in order, he makes out a deposit ticket, carries the receipts to the bank, and deposits them. The bank gives the cashier a <u>bank receipt</u> (deposit ticket) which shows the amount deposited.

The cashier then gives the bank deposit ticket and his adding machine tapes generated thus far to a company accountant or bookkeeper. Before the daily totals are entered, the accountant must make sure that the receipts totaled on the register tape plus the total of the mailed receipts are equal to

_____

- - - - - - - - - - - - - -

the total of the bank deposit tickets

19. Only when the accountant or bookkeeper has made sure that the proper amount has been deposited in the bank can he _____

_____

- - - - - - - - - - - - - -

enter the cash receipts on the company books (or equivalent answer)

20. Monthly the bank statement is forwarded to the accountant. He compares the deposits shown on the bank statement with _____

_____.

- - - - - - - - - - - - - -

the receipts recorded on the company books (in the Cash Receipts Journal)

Self-Teaching Section C

CONTROL OF DISBURSEMENTS

21. All businesses, regardless of size, must have some way of making sure that when cash is disbursed (paid to outsiders) the business is receiving goods or services in an equal value. The cash disbursement system is designed to assure this. In the Mickey Mouse Company (which only has two employees), the owner, a Mr. Disney, considers each and every purchase before he writes a check to pay for the item. In effect, Mr. Disney's check of items prior to check writing is a _____.

- - - - - - - - - - - - - -

cash disbursement system (an internal control)

22. In order to make sure that no unjustified disbursement is made, many businesses use a cash disbursement system called a voucher system. The voucher system can be time consuming and expensive, so businesses need to carefully consider if their needs justify the use of this cash disbursement system. In the voucher system, a document called a voucher is prepared, requesting that a check be drawn for a cash disbursement. It is only when

the voucher has been approved that _____.

– – – – – – – – – – – – – – – –

cash may be disbursed, or payment can be made (or equivalent)

23. For a voucher system to be most effective for internal control, a voucher should be prepared and approved for each and every payment that is made. Which of the following would have been requested through the preparation of a voucher?

_____ a. the payment for supplies
_____ b. the ordering of supplies
_____ c. the payment of salaries
_____ d. the payment for merchandise
_____ e. the payment of utilities expense

– – – – – – – – – – – – – – –

   (a); (c); (d); (e)

24. The main characteristic of the voucher system is that cash, in the form of check payments, may be disbursed only after the voucher has been approved by the appropriate individual--usually the financial officer of the company. Planning is also important to this system, so that cash is not disbursed before necessary.
     The steps in disbursing cash through the voucher system are as follows:

    When an invoice has been received and it has been determined that
    the items on the invoice have been delivered,
    (a) a voucher is prepared
    (b) the voucher is approved
    (c) the voucher is entered into a special journal called the Voucher
         Register
    (d) the voucher is placed in an unpaid voucher file
    (e) a bookkeeper goes through the file and prepares a check in the
         amount of each voucher
    (f) the checks are entered in a book called the Check Register.

Since the voucher system exerts most control when all requests for cash payments are put through the sequence above, it is safe to assume that in a company using the voucher system, all payments are made by _____.

– – – – – – – – – – – – – – –

check

25. Suppose you are a clerk for Criterion Optics, Inc. On August 28 the following invoice came to your desk:

```
┌─────────────────────────────────────────────────────────────────┐
│                      ALLIED SUPPLIES                              │
│                      2740 9th Street                              │
│                      New York, N.Y.                               │
│                                                                   │
│                          Invoice                                  │
│                                                                   │
│                               Number   894                        │
│                                                                   │
│   Sold to:  Criterion Optics, Inc.    Date Shipped:   8/9/8-      │
│             567 Marshal Street                                    │
│             Hampstead, Ga.            Salesman:  EBR              │
│                                                                   │
│   Pieces             Description                   Price          │
│     1        Grinding Machine - Model IV        $3,500.00         │
│              (I.D. #604849)                                       │
└─────────────────────────────────────────────────────────────────┘
```

Your first step would be to:

_____ a. draw a check in the amount of $3500
_____ b. find out if the grinding machine had, in fact, been
          delivered in good condition

– – – – – – – – – – – – – – – –

   (b)

26. After making sure the machine was delivered, the next step would be to fill out a voucher. Below is a blank voucher. In practice, the information required on the bottom (or back) of a voucher varies widely, though it usually includes the items on the voucher reproduced on the following page. Use the information on the invoice above to fill in the top half of the voucher:

```
                              VOUCHER


        Date: _____       Voucher Number: _476_____

        Payee: _____       Item: _____

        Address: _____       Invoice Number: _____

               _____       Payment Date: _____

     _____

     Account To Be Debited   Amount   Account Distribution
     _____       $___     Approved: _____

     _____      ____    Entered in Voucher
                                         Register: _____
     _____     ====     Approved for
     Total Voucher Payable               Payment: _____
       Credit                 ____     Check Number: _____

                                       Entered in Check
                                         Register: _____
```

```
                              VOUCHER


     Date: _8/28/8-_____       Voucher Number: __476_____
     Payee: _Allied Supplies_       Item: _Grinding Machine____
     Address: _2740-9th Street      Invoice Number: __894_____
             _New York, N.Y.__      Payment Date: _____
```

27. Your next step, as the clerk for Criterion Optics, is to

     ____ a. file the voucher in the unpaid voucher file
     ____ b. enter the Voucher Register
     ____ c. send the voucher to the financial officer for approval

(c)

28. Once the financial officer approves the purchase and signs the voucher, the information on the voucher is entered in a Voucher Register. Since a voucher is entered whenever there is a request for any payment, the Voucher Register can be thought of as taking the place of

    ____ a. the Cash Disbursements Journal

    ____ b. the Purchases Journal

- - - - - - - - - - - - - - -

(b) (Note that the Cash Disbursements Journal is <u>not</u> replaced by the Voucher Register, because the Voucher Register records only <u>requests</u> for disbursement, not the actual disbursement of cash.)

29. Since a voucher is a request for payment, be it for merchandise, salary, services, or supplies, the Voucher Register is often thought of as an <u>expand-ed Purchases Journal</u>.

Below is the Voucher Register for Criterion Optics. Study it carefully.

VOUCHER REGISTER							
Date	Payee	Voucher Number	Vouchers Payable Credit	Purchases Debit	Sundry Debit		
					Account	p.r.	Amount

Notice that the register has columns for

(a) payee--the person or firm to which the requested check will be drawn,

(b) the date, the voucher number, a p.r. column, and

(c) three money columns in which the amounts of the transaction are written.

Since each request for a check to be drawn goes through the voucher system, you would expect that the amounts of <u>all</u> requested payments be entered in the

column headed _____.

- - - - - - - - - - - - - - -

vouchers payable credit

30. When a voucher is prepared the amount is credited to an account called
<u>vouchers</u> <u>payable</u>. Thus, the vouchers payable account will record all of the
short-term debts of a business. This being the case, the vouchers payable
account must be classified as

       ____ a. an asset account
       ____ b. a liability account
       ____ c. an owner's equity account

- - - - - - - - - - - - - - -

  (b)

31. When a check is actually prepared in payment of a voucher, a <u>decrease</u>
in the vouchers payable account must be recorded. This will be done through

a _____ entry to the vouchers payable account.
 (debit/credit)

- - - - - - - - - - - - - - -

  debit

32. The <u>purchases</u> <u>debit</u> <u>column</u> is used for

       ____ a. purchases of office supplies
       ____ b. purchases of merchandise
       ____ c. both of the above

- - - - - - - - - - - - - - -

  (b) (Remember "purchases" means purchases of <u>merchandise</u>.)

33. Use the information on the voucher in Frame 26 to make an entry into
the Voucher Register in Frame 29.

- - - - - - - - - - - - - - -

VOUCHER REGISTER								
Date	Payee	Voucher Number	Vouchers Payable Credit	Purchases Debit	Sundry Debit			
					Account	p.r.	Amount	
Aug 28	Allied Supplies	476	3,500 00		Equipment		3,500 00	

34. Here are two more transactions. Enter each of them on the Voucher Register in Frame 29.

- On August 29, the financial officer approves voucher number 477 which requested that a $400 check be drawn payable to Clearview Optics, Inc., for merchandise purchased that same day.

- On August 30, voucher number 478 is approved. It requests payment of $60 be made for a cash purchase of supplies from Carter Stationers.

- - - - - - - - - - - - - - - -

VOUCHER REGISTER								
Date	Payee	Voucher Number	Vouchers Payable Credit	Purchases Debit		Sundry Debit		
						Account	p.r.	Amount
Aug 28	Allied Supplies	476	3,500 00			Equipment		3,500 00
29	Clearview Optics	477	400 00	400 00				
30	Carter Stationers	478	60 00			Supplies		60 00

35. All requests for payment go through the voucher system. Therefore, the amounts of all payments requested will eventually be posted as credits to the vouchers payable account. The vouchers payable account is debited only when _____.

- - - - - - - - - - - - - - - -

the check is drawn, or when the voucher is paid (or equivalent)

36. As soon as the voucher is entered into the Voucher Register, it is filed in the unpaid voucher file, usually according to the date when the voucher must be paid. When a voucher comes due, it is removed from the unpaid voucher file and a check is prepared (drawn). As soon as the check is drawn, the check number, the amount, the payee, and the accounts affected are recorded in the Check Register. All entries to the Check Register involve a

_____ to the _____ account.
(debit/credit)

- - - - - - - - - - - - - - - -

debit; vouchers payable

37. On the following page are the headings from a simple form of Check Register:

CHECK REGISTER						
Date	Payee	Voucher Number	Check Number	Vouchers Payable Debit	Purchases Credit	Cash Credit

Since all payments are made by check, and all checks are entered in the Check Register, the Check Register can replace what other special journal?

_____

– – – – – – – – – – – – – – –

the Cash Disbursements Journal

38. In the voucher system described in this chapter, there are no individual customer accounts maintained. Hence there is no need for

_____ a. an Accounts Receivable Subsidiary Ledger
_____ b. a General Ledger
_____ c. an Accounts Payable Subsidiary Ledger

– – – – – – – – – – – – – – –

(c)

39. The amount due on each voucher is often thought of in the same way as a credit balance in an Accounts Payable Subsidiary Ledger. Hence, when the voucher system is used, the Accounts Payable Subsidiary Ledger is replaced by

_____ a. the unpaid voucher file   _____ c. the Voucher Register
_____ b. the Check Register   _____ d. the paid voucher file

– – – – – – – – – – – – – – –

(a) (not (c), since at any given time the Voucher Register will include paid as well as unpaid vouchers)

40. When a check is sent, the voucher is marked "paid." The "paid" voucher is then placed in a file called the _____ file.

– – – – – – – – – – – – – – –

paid voucher

41. Several events in the voucher system are listed below. Number the events in order of their occurrence:

    ____ a. the voucher is prepared
    ____ b. the check is prepared
    ____ c. the invoice is received
    ____ d. an entry is made into the Voucher Register
    ____ e. the voucher is filed in the unpaid voucher file
    ____ f. the voucher is filed in the paid voucher file
    ____ g. the voucher is approved
    ____ h. an entry is made in the Check Register

— — — — — — — — — — — — — —

    (a) 2; (b) 6; (c) 1; (d) 4; (e) 5; (f) 8; (g) 3; (h) 7

42. Edward Collins, the delivery man at Criterion Optics, has to go clear across town to make a delivery to a customer. He expects that Criterion will pay for his transportation. He returns with a receipt from the bus driver which shows that Edward paid 20¢ for transportation. What will Edward do now?

    ____ a. request that a voucher be prepared and that a check subsequently be issued to him for 20¢
    ____ b. there must be an easier way to obtain small amounts of cash

— — — — — — — — — — — — — —

    (b)

43. The voucher system for disbursing cash is quite adequate for the day-to-day purchases made by a company. For very small, or for emergency expenditures, however, the voucher system could become quite unwieldy. In these cases, small amounts of cash are disbursed by a company employee called the petty cashier, through a system called the petty cash system.

    Edward would get his bus fare from the _____.

— — — — — — — — — — — — — —

    petty cashier

44. In order to get the fare, Edward fills out a petty cash voucher--a small slip of paper that gives the amount of cash he needs, the way it will be spent, his signature, and the signature of his supervisor (or whoever is authorized to sign petty cash vouchers). After Edward returns from his trip he must offer some proof that he has spent the money in the approved manner. What

kind of proof will Edward offer? _____

— — — — — — — — — — — — — —

    a receipt from the bus driver (or equivalent answer)

45. Most petty cash systems are established by drawing a check payable to the petty cashier in some specified amount. This employee cashes the check and keeps the cash in his or her office ready to disburse it when presented

with _____.
– – – – – – – – – – – – – – – –
an approved petty cash voucher

46. If the check establishing the petty cash fund was disbursed through a voucher system, a record of the check will be found in both the

_____ and the _____.
– – – – – – – – – – – – – – –
Check Register; Voucher Register

47. When the petty cash fund was established at Criterion Optics, it was felt that $20 would be adequate for the total fund. When, in the course of time the fund drops below a certain minimum ($5 at Criterion), the petty

cashier will _____.
– – – – – – – – – – – – – – –
request that another check be drawn, or prepare a voucher (if voucher system is used)

48. Before the financial officer will approve the drawing of a check to the petty cashier, he must be satisfied that all of the money drawn out of the petty cash fund in the past was spent in a justifiable manner. He is assured of this because

_____ a. the cashier requires anyone who makes an expenditure through the fund to return a receipt for this expenditure
_____ b. all petty cash expenditures are recorded in the Voucher Register and in the Check Register
_____ c. petty cashiers are chosen for their long time records for honesty

– – – – – – – – – – – – – –
(a)

49. If Criterion's petty cash fund dropped to $3.50, what should be the total value of the receipts accumulated by the petty cashier? $_____

– – – – – – – – – – – – – –
$16.50

50. In a petty cash system, the total amount of receipts plus _____

_____ should be equal to the total amount of the petty cash

fund.

— — — — — — — — — — — — — — —

the cash left in the fund (or equivalent answer)

Self-Teaching Section D

THE BANK ACCOUNT

51. Most businesses use a bank to hold and protect their cash assets. Each
check that is written eventually finds its way back to the bank in which the
company has its account. At the bank, the amount of the check is deducted
from the total balance in the company's account. Each month, the bank reports on the transactions it has made for the company by means of a <u>bank</u>
statement. The diagram on the following page shows the route that a check
might take.
     What does the firm do when it receives the bank statement? _____

_____

— — — — — — — — — — — — — — —

the firm checks the statement by comparing it with the company records
to be sure it is accurate (or equivalent answer)

52. When a checkbook is used, it serves as the company's record of all
payments made by check. If the company is using the voucher system of
cash disbursement, the company would compare the bank statement with

what record? _____.

— — — — — — — — — — — — — — —

Check Register

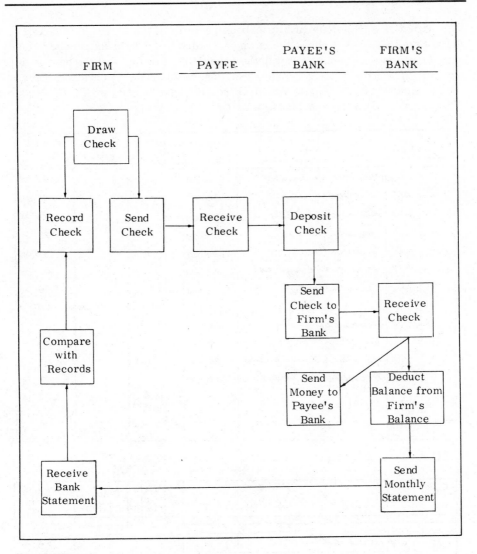

53. Below is a page from the checkbook record of Pachyderm Ice Cream, Inc. Note that when a check is drawn, a record is made of the number, the date on which the check is drawn, the payee, the amount, and the new balance resulting from the check's being drawn. On October 24, Pachyderm issued check number 112 payable to Pacific Electric in the amount of $2.00. Record this transaction in the checkbook below:

Check No.	Date	Payee	Amount of Check	✓	Date of Dep.	Amount of Dep.	Balance
							167 00
101	10/2	Harold Frazer	2 00				165 00
102	10/3	Waltham, Inc.	30 00				135 00
103	10/3	Starnes Realty	39 00				96 00
104	10/4	Harold Frazer	21 00				75 00
105	10/8	Arling Corp.	24 00				51 00
106	10/9	Sanford Supplies	10 00				41 00
107	10/10	Rex Stationers	5 00				36 00
					10/11	18 00	54 00
108	10/14	Starnes Realty	12 00				42 00
109	10/15	Harold Frazer	9 00				33 00
110	10/15	Western Telephone	20 00				13 00
111	10/22	Mandrake Supplies	6 00				7 00
					10/22	20 00	27 00

- - - - - - - - - - - - - - - - - -

Check No.	Date	Payee	Amount of Check	✓	Date of Dep.	Amount of Dep.	Balance
112	10/24	Pacific Electric	2 00				25 00

54. Whenever a deposit is made at the bank, it is recorded in the checkbook by

_____ a. adding the amount of the deposit to the balance
_____ b. subtracting the amount of the deposit from the balance

- - - - - - - - - - - - - - - -

(a)

55. On a specified date each month the bank sends to each depositor a record of transactions that the bank has processed for that depositor. This bank statement will include:

- the amount of each check paid by the bank

- the amount of each deposit made to the account

- the amounts of any additions to the account made as a result of special services performed by the bank, such as collecting a note due to the depositor

- the amounts of any deductions resulting from special charges

The statement will also include the balance of the account recorded on the day that the statement was prepared. When will all checks cashed <u>after</u> the preparation of the monthly statement be reported by the bank?

_ _ _ _ _ _ _ _ _ _ _ _ _ _ _

next month, or on the next statement (or equivalent answer)

56. Here is the bank statement of Pachyderm Ice Cream listing the amounts of all checks paid by the bank:

STATEMENT OF ACCOUNT WITH   **BANK OF PIGGY**

BANK OF PIGGY

DOWNTOWN BRANCH

PERIOD ENDING
OCT. 22, 1986

ACCOUNT NO.
0449201131

PACHYDERM ICE CREAM, INC.

11 BIG ROCK CANDY MT. ROAD

OZVILLE, NEW YORK 01001

↟ Clip along this line when sending a change of address

CHECKS--LISTED IN ORDER OF PAYMENT					DEPOSITS	DATE	BALANCE
2 00	5 00					OCT 11	160 00
30 00						OCT 12	130 00
39 00						OCT 13	91 00
21 00	24 00				18 00	OCT 15	64 00
12 00						OCT 18	52 00
10 00	9 00	20 00	1 00 S			OCT 22	12 00

SUMMARY OF ACTIVITY

BALANCE FORWARD	DEBITS		CREDITS		SERVICE CHARGE		NEW BALANCE
	number	amount	number	amount	items	amount	
167 00	10	172 00	1	18 00	17	1 00	12 00

ENCLOSURES 10

EXPLANATION OF SYMBOLS

R	Reversing Entry	F	Follow Sheet	A	Automatic Payroll Entry
M	Miscellaneous Entry	S	Service Charge	NSF	Nonsufficient Funds
N	No Ticket Entry	T	Tenplan Charge	B	Instant Cash Entry

Notice that the "new balance" reported on the bank statement and the last balance recorded in Pachyderm's checkbook (Frame 53), <u>as of</u> <u>the date of the statement</u> differ by the amount of \$_____. (Since the \$2.00 check written on the 24th comes after the date of the statement, we won't count it.)

— — — — — — — — — — — — — —

\$27 − 12 = \$15

57. Because of the time lag between the preparation of the bank statement and the receipt of the statement by the depositor, the balance on the state-ment may not agree with the balance in the checkbook. To see whether or not the bank records agree with the company records it is necessary to up-date both of these documents in a procedure known as <u>reconciliation of the account</u>. When the bank statement is received, the account is reconciled by bringing up to date the balance in the _____ as well as the balance in the _____ .

— — — — — — — — — — — — — —

checkbook; bank statement (in either order)

58. If, after bringing the balance of both records up to date, the totals agree, the account is said to be _____ .

— — — — — — — — — — — — — —

reconciled

59. On the 27th of the month, Pachyderm Ice Cream received a bank state-ment dated for the 22nd of the month which reports a balance of \$12. The balance in Pachyderm's checkbook <u>as of the</u> <u>22nd</u> was \$27. Which of the fol-lowing might be a reason for the discripancy?

_____ a. From the 23rd to the 27th, Pachyderm drew checks that did not reach the bank in time to be included on the statement.
_____ b. An error was made in recording the check in the checkbook.
_____ c. The bank made charges to Pachyderm's account that were not recorded in the checkbook.
_____ d. The bank made an error in debiting Pachyderm's account by too large an amount.

— — — — — — — — — — — — — —

(b), (c), and (d) (<u>a</u> would only be possible where the bank statement bal-ance is <u>larger</u> than the checkbook balance)

60. A discrepancy between a checkbook balance and a bank statement balance may occur for a number of reasons, such as:

- a firm may record checks in the checkbook which have not reached the bank in time to be included in the monthly statement

- a firm may record deposits in the checkbook which have not reached the bank in time to be included in the monthly statement

- the bank statement may record additions or subtractions to the firm's account which are not yet recorded in the checkbook, even though the firm is aware of them

- errors may have been made, either at the bank or at the firm

Reconciliation procedures will adjust for the first three reasons above. After these procedures have been carried out, if the bank-statement balance and the checkbook balance still do not agree, we may assume the discrepancy is caused by some error.

The accountant for Pachyderm compares the check amounts given on the bank statement with the amounts recorded in the company checkbook. (In actual practice, the bank sends the paid checks along with the statement. These checks, as well as the amounts given in the statement, are compared with the checkbook record.) He finds that a check for $6 was drawn on the 22nd, and did not reach the bank in time to be included on the bank statement. The special name given to checks that do not reach the bank in time to be included on the statement is checks outstanding, or outstanding checks. To see whether the bank's records and the checkbook agree, the accountant will subtract the total amount of the checks outstanding from the

_____ balance.
(statement/checkbook)

- - - - - - - - - - - - - - - -

statement

61. Assume you are the bookkeeper for Pachyderm Ice Cream. You are to reconcile the bank statement. Using Frame 53 (the company checkbook record) and the bank statement in Frame 56, fill in the blanks below to adjust the balance:

Balance on the statement . . . . $_____ (a)

Minus Checks outstanding . . . . − $_____ (b)

Equals Adjusted statement balance . . . . = $_____ (c)

- - - - - - - - - - - - - - - -

(a) $12; (b) $6; (c) $6

62. The adjusted statement balance of $6 still does not agree with the check-book balance as of the 22nd. A possible reason for this is that (more than one may be correct):

_____ a. The bank has made charges to Pachyderm's account that have not yet been entered into Pachyderm's checkbook
_____ b. An error has been made
_____ c. Pachyderm has made deposits which are included in the checkbook but not on the bank statement

— — — — — — — — — — — — — — —

  (a), (b), and (c)

63. Look at Pachyderm's checkbook record in Frame 53. In the space below, write the amounts of any deposits that were made as of the 22nd, but are not included in the statement in Frame 56. $_____

— — — — — — — — — — — — — — —

  $20

64. On the 22nd of October, Pachyderm mailed a deposit of $20 to the bank which did not arrive in time for inclusion in the bank statement. In order to bring the bank statement balance more up to date, the accountant will have to not only subtract outstanding checks from the statement balance, but will also have to _____ the amount of the deposit.
          (add/subtract)

— — — — — — — — — — — — — — —

  add

65. Adjust the bank statement balance as described above and write the ad-justed balance in the space below. Also, write the checkbook balance in the space below:

balance reported on bank statement . . . . $_____ (a)

outstanding checks . . . . $_____ (b)

deposit not included in statement . . . . . $_____ (c)

adjusted bank statement balance . . . . . . $_____ (d)

actual checkbook balance (from Frame 53). . . . . . . $_____ (e)

    Is the account reconciled? _____ (f)

— — — — — — — — — — — — — — —

  (a) $12; (b) $6; (c) $20; (d) $26; (e) $27; (f) no

66. Even though the bank-statement balance has been brought up to date (as of the 22nd), its balance still does not agree with the balance recorded in the checkbook. What could be responsible for the difference?

_____

_____

— — — — — — — — — — — — — — — —

The bank could have made additions or subtractions from the account which are not yet recorded in the checkbook, or there may have been an error.

67. Banks usually make routine additions and subtractions from an account balance that are not usually recorded in the checkbook until the statement is reconciled. The depositor knows about these charges; for example, one is a deduction of a <u>service</u> <u>charge</u> from the account. Look back to Pachyderm's bank statement in Frame 56. Notice the last charge under the checks column

--it is the service charge. The entry is written as _____.

— — — — — — — — — — — — — — — —

1.00S

68. In order to account for this service charge, the amount will have to be

_____ the checkbook balance.
(added to/subtracted from)

— — — — — — — — — — — — — — — —

subtracted from

69. Balance in the checkbook . . . . $_____ (a)

Minus Service charge . . . . $_____ (b)

Equals Adjusted checkbook balance . . . . . . $_____ . (c)

After filling in these blanks, we can now say that Pachyderm's account is

(d) _____.

— — — — — — — — — — — — — — — —

(a) $27; (b) $1; (c) $26; (d) reconciled

70. Fill in the blanks in the statements that follow to give the correct reconciliation procedure:

(a) Balance in checkbook _____ the service charge equals the
                              (+/−)
     adjusted checkbook balance.

(b) Balance in bank statement_____ checks outstanding_____
$$\overline{(+/-)(+/-)}$$
deposits not included in the statement equals the adjusted
statement balance.

_ _ _ _ _ _ _ _ _ _ _ _ _ _ _ _

(a) -; (b) -, +

71. As we have said, a bank will usually deduct a service charge from the
account of a depositor. Another kind of deduction is a NSF charge (nonsuf-
ficient funds charge). An NSF charge is deducted for handling the return of
any check that was drawn on a balance which was not large enough to cover
it. Which of the following situations would result in an NSF charge?

____ a. the bank is asked to cash a check for $46; there is $23
in the payer's account
____ b. the bank is asked to cash a check for $32; there is $39
in the payer's account

_ _ _ _ _ _ _ _ _ _ _ _ _ _ _ _

(a)

72. In reconciling an account when the statement records an NSF charge,

the amount of the charge must be (a)_____ the
$$\text{(added to/subtracted from)}$$
(b) _____ balance.
(bank statement/checkbook)

_ _ _ _ _ _ _ _ _ _ _ _ _ _ _ _

(a) subtracted from; (b) checkbook

73. In addition to automatically deducting charges from a depositor's
account, a bank may give other services which cause additions to be made
to the account. One of these services is the collection of installment payments made by customers of the depositor. Harold James, for example,
has purchased $1000 of equipment from Ace Plumbing. He is paying the
amount in monthly installments of $200 to Ace's bank. When the bank re-
ceives the payment each month, it deposits the $200 to Ace's account. On
the day James pays the bank, does this automatic deposit appear in Ace's

checkbook? (a) _____ Does it appear on Ace's bank statement? (b) _____

_ _ _ _ _ _ _ _ _ _ _ _ _ _ _ _

(a) no; (b) yes

74. In order to take this automatic deposit into account when adjusting the
checkbook balance, the accountant will have to _____ the amount
                                                (add/subtract)
_____ the balance in the checkbook.
(from/to)

- - - - - - - - - - - - - - -

   add; to

75. Use the following information to bring the checkbook balance of $732 up
to date.

   Collection of Harold James' note: $200
   Service charge: $2
   NSF charge: $2

- - - - - - - - - - - - - - -

   checkbook balance: $732
                       + 200 the collected note
                          932
                       -    4 the NSF ($2) and the service charge ($2)
                        $928 adjusted checkbook balance

76. In this example you are required to reconcile a bank account. Read it
carefully:

   The Further Book Store receives its bank statement on July 24th.
   The statement is dated July 17th. In comparing the checks listed
   in the statement with those recorded in the checkbook, Further's
   accountant finds that two checks, one for $150 and one for $95,
   did not reach the bank in time to be recorded on the statement.
   In addition, a $300 mail deposit was sent on the 17th of the month.
   The statement includes a service charge of $2 and two NSF
   charges of $2 each. The bank collected an installment payment
   made to Further in the amount of $75. The statement balance
   is $439 and the checkbook balance on July 24th is $425.

Reconcile the account:

BANK STATEMENT			CHECKBOOK	
statement balance	$439		$425	checkbook balance
checks outstanding	− 245		+ 75	collected note
	194		500	
deposits not included	+ 300		− 6	charges
adj. statement balance	$494		$494	adj. checkbook balance

SELF-TEST

This Self-Test will show you whether or not you have mastered the chapter objectives and are ready to go on to the next chapter. Answer each question to the best of your ability. Correct answers and instructions are given at the end of the test.

1. What are two reasons for the separation of the record keeping for an asset from the custody of that asset?

(a) _____

(b) _____

2. Very small businesses with only one employee (the owner) do not need to be concerned with internal control procedures. True or false? _____

3. What general rule of internal control is being broken in the following example:

> At the end of each working day at the Hallmark Department Store, all of the checkers bring their cash drawers and their register tapes to Harold Wilson, the company bookkeeper. Wilson counts the cash and makes sure that the tapes agree with the total. He then enters the total cash receipts into the company books and deposits the money in the bank.

_____

_____

4. In a cash receipts control system composed of (1) an accountant and (2) a cashier, who would be responsible for the following activities?

_____ a. preparation of deposit slips

_____ b. reconciling the bank statement

_____ c. entering information in the books at the end of the day

_____ d. making the deposit at the bank

5. Which of the following items would be paid for out of petty cash?

____ a. a company car   ____ c. an office desk
____ b. postage   ____ d. a water cooler

6. In a petty cash system, paid vouchers (receipts) + _____ = total petty cash fund.

7. What fundamental protection is given by the voucher system?

_____

_____

8. Below are several events connected with the purchase of a sofa for the Martin Realty Company. They are not necessarily arranged in the order in which they occurred. Write the numbers in the blanks to show the order in which the events occurred. Use "1" for the earliest event and "8" for the last.

_____ a. the invoice for the sofa was received
_____ b. a check was prepared
_____ c. the financial officer approved the voucher
_____ d. the voucher was filed in the unpaid voucher file
_____ e. the check was entered in the Check Register
_____ f. the voucher was recorded in the Voucher Register
_____ g. the voucher was prepared
_____ h. it was confirmed that the sofa arrived in good condition

9. Crawford Furniture Distributors replaced its usual cash disbursement system with a voucher system which includes a Voucher Register and a Check Register. What two special journals are no longer needed by Crawford?

(a) _____   (b) _____

10. Reconcile the bank account of Supreme Printing Company, Inc., using the following information:

Balance on bank statement	$3023
Balance in checkbook	3219
Deposit (not recorded on statement)	448
Checks outstanding	
to Evans Print Supplies	150
to Eastern Telephone Co.	56
Service Charge	2
Nonsufficient funds charge	2
Note automatically collected	50

Self-Test Answers

Compare your answers to the Self-Test with the correct answers given below.
If all of your answers are correct, you are ready to go on to the next chapter. If you missed any questions, study the frames indicated in parentheses
following the answer. If you miss many questions, go over the entire chapter
carefully.

1. (a) To protect the assets, or equivalent answer
   (b) To assure accurate record keeping, or equivalent answer
   (Frames 1-12)

2. False (Frames 1-12)

3. The assets are not as securely protected as they would be if the custody
function were separated from the record-keeping function. This could be
solved by having Wilson give each checker a receipt for the money received.
(Frames 1-12)

4. (a) 2-cashier; (b) 1-accountant; (c) 1-accountant; (d) 2-cashier
   (Frames 13-20)

5. (b) (Frames 42-50)

6. Cash remaining in the fund (Frames 47-50)

7. It assures that no unwarranted expenditures are made because the voucher is checked by supervisory personnel. (Frames 21-41)

8. (a) 1; (b) 7; (c) 4; (d) 6; (e) 8; (f) 5; (g) 3; (h) 2 (Frames 21-41)

9. (a) Cash Disbursements Journal; (b) Purchases Journal (in either order)
   (Frames 21-41)

10.

statement balance	$3023	$3219	checkbook balance
checks outstanding	- 206	+ 50	note collected
	2817	3269	
deposits not included	+ 448	- 4	charges
adjusted statement bal.	$3265	$3265	adjusted checkbook bal.

(Frames 51-76)

CHAPTER NINE

Payroll Accounting

OBJECTIVES

When you complete this chapter you will be able to

- state and use the formula for net earnings
- give examples of mandatory and optional deductions
- compute employee's and employer's FICA taxes
- compute employer's unemployment taxes
- determine federal income tax deductions from employee's gross earnings
- complete and use the Payroll Register and the Employee's Earnings Record

If you feel that you have already mastered these objectives and might skip all or part of this chapter, turn to the end of the chapter and take the Self-Test. The results will tell you what frames of the chapter you should study. If you answer all questions correctly, you are ready to begin the next chapter.

If this material is new to you, or if you choose not to take the Self-Test now, turn to the Overview and Self-Teaching Sections that follow.

CHAPTER OVERVIEW

Businesses often spend significant amounts of time and money on matters related to the payment of wages. For the sake of clarity, we have not emphasized these matters in earlier chapters. But in this chapter we will discuss those aspects of bookkeeping and accounting that are most directly related to the making and keeping of payroll records.

EMPLOYEE'S DEDUCTIONS AND EMPLOYEE'S EARNINGS RECORD

The total amount that an employee earns is called the <u>gross</u> <u>earnings</u> of that employee. Government regulations require that businesses deduct amounts from the gross earnings of their employees and make tax payments on behalf of those employees. These amounts are called deductions. Two of the taxes deducted from gross earnings are as follows:

1. Employee's FICA (Federal Insurance Contributions Act) Tax

The FICA tax funds are eventually disbursed by government in the form of old age or disability payments. It is up to the business to calculate for each employee the amount of FICA tax that must be paid. The basis for the tax varies from year to year. In this book, we assume that the tax is applied to the first $36,000 earned by an employee in a year. We assume that the percentage of gross earnings deducted is 9%.

2. Employee's Federal Income Tax

All employers are required to calculate the amount of federal income tax payable by an employee and to deduct this amount from gross earnings each time the employee is paid. There are many ways to make this determination. In this chapter we will use a <u>tax</u> <u>table</u>. The amount of federal income tax withheld depends on the gross wages of the employee, the marital status of the employee, the frequency with which the payroll is paid (weekly, monthly, etc.), and the number of persons that the employee claims as dependents.

The federal income tax and the FICA tax are fairly standard deductions. Other taxes that may be deducted depending on the city or state in which the person is employed are:

(a) a state income tax
(b) a city income tax

Other nontax deductions which may be required in certain cases are:

(a) state disability insurance
(b) union dues
(c) employee's share of accident, health, or life insurance
(d) employee's share of pension plan

In addition to these deductions, which are mandatory, there are other optional or voluntary deductions that a business might subtract from the gross wages of an employee. Examples of these are:

(a) deductions for the purchase of U.S. savings bonds
(b) deductions of amounts to be deposited into the employee's personal savings account

Government regulations also require that an employer keep separate payroll records for each employee, including gross and cumulative earnings, and all deductions for each pay period. This information is entered in an Employee's Earnings Record each time the employee is paid.

Employee deductions will vary widely from one business to another. We will not attempt to cover all possibilities. Instead we will concentrate on the general procedures of payroll accounting as applied to the payments most widely required.

THE PAYROLL REGISTER AND THE EMPLOYER'S PAYROLL TAX EXPENSES

In addition to collecting taxes from employees, a business is required to pay taxes itself on the wages of its employees. Two of these taxes are outlined below:

1. Unemployment Tax

The amount of unemployment tax that an employer must pay depends on the earnings of his employees, and in some states on the firm's employment record. The employer must pay the tax on each employee's earnings up to $7,000. Though the rate at which the unemployment tax is applied to this $7,000 changes from year to year, we are assuming in this chapter a rate of 2.7%. States may also levy an unemployment tax. However, we will only cover the federal tax thoroughly.

2. Employer's FICA Tax

A business must pay an FICA tax that is equal to the FICA tax paid by employees of the business. For our purposes, this means that an employer must pay 9% of the first $36,000 earned by each of his employees in a year.

The record from which employer's taxes are determined is called the Payroll Register. The Payroll Register lists all employees of the business, their gross and cumulative earnings, the amount of these earnings subject to employer's taxes, all of the deductions from each employee's earnings, and their net earnings.

JOURNALIZING PAYROLL EXPENSE AND SALARY EXPENSE

The expenditures related to payroll are recorded in a General Journal. This involves two separate journal entries.

(a) The entry for salary expense shows how gross earnings are disbursed among the various deductions and net earnings of the employee.

(b) The entry for payroll tax expense shows which employer taxes are payable and in what amounts.

Self-Teaching Section A

EMPLOYEE'S DEDUCTIONS AND EMPLOYEE'S EARNINGS RECORD

1. Many businesses expend significant amounts of time and money on matters relating to the payment of wages to employees. In addition to paying these wages, a business must also pay taxes on these wages to government agencies. The law also requires that the business collect tax payments from employee's themselves, in the form of wage deductions. These collected amounts are then remitted to the government periodically. The legal burdens placed on businesses that employ individuals make necessary very specific record-keeping procedures. This chapter deals with those procedures established to account for payroll and payroll-related expenditures.

2. The government requires businesses that employ individuals to keep accurate records reporting amounts earned by employees. One of these records is called the Employee's Earnings Record. A business will keep one Employee's Earnings Record for each person it employs. Below is the Employee's Earnings Record for Kenneth Ball, one of the employees of The Bright Light Shop.

EMPLOYEE'S EARNINGS RECORD

Name _Ball, Kenneth_

Address _1843-10th Street_
Hereville, La.

Social Security Number _123-45-6789_

Married _X_   Number of
Single _____   Exemptions _4_

Weekly Rate $ _800.00_

Pay Period Ending	Gross Earnings		Deductions				Net Earnings
	For Period	Cumu-lative	FICA	Federal Wthldng.	Misc.	Total	

The top portion of Kenneth Ball's Employee's Earnings Record has been filled in (do not worry if some of the terms on this form are not yet familiar to you).

What amount of money does Ball earn per week? $_____

- - - - - - - - - - - - - - -

$800.00

3. In previous chapters, we showed that the total amount of wages paid to an employee is included in a debit entry to the salary expense account. The amount of total wages earned by an employee is called the <u>gross earnings</u> of that employee. The period of time over which this amount is earned is called the <u>pay period</u> (not to be confused with the accounting period, though the two may coincide). Entries are made in the Employee's Earnings Record as of the last day of each pay period. The arrows on the form on page 265 show that the Employee's Earnings Record calls for the last date of the pay period, as well as the gross earnings for the period and the cumulative (total) gross earnings for all periods of the current year. Kenneth Ball earned $800 for the pay period ending January 7, the first pay period of the year. In the Employee's Earnings Record in Frame 2, show the entry that The Bright Light Shop's accountant would make to record this information.

- - - - - - - - - - - - - - -

Pay Period Ending	Gross Earnings	
	For Period	Cumulative
January 7	800.00	800.00

4. The Bright Light Shop is a rather small business employing only one other person besides Kenneth Ball. The Employee's Earnings Record for Martin Manners, the other employee, is shown below with the gross earnings filled in for the period ending January 7.

EMPLOYEE'S EARNINGS RECORD

Name *Manners, Martin*   Social Security Number *987-65-4321*

Address *743 Main Street*   Married ____   Number of
Thereville, La.   Single _X_   Exemptions *1*

Weekly Rate $*575.00*

Pay Period Ending	Gross Earnings		Deductions				Net Earnings
	For Period	Cumulative	FICA	Federal Wthldng.	Misc.	Total	
January 7	575.00	575.00					

Manners earned another $575.00 for the next period (ending January 14). Record this information in the form on the previous page.

- - - - - - - - - - - - - - - -

| Pay Period Ending | Gross Earnings | |
	For Period	Cumu- lative
January 7	575.00	575.00
January 14	575.00	1150.00

5. An employee does not receive all the money that he earns. This is because the business for which he works will make <u>deductions</u> from his gross earnings. The amount remaining after all these deductions have been made is called the employee's <u>net earnings</u>. That is,

net earnings = gross earnings − deductions

If an employee has gross earnings of $250, and deductions amounting to $53, then his net earnings are $_____.

- - - - - - - - - - - - - - -

$197

6. Looking back to the Employee's Earnings Record in Frame 4 notice that under the section headed "Deductions" are four columns headed "FICA," "Federal Wthldng.," "Misc.," and "Total." In these columns will be entered the amount of the deductions from Manner's gross earnings. There are two general types of deductions:

(a) <u>mandatory</u> deductions, that an employer <u>must</u> make
(b) <u>optional</u> or voluntary deductions, that an employer <u>may</u> make at the discretion of the employee

Which of the following deductions do you think are of the <u>mandatory</u> type?

____ a. deductions for federal income tax
____ b. deductions for the purchase of savings bonds
____ c. deductions for the deposit of amounts in employee's personal savings account

- - - - - - - - - - - - - - -

(a)

7. Government agencies require that an employer make deductions from employee's wages for the payment of taxes. In this sense, all employers may be considered tax collectors for the government. The employer will accumulate the amounts collected in this way and at periodic intervals will remit the funds to the taxing agency.

Two such taxes that are almost universally collected in this way are:

(a) FICA (Federal Insurance Contributions Act) taxes
(b) federal income taxes

If an employee earned $300 for the pay period and his employer deducted $12.50 for the FICA taxes and $29.30 for the federal income tax, what were the employee's <u>net earnings</u> for the period? $_____

— — — — — — — — — — — — — — —

$258.20   ($300.00 − $12.50 − $29.30)

8. How does an employer determine how much FICA tax to deduct from each employee's gross earnings? While all employees must pay the FICA tax, the tax <u>may</u> not apply to all of the earnings of an employee. In this chapter we assume that an employee must pay the FICA tax on only the <u>first</u> $36,000 earned in any year. If an employee earns $40,000 in one year, the amount of gross earnings that he <u>does</u> <u>not</u> have to pay on the FICA tax is $_____.

— — — — — — — — — — — — — — —

$4,000

9. Last year, Martin Manners earned a total of $29,900 (gross earnings). On how much of his gross earnings did Manners have to pay the FICA tax?
$_____.

— — — — — — — — — — — — — —

all of it, or $29,900

10. The amount of gross earnings of an employee that are subject to a tax are called the <u>taxable earnings</u> of that employee. Give the <u>FICA taxable earnings</u> of the three employees below (yearly gross earnings are given).

        (a) $45,000 $ _____
        (b) $36,500 $ _____
        (c) $28,000 $ _____

— — — — — — — — — — — — — —

(a) $36,000 (b) $36,000 (c) $28,000

11.   The rate at which the FICA tax is applied (i.e., the percentage of gross earnings that goes to pay the tax) varies from year to year in accordance with a schedule set forth by Congress.   For our purposes we will assume that the rate is 9%.   This means that the maximum FICA tax an employee will have to pay in any year is 9% of $_____ or a total amount of $_____ .

- - - - - - - - - - - - - - - -

   $36,000; $3,240

12.   The FICA tax is computed and withheld each time that an employee receives wages.   Kenneth Ball earns $800 per week.   For the first pay period of the year, Ball's employer must deduct from Ball's gross earnings 9% of his $800 salary (or $72) for payment of Ball's FICA tax.   After 45 weeks of the year have gone by, Ball will have earned a total of $36,000.   On gross earnings of the 46th week of the year, Ball:

_____ a.   will pay another $72 in FICA tax
_____ b.   will not have to pay any FICA tax at all

- - - - - - - - - - - - - - - -

   (b)

13.   If a wage payment causes an employee's cumulative wages for the year to exceed $36,000, the employee need pay the FICA tax only on that portion of the wage included in the first $36,000 earned.   Here is the payroll information for an employee:

   (a) cumulative gross earnings through the 51st pay period of the
        year: $35,500
   (b) gross earnings for the 52nd pay period: $700
   (c) cumulative gross earnings through the 52nd pay period of the
        year: $36,200

How much of the gross earnings for the 52nd pay period are subject to the FICA tax? $_____ .

- - - - - - - - - - - - - - - -

   $500 ($36,000 - 35,500), or all but $200 ($36,200 - 36,000)

14.   On the following page is payroll information on three employees working for Dunn's Floor Finishers.   For each employee, compute the FICA taxable earnings for the current period and the amount of FICA tax that will be deducted from wages for the current period.

Employee	Cumulative wages as of the last period	Wages for current period	FICA taxable earnings	FICA tax deducted from employee's wages
Andrews	$37,000	$900	_____	_____
Burke	$35,900	$500	_____	_____
Carson	$24,000	$400	_____	_____

- - - - - - - - - - - - - -

Employee	FICA taxable earnings	FICA tax deducted from employee's wages
Andrews	$ 0	$0
Burke	$400	$36
Carson	$400	$36

15. Below are the Employee's Earnings Records for Ball and Manners. For each, fill in the amount of FICA tax to be deducted for the first two pay periods.

EMPLOYEE'S EARNINGS RECORD

Name _Ball, Kenneth_   Social Security Number _123-45-6789_

Address _1843 - 10th Street_   Married _X_   Number of

Hereville, La.   Single _____   Exemptions _4_

Weekly Rate $ _800.00_

Pay Period Ending	Gross Earnings		Deductions				Net Earnings
	For Period	Cumu- lative	FICA	Federal Wthldng.	Misc.	Total	
January 7	800.00	800.00					
January 14	800.00	1,600.00					

EMPLOYEE'S EARNINGS RECORD

Name *Manners, Martin*   Social Security Number 987-65-4321

Address *743 Main Street*   Married _____   Number of
         Thereville, La.   Single _X_   Exemptions _1_

                                  Weekly Rate $ 575.00

Pay Period Ending	Gross Earnings		Deductions				Net Earnings
	For Period	Cumu-lative	FICA	Federal Wthldng.	Misc.	Total	
January 7	575.00	575.00					
January 14	575.00	450.00					

- - - - - - - - - - - - - - - -

Ball:

FICA
72.00
72.00

Manners:

FICA
51.75
51.75

16. Another tax that an employer must withhold from an employee's wages is <u>federal income tax</u>. This tax is a progressive tax, which means that the rate at which the tax is applied increases as the employee's gross wages increase. All other things being equal, therefore, an employee who earns

more money will have to pay a _____ tax than an employee who
                                  (higher/lower)
earns less money.

- - - - - - - - - - - - - - - -

    higher

17. Which of the following employees will probably have to pay the <u>higher</u> tax?

    _____ a. John, who earns $1,200 a week and reports that he is supporting a wife and a child

    _____ b. Harry, who also earns $1,200 a week and reports that he is supporting his wife, his six children, and his aged mother-in-law

- - - - - - - - - - - - - - - -

    (a), since John is presumably more able to pay a higher tax, all other things being equal

18. The amount of income tax to be paid depends, for one, on the <u>marital</u> status of the employee. All other things considered equal, a worker who is married will pay a <u>lower</u> federal income tax than an employee who is single. Frames 16 and 17 suggest two other things on which the amount of income tax will depend. These are:

(a) _____

(b) _____

- - - - - - - - - - - - - - - -

(a) the number of individuals an employee claims to be supporting (or equivalent answer); (b) the amount of wages earned by the employee in a given period of time (or equivalent answer)

19. The number of persons an employee <u>claims</u> as dependents for tax purposes are called the exemptions of that employee. The number of exemptions claimed by an employee are not necessarily the same as the number of <u>dependents</u> that he has. Dependents are persons that an employee is <u>actually</u> supporting. However since there are certain tax advantages in claiming fewer dependents as tax exemptions, the number of employee exemptions will not always be the same as the number of employee dependents. Be careful not to confuse these terms. Harry is actually supporting himself, his wife, his six children, and his aged mother-in-law; at work, he <u>claims</u> to be supporting only himself, his wife, and his mother-in-law.

(a) How many <u>exemptions</u> does Harry claim? _____

(b) How many <u>dependents</u> does Harry have? _____

- - - - - - - - - - - - - - - -

(a) 3; (b) 9

20. What are three things that determine the amount of federal income tax an employee must pay?

(a) _____

(b) _____

(c) _____

- - - - - - - - - - - - - - -

(a) his marital status; (b) the amount of his wages (and how often he is paid); (c) the number of his exemptions (or equivalent, in any order)

21. One common way to compute the amount of federal income tax to be withheld from an employee's wages is to use a tax table. Howard Andrews, who is married and claims himself and his wife as exemptions, earned $700 for the pay period ending March 27. See the Tax Table on the next page that is used to determine the federal income tax payable by married employees.

MARRIED Persons–WEEKLY Payroll Period

(For Wages Paid After December 1984)

And the wages are–		And the number of withholding allowances claimed is–										
At least	But less than	0	1	2	3	4	5	6	7	8	9	10
		The amount of income tax to be withheld shall be–										
$490	$500	$75	$70	$66	$61	$57	$52	$48	$45	$41	$38	$34
500	510	78	73	68	63	59	55	50	47	43	39	36
510	520	80	75	70	66	61	57	52	48	45	41	38
520	530	83	78	73	68	63	59	55	50	47	43	39
530	540	85	80	75	70	66	61	57	52	48	45	41
540	550	88	83	78	73	68	63	59	55	50	47	43
550	560	90	85	80	75	70	66	61	57	52	48	45
560	570	93	88	83	78	73	68	63	59	55	50	47
570	580	95	90	85	80	75	70	66	61	57	52	48
580	590	98	93	88	83	78	73	68	63	59	55	50
590	600	101	95	90	85	80	75	70	66	61	57	52
600	610	103	98	93	88	83	78	73	68	63	59	55
610	620	106	101	95	90	85	80	75	70	66	61	57
620	630	109	103	98	93	88	83	78	73	68	63	59
630	640	112	106	101	95	90	85	80	75	70	66	61
640	650	115	109	103	98	93	88	83	78	73	68	63
650	660	117	112	106	101	95	90	85	80	75	70	66
660	670	120	115	109	103	98	93	88	83	78	73	68
670	680	123	117	112	106	101	95	90	85	80	75	70
680	690	126	120	115	109	103	98	93	88	83	78	73
690	700	129	123	117	112	106	101	95	90	85	80	75
700	710	132	126	120	115	109	103	98	93	88	83	78
710	720	136	129	123	117	112	106	101	95	90	85	80
720	730	139	132	126	120	115	109	103	98	93	88	83
730	740	142	136	129	123	117	112	106	101	95	90	85
740	750	146	139	132	126	120	115	109	103	98	93	88
750	760	149	142	136	129	123	117	112	106	101	95	90
760	770	152	146	139	132	126	120	115	109	103	98	93
770	780	155	149	142	136	129	123	117	112	106	101	95
780	790	159	152	146	139	132	126	120	115	109	103	98
790	800	162	155	149	142	136	129	123	117	112	106	101
800	810	165	159	152	146	139	132	126	120	115	109	103
810	820	169	162	155	149	142	136	129	123	117	112	106
820	830	172	165	159	152	146	139	132	126	120	115	109
830	840	175	169	162	155	149	142	136	129	123	117	112
840	850	179	172	165	159	152	146	139	132	126	120	115
850	860	182	175	169	162	155	149	142	136	129	123	117
860	870	185	179	172	165	159	152	146	139	132	126	120
870	880	188	182	175	169	162	155	149	142	136	129	123
880	890	192	185	179	172	165	159	152	146	139	132	126

To use this table, <u>first</u>, find the <u>row</u> that corresponds to Howard's wages. It is the row that says that the employee's wages are at least $_____, but less than $_____.

- - - - - - - - - - - - - - -

$700; $710

22. Now, move your finger across this row until it comes to the <u>column</u> that gives the number of exemptions claimed by Howard. This is the column headed by the number _____.

- - - - - - - - - - - - - -

2

23. The amount located at the intersection of the "wages" row and the "exemptions" column is the amount of federal income tax to be deducted from

Howard's wages. This amount is $_____.

- - - - - - - - - - - - - -

   $120.00

24. Charles Burke is a co-worker of Howard's. He also earned $700 for the pay period. Burke, however, is single and claims only one exemption, himself. Use the Tax Table for single persons below to determine the amount of federal income tax to be deducted from Burke's wages for the period.

$_____

- - - - - - - - - - - - -

   $159.00

SINGLE Persons–WEEKLY Payroll Period

(For Wages Paid After December 1984)

And the wages are–		And the number of withholding allowances claimed is–										
At least	But less than	0	1	2	3	4	5	6	7	8	9	10
		The amount of income tax to be withheld shall be–										
$380	$390	$65	$60	$55	$50	$46	$41	$37	$33	$29	$26	$22
390	400	68	63	58	53	48	43	39	35	31	27	24
400	410	71	65	60	55	50	46	41	37	33	29	26
410	420	73	68	63	58	53	48	43	39	35	31	27
420	430	76	71	65	60	55	50	46	41	37	33	29
430	440	78	73	68	63	58	53	48	43	39	35	31
440	450	81	76	71	65	60	55	50	46	41	37	33
450	460	84	78	73	68	63	58	53	48	43	39	35
460	470	87	81	76	71	65	60	55	50	46	41	37
470	480	90	84	78	73	68	63	58	53	48	43	39
480	490	93	87	81	76	71	65	60	55	50	46	41
490	500	96	90	84	78	73	68	63	58	53	48	43
500	510	99	93	87	81	76	71	65	60	55	50	46
510	520	102	96	90	84	78	73	68	63	58	53	48
520	530	105	99	93	87	81	76	71	65	60	55	50
530	540	108	102	96	90	84	78	73	68	63	58	53
540	550	111	105	99	93	87	81	76	71	65	60	55
550	560	114	108	102	96	90	84	78	73	68	63	58
560	570	117	111	105	99	93	87	81	76	71	65	60
570	580	121	114	108	102	96	90	84	78	73	68	63
580	590	124	117	111	105	99	93	87	81	76	71	65
590	600	127	121	114	108	102	96	90	84	78	73	68
600	610	131	124	117	111	105	99	93	87	81	76	71
610	620	134	127	121	114	108	102	96	90	84	78	73
620	630	138	131	124	117	111	105	99	93	87	81	76
630	640	141	134	127	121	114	108	102	96	90	84	78
640	650	144	138	131	124	117	111	105	99	93	87	81
650	660	148	141	134	127	121	114	108	102	96	90	84
660	670	151	144	138	131	124	117	111	105	99	93	87
670	680	155	148	141	134	127	121	114	108	102	96	90
680	690	159	151	144	138	131	124	117	111	105	99	93
690	700	162	155	148	141	134	127	121	114	108	102	96
700	710	166	159	151	144	138	131	124	117	111	105	99
710	720	170	162	155	148	141	134	127	121	114	108	102
720	730	173	166	159	151	144	138	131	124	117	111,	105
730	740	177	170	162	155	148	141	134	127	121	114	108
740	750	181	173	166	159	151	144	138	131	124	117	111
750	760	184	177	170	162	155	148	141	134	127	121	114
760	770	188	181	173	166	159	151	144	138	131	124	117
770	780	192	184	177	170	162	155	148	141	134	127	121

25.

EMPLOYEE'S EARNINGS RECORD

Name *Ball, Kenneth*

Address *1843 - 10th Street*
Hereville, La.

Social Security Number *123-45-6789*

Married _X_ Number of
Single ____ Exemptions _4_

Weekly Rate $ ~~800.00~~ *850.00*

Pay Period Ending	Gross Earnings		Deductions				Net Earnings
	For Period	Cumu-lative	FICA	Federal Wthldng.	Misc.	Total	
January 7	800.00	800.00	72.00	139.00			
January 14	800.00	1600.00	72.00	139.00			
January 21	850.00	2450.00	76.50				

EMPLOYEE'S EARNINGS RECORD

Name *Manners, Martin*

Address *743 Main Street*
Hereville, La.

Social Security Number *987-65-4321*

Married ____ Number of
Single _X_ Exemptions _1_

Weekly Rate $ ~~575.00~~ *600.00*

Pay Period Ending	Gross Earnings		Deductions				Net Earnings
	For Period	Cumu-lative	FICA	Federal Wthldng.	Misc.	Total	
January 7	575.00	575.00	51.75	114.00			
January 14	575.00	1150.00	51.75	114.00			
January 21	600.00	1,750.00	54.00				

Above are the Employee's Earnings Records of Ball and Manners. Notice that both men have been given raises. Use the information at the top of the forms as well as the Tax Tables to determine the federal income tax to be withheld from each employee's gross earnings for the pay period ending January 21. Enter these on the records above.

- - - - - - - - - - - - - - -

Ball:

Federal Wthldng.
139.00
139.00
155.00

Manners:

Federal Wthldng.
114.00
114.00
124.00

26. In addition to federal income tax and the FICA tax, there may be other taxes deducted from an employee's wages. In some states, a state income tax may be applied. There are even some cities that require the payment of a city income tax. Wherever the law requires, an employer will make deductions from employee's wages for these items. Since the methods for determining the amount of these taxes is pretty much the same as that for federal income tax (though the amounts will differ from place to place), we will not go into detail on state or city income taxes here.

27. In addition to the <u>mandatory</u> deductions, there are other <u>optional</u> or voluntary deductions an employee may request. Which of the following deductions are optional?

     ____ a. a deduction for the payment of state income taxes
     ____ b. a deduction for the purchase of a savings bond
     ____ c. a deduction for the payment of an FICA tax
     ____ d. a deduction for the deposit of money into an employee's savings account

- - - - - - - - - - - - - - -

(b) and (d)

28. Separate columns should be added to the Employee's Earnings Record to record each deduction required in a particular business. In the Employee's Earnings Record which we are using, optional deductions are entered in the column headed "Misc." Usually some notation is also entered to show what the deduction is for. Ball has requested that his employer deduct $10 per week and deposit this money into his personal savings account. Manners has requested that his employer deduct $18.75 each week for the purchase of a U.S. Savings Bond. These optional deductions have been entered for the first two pay periods on the forms below. Enter the optional deductions for each employee for the pay period ending January 21.

Ball:

Pay Period Ending	Gross Earnings		Deductions				Net Earnings
	For Period	Cumu-lative	FICA	Federal Wthldng.	Misc.	Total	
January 7	800.00	800.00	72.00	139.00	10.00 SA		
January 14	800.00	1,600.00	72.00	139.00	10.00 SA		
January 21	850.00	2450.00	76.50	155.00			

Manners:

Pay Period Ending	Gross Earnings		Deductions				Net Earnings
	For Period	Cumu-lative	FICA	Federal Wthldng.	Misc.	Total	
January 7	575.00	575.00	51.75	114.00	18.75 SB		
January 14	575.00	450.00	51.75	114.00	18.75 SB		
January 21	600.00	1,750.00	54.00	124.00			

- - - - - - - - - - - - - - - -

Ball:

Misc.
10.00 SA
10.00 SA
10.00 SA

Manners:

Misc.
18.75 SB
18.75 SB
18.75 SB

29. The Employee's Earnings Record also calls for the total amount of deductions from gross earnings (in the "total" column) as well as the amount of net earnings of the employee. Total the deductions for each employee for each pay period and enter the amounts in the correct places on the records in Frame 28. Now determine the net earnings for each employee for each pay period, and enter these amounts. (If you have forgotten how to compute net earnings, refer to the formula in Frame 5.)

- - - - - - - - - - - - - - - -

Ball:

Total	Net Earnings
221.00	579.00
221.00	579.00
241.50	608.50

Manners:

Total	Net Earnings
184.50	390.50
184.50	390.50
196.75	403.25

Self-Teaching Section B

THE PAYROLL REGISTER AND THE EMPLOYER'S PAYROLL TAX EXPENSES

30. Another important payroll record which a business should keep is the Payroll Register. This record, shown on the following page, records much of the same information as is found on the Employee's Earnings Record. Study it carefully.

PAYROLL REGISTER (Week Ending _____)									
Name	Gross Earnings	Taxable Earnings		Deductions					Net Earnings
		Unem-ployment	FICA	FICA	Federal Wthldng.	Misc.	Total		

The Payroll Register requires that entries be made for each pay period. Which of the following statements is true?

    ____ a. At each pay period, information for <u>all</u> employees is entered onto the <u>same</u> Payroll Register.

    ____ b. At each pay period, information for each employee is entered into <u>individual</u> Payroll Registers.

– – – – – – – – – – – – – – – –

  (a) (Some firms may keep a confidential register for executives.)

31. The Payroll Register is useful in determining the <u>payroll tax expense</u> of a business. So far, we have been discussing taxes that are deducted from the employee's gross earnings, and remitted to the government by the business. There are also taxes on wages that must be paid <u>by the business</u>. One such tax is the federal unemployment insurance tax. The rate at which this tax is applied varies according to a schedule set forth by Congress. For our purposes, we will assume that the federal unemployment tax is applied at a rate of 2.7% of the first $7,000 earned by each employee in a year. This means that if an employee has accumulated gross earnings of $8,000

    ____ a. the business need not pay any unemployment tax on that employee's wages for the remainder of the year

    ____ b. the business must continue to pay the unemployment tax on that employee's wages for the remainder of the year

– – – – – – – – – – – – – – – –

  (a)

32. On the next page is payroll information on the three employees of Dunn's Floor Finishers. For each, compute the earnings subject to unemployment insurance <u>for the current period</u>. Then compute the total amount of unemployment tax that the business must pay <u>for the current period</u> (remember, we are assuming a rate of 2.7% of the first $7,000 in earnings of each employee).

Employee	Cumulative wages as of last period	Current period's wages	Unemployment insurance taxable earnings
Andrews	$8,500	$900	_____
Burke	$6,900	$500	_____
Carson	$6,800	$400	_____

Total unemployment insurance tax payable by Dunn for this period: $_____

- - - - - - - - - - - - - - -

Employee	Unemployment insurance taxable earnings
Andrews	$ 0
Burke	$100
Carson	$200

Total unemployment insurance tax payable by Dunn's for this period is $8.10
(2.7% of $100 + $200 = $8.10)

33. Below is the Payroll Register for The Bright Light Shop for the pay period ending January 21. The gross earnings of both Ball and Manners have been entered. Determine the earnings subject to unemployment insurance tax and enter the amount in the appropriate place on the form. Then compute the total unemployment tax payable by the business for the period.

| | | Taxable Earnings | | Deductions | | | | Net Earnings |
Name	Gross Earnings	Unemployment	FICA	FICA	Federal Wthldng.	Misc.	Total	
Ball, Kenneth	850.00	850.00	850.00					
Manners, Martin	600.00	600.00	600.00					

PAYROLL REGISTER (Week Ending *January 21, 19—*   )

Total unemployment tax payable for the period: $_____

- - - - - - - - - - - - -

Unemployment
850.00
600.00

Total unemployment tax payable for the period: $39.15 (2.7% of $1,450.00)

34. In addition to the unemployment tax, a business must pay an FICA tax on the wages of all of its employees. For our purposes, we will assume that the tax is applied at a rate of 9% of the total FICA taxable earnings of all employees together. This means that the tax payable by the business is equal to the FICA tax paid by all of its employees together. Now go back to Frame 33 and enter the FICA taxable earnings of the two employees, and then compute the FICA tax payable by the business.

FICA tax payable: $_____

- - - - - - - - - - - - - - -

FICA
850.00
600.00

The total FICA tax payable for the period is $130.50 (9% of $1,450.00). Note that this acts as a check on the computation of the individual FICA tax payable by employees. That is, (9% of $850) + (9% of $600) should equal 9% of ($850 + $600).

35. Here is a portion of a business's Payroll Register. Gross earnings for its two employees have been entered. Assuming that the cumulative gross earnings of the employees as of the last payroll period were

Adams: $6,950.00
Baker: $35,985.00

enter the unemployment and FICA taxable earnings of the two employees. Then determine the unemployment and FICA taxes payable by the business for the period.

PAYROLL REGISTER (Week Ending *March 16, 19—*   )

Name	Earnings	Taxable Earnings		Deductions					Net Amount
		Unem-ployment	FICA	FICA	Federal Wthldng.	Misc.	Total		
Adams	300.00								
Baker	950.00								

Unemployment tax payable: $_____; FICA tax payable: $_____

- - - - - - - - - - - - - -

PAYROLL ACCOUNTING 281

		Taxable Earnings		Deductions				Net
Name	Gross Earnings	Unem-ployment	FICA	FICA	Federal Wthldng.	Misc.	Total	Earnings
Adams	300.00	50.00	300.00					
Baker	950.00	0.00	15.00					

PAYROLL REGISTER (Week Ending *March 16, 19—*)

Unemployment tax payable: $1.35; FICA tax payable: $28.35

36. The remainder of the Payroll Register may be copied from each Employee's Earnings Record. Here is the Payroll Register of the Bright Light Shop for the period ending January 21. It includes all of the information that you have entered. Refer to the completed Employee's Earnings Records in Frame 28 to complete the Payroll Register. Sum the columns under "Deductions."

PAYROLL REGISTER (Week Ending *January 21, 19—*)

		Taxable Earnings		Deductions				Net
Name	Gross Earnings	Unem-ployment	FICA	FICA	Federal Wthldng.	Misc.	Total	Earnings
Ball, Kenneth	850.00	850.00	850.00					
Manners, Martin	600.00	600.00	600.00					

- - - - - - - - - - - - - -

		Taxable Earnings		Deductions				Net
Name	Gross Earnings	Unem-ployment	FICA	FICA	Federal Wthldng.	Misc.	Total	Earnings
Ball, Kenneth	850.00	850.00	850.00	76.50	153.00	10.00 SA	241.50	608.50
Manners, Martin	600.00	600.00	600.00	54.00	124.00	18.75 SB	196.75	403.25
				130.50	279.00	10.00 SA	438.25	1,011.75
						18.75 SB		

Self-Teaching Section C

JOURNALIZING PAYROLL EXPENSE AND SALARY EXPENSE

37. Expenditures related to payroll may be recorded in the General Journal. From the business's point of view, there are two types of expenses that must be accounted for:

> (a) Salary Expense--that is, gross earnings of the employees. This item includes not only net earnings payable to employees, but also taxes deducted from employee's earnings that are payable to the government by the business, as well as optional deductions also payable by the business.
>
> (b) Payroll Tax Expense--that is, taxes based on employees' gross earnings levied against the business.

Salary expense includes:

> • net earnings payable to the employees
> • FICA taxes on employees, deducted by the business
> • federal income tax on employees, deducted by the business
> • optional deductions from employees' earnings, deducted by the business

Since, at the time these salary expenses are recorded, no cash has actually been paid out, the items payable on behalf of employees are considered to be

> _____ a. assets of the business
> _____ b. liabilities of the business

– – – – – – – – – – – – – – – –

>   (b)

38. Gross salaries would be recorded in the journal as a _____ to

the _____ account.   (debit/credit)

– – – – – – – – – – – – – – –

>   debit; salary expense

39. Since the items which make up the salary expense of a business are all considered liabilities of the business, they would all be journalized as

_____ .

(debits/credits)

– – – – – – – – – – – – – – –

>   credits

40. Here are all the account titles and amounts recorded in a General Journal entry for salary expense. Rearrange them as they would appear in a simplified journal entry:

Employee's federal income tax payable: $800.00
Employee's FICA tax payable: $350.00
Salary expense: $8500.00
Savings bond deductions payable: $625.00
Salaries payable: $6725.00

Salary expense $8500.00
    Employee's FICA taxes payable . . . . $ 350.00
    Employee's federal income tax payable 800.00
    Savings bond deduction payable 625.00
    Salaries payable 6725.00

(Note: the order of the "credits" in the journal entry is not standard, except that salaries payable is usually shown last.)

41. A firm has the following payroll-related expenses for the period ending April 21:

Employee's FICA taxes: $35
Employee's federal income taxes: $120
Employee's net earnings: $520
Savings account deduction: $60

What is the simplified journal entry to record the salary expense?

Salary expense $735
    Employee's FICA tax payable . . . . $ 35
    Employee's federal income tax payable 120
    Savings account deduction payable 60
    Salaries payable 520
        Payroll for week ended April 21

42. The other important General Journal entry records the expenses that come about as a result of payroll taxes on the business itself. For the pay period ending January 14, Dunn's Floor Finishers' payroll tax expense is $6 for unemployment insurance taxes and $30 for FICA taxes, for a total payroll tax expense of $36. The General Journal entry for payroll tax expense is shown as a $36 debit to payroll tax expense. The account(s) credited will be:

    ____ a. FICA tax payable only
    ____ b. FICA tax payable and unemployment insurance tax payable
    ____ c. FICA tax expense and unemployment tax expense
    ____ d. Unemployment tax expense only

- - - - - - - - - - - - - - - -

(b)

43. Give the simplified journal entry for Dunn's Floor Finishers' payroll tax expense for the pay period ending January 14th (assume that only FICA taxes and federal unemployment taxes are paid):

- - - - - - - - - - - - - - - -

Payroll tax expense $36
    FICA tax payable $30
    Federal unemployment tax payable 6
        Payroll taxes for the week ended January 14

44. For the pay period ending May 29th, a firm has the following taxes to pay:
    FICA tax: $45
    Federal unemployment tax: $9
    State unemployment tax: $5

Give the General Journal entry to record payroll tax expense for this period.

- - - - - - - - - - - - - - - -

```
Payroll tax expense . . . . . . . . . . . . . . . . $59
    FICA tax payable. . . . . . . . . . . . . . . . . . $45
    Federal unemployment tax payable . . . . . . . . .  9
    State unemployment tax payable . . . . . . . . . .  5
```

45. Refer to Frames 33 and 36 for the payroll information for the Bright Light Shop. Using this information,

(a) Give the journal entry to record salary expense

(b) Give the journal entry to record payroll tax expense

- - - - - - - - - - - - - - - -

```
(a)  Salary expense . . . . . . . . . . . . . . . . . . $405.00
         Employee's FICA tax payable . . . . . . . . . . . . $ 20.25
         Employee's federal income tax payable . . . . . . .   54.10
         Employee's savings account payable . . . . . . . .   10.00
         Savings bond payable. . . . . . . . . . . . . . . .   18.75
         Salary payable . . . . . . . . . . . . . . . . . .  301.90

(b)  Payroll tax expense . . . . . . . . . . . . . . $24.30
         FICA tax payable. . . . . . . . . . . . . . . . . . $20.25
         Unemployment tax payable. . . . . . . . . . . . . .   4.05
```

SELF-TEST

This Self-Test will show you whether or not you have mastered the chapter objectives and are ready to go on to the next chapter. Answer each question to the best of your ability. Correct answers and instructions are given at the end of the test.

1. Gross earnings — total deductions is the formula for _____.

2. Name two deductions from employee's gross earnings that an employer must make:

    (a) _____

    (b) _____

3. On what three things does the amount of federal income tax deducted from gross earnings depend?

    (a) _____

    (b) _____

    (c) _____

4. National Auto Supplies has three employees. The Employee's Earnings Records of these employees appear on the next page. Using the following payroll data, the Tax Tables on pages 273 and 274, and the information on the upper part of the Employee's Earnings Records, complete the Employee's Earnings records for the pay period ending September 15.

Additional data:

    Cumulative gross earnings through last period:
        Crosby - $25,000
        Mason - $32,450
        Stamm - $35,800

    Optional deductions:
        Crosby - $15 (savings account deposit)
        Mason - $25 (savings account deposit)
        Stamm - none

EMPLOYEE'S EARNINGS RECORD

Name *Crosby, Henry*

Address *204 Adams Street*
Hereville, La.

Social Security Number *246-81-3570*

Married *X*   Number of
Single _____   Exemptions *2*

Weekly Rate $ *500.00*

Pay Period Ending	Gross Earnings		Deductions				Net Earnings
	For Period	Cumu- lative	FICA	Federal Wthldng.	Misc.	Total	

EMPLOYEE'S EARNINGS RECORD

Name *Mason, Matthew*

Address *101 - 10th Street*
Shereville, La.

Social Security Number *010-10-1010*

Married *X*   Number of
Single _____   Exemptions *5*

Weekly Rate $ *550.00*

Pay Period Ending	Gross Earnings		Deductions				Net Earnings
	For Period	Cumu- lative	FICA	Federal Wthldng.	Misc.	Total	

EMPLOYEE'S EARNINGS RECORD

Name *Stamm, Charles*

Address *5043 - 8th Street*
Hereville, La.

Social Security Number *100-00-0000*

Married _____   Number of
Single *X*   Exemptions *1*

Weekly Rate $ *700.00*

Pay Period Ending	Gross Earnings		Deductions				Net Earnings
	For Period	Cumu- lative	FICA	Federal Wthldng.	Misc.	Total	

5. Here is National Auto Supplies' Payroll Register. Complete it for the period ending September 15.

| | | Taxable Earnings | | Deductions | | | | Net |
Name	Gross Earnings	Unem-ployment	FICA	FICA	Federal Wthldng.	Misc.	Total	Earnings

PAYROLL REGISTER (Week Ending _September 15, 19—_)

6. (a) What is the total unemployment tax payable by National for the pay period ending September 15? $_____

(b) What is the total FICA tax payable by National for the pay period ending September 15? $_____

7. Show the General Journal entry to record National's
    (a) Salary expense

    (b) Payroll tax expense

Self-Test Answers

Compare your answers to the Self-Test with the correct answers given below. If all of your answers are correct, you are ready to go on to the next chapter. If you missed any questions, study the frames indicated in parentheses following the answer. If you miss many questions, go over the entire chapter carefully.

1. Net earnings (Frame 5)

2. (a) FICA tax; (b) Federal income tax (Frames 6-7)

3. (a) marital status and number of exemptions claimed; (b) length of payroll period; (c) gross earnings (Frames 16-20)

4. Crosby:

Pay Period Ending	Gross Earnings		Deductions				Net Earnings
	For Period	Cumu-lative	FICA	Federal Wthldng.	Misc.	Total	
September 15	500.00	25,500.00	45.00	68.00	15.00 SA	128.00	372.00

Mason:

Pay Period Ending	Gross Earnings		Deductions				Net Earnings
	For Period	Cumu-lative	FICA	Federal Wthldng.	Misc.	Total	
September 15	550.00	3,300.00	49.50	66.00	25.00 SA	140.50	409.50

Stamm:

Pay Period Ending	Gross Earnings		Deductions				Net Earnings
	For Period	Cumu-lative	FICA	Federal Wthldng.	Misc.	Total	
September 15	700.00	36,500.00	18.00	159.00	0	177.00	523.00

The frame references for this question have been entered into the appropriate spaces on the Employee's Earnings Record below.

Pay Period Ending	Gross Earnings		Deductions				Net Earnings
	For Period	Cumu-lative	FICA	Federal Wthldng.	Misc.	Total	
f. 1-4	f. 1-4	f. 1-4	f. 8-15	f. 21-25	f. 27-28	f. 29	f. 29

5.

| | | PAYROLL REGISTER (Week Ending _September 15, 19—_) | | | | | | |

Name	Gross Earnings	Taxable Earnings		Deductions				Net Earnings
		Unem-ployment	FICA	FICA	Federal Wthldng.	Misc.	Total	
Crosby, Henry	500.00	0	500.00	45.00	68.00	15.00 SA	128.00	372.00
Mason, Matthew	550.00	550.00	550.00	49.50	66.00	25.00 SA	140.50	409.50
Stamon, Charles	700.00	0	200.00	18.00	159.00	0	177.00	523.00
	1,750.00	550.00	1,250.00	112.50	293.00	40.00 SA	445.50	1304.50

The frame references for this question have been entered into the appropriate spaces in the Payroll Register below.

Name	Gross Earnings	Taxable Earnings		Deductions				Net Earnings
		Unem-ployment	FICA	FICA	Federal Wthldng.	Misc.	Total	
	f. 1-4	f. 30-33	f. 34-35	f. 36	f. 36	f. 36	f. 36	f. 36

6. (a) $14.85   (Frames 30-33)
    (b) $112.50   (Frames 34-35)

7. (a) Salary expense $1,750.00
     Employee's FICA tax payable . . . . $ 112.50
     Employee's federal income tax payable 293.00
     Savings account deposits payable 40.00
     Salaries payable 1,304.50
     Payroll for week ending September 15

                     (Frames 37-40)

    (b) Payroll tax expense $127.35
     Unemployment tax payable . . . . $ 14.85
     FICA tax payable 112.50
     For week ending September 15

                     (Frames 42-45)

CHAPTER TEN
Evaluating Financial Statements

OBJECTIVES

When you complete this chapter, you will be able to compute
a business's

- working capital,

- current ratio,

- acid-test ratio,

- cost of goods sold percentage,

- gross profit percentage,

- operating expense percentage, and

- after-tax net income percentage (for corporations only).

If you feel you have already mastered these objectives and
might skip all or part of this chapter, turn to the end of the chapter and take the Self-Test. The results will tell you what frames
of the chapter you should study. If you answer all questions correctly, you will have completed this book.

If this material is new to you, or if you choose not to take the
Self-Test now, turn to the Overview and Self-Teaching Sections
that follow.

CHAPTER OVERVIEW

EVALUATING FINANCIAL STATEMENTS

In this last chapter we will look at financial statements from the viewpoint of the manager, the investor, and the lender.

We have stressed that through the use of bookkeeping and accounting systems the accountant takes inputs in the form of business transactions and, by sorting, recording, and summarizing these inputs, he produces financial-statement outputs valuable to managers, investors, lenders, and others who might be concerned with the overall direction and future of a particular business. In this chapter we will discuss some of the ways in which accountants develop figures, ratios, and percentages from the financial statements they use in evaluating the business and its performance. In a sense, this chapter is a good summary because it shows the use and value of the bookkeeping and accounting effort.

Analyzing financial statements can be very complex--whole books have been written on the subject. All we will be able to do in this chapter is provide you with an introduction to seven measures commonly used in the analysis of financial statements. (There are, of course, many others.) Three of these are concerned with Balance Sheet analysis; four with Income Statement analysis.

Before considering these measures, however, we need to define some new terms:

Marketable Securities: Investments in stocks, bonds, and notes which are readily marketable and which the company does not intend to hold permanently.

Net Receivables: Accounts receivable minus an estimated amount that the company thinks will not be collected. Different businesses use different formulas or histories in calculating the amount of accounts receivable that will probably not be collected.

Liquid Assets: All current assets except inventories.

Net Sales: Income from all sales (gross) minus the price of any returned goods and the amount of any discounts given to customers.

Cost of Goods Sold: The cost of the merchandise given to the customer when a sale is made.

Gross Profit: Net sales minus cost of goods sold.

Operating Expenses: All costs of doing business other than the cost of goods sold. This includes selling and administrative costs such as salaries and wages, rent, utilities, payroll taxes, property taxes, insurance, and depreciation.

Operating Profit: Gross profit minus operating expenses.

Income after Federal Income Taxes: This is found only on corporation statements because sole proprietorship and partnerships are not taxable entities (the owners take up their share of the income of the business on their individual income tax return). This is the operating profit minus nonoperating income (interest or divident income) or expense (interest expense), extraordinary adjustments to income and expense, and federal income taxes of the corporation.

The seven measures for financial statement analysis are presented in the chart on the following page. Study it carefully before beginning the self-teaching section. Remember that the interpretation of these measures will vary widely in practice depending on many other factors in the business situation.

Self-Teaching Section A

EVALUATING FINANCIAL STATEMENTS

1. Imagine that you are a newly appointed loan officer at a bank. You've been asked by the president of the Whiz-Bang Corporation about the possibility of a loan. Among the things the bank wants you to do is to secure financial statements for analysis. You are to make an analysis to submit to the loan committee as part of your recommendation about the loan.

The two financial statements you examine are (1) the Balance Sheet, and (2) the Income Statement. There are seven common measures you can use:

From the Balance Sheet you can calculate:

  (a) working capital
  (b) current ratio
  (c) acid-test ratio

From the Income Statement you can calculate:

  (a) cost of goods sold as a percentage of net sales
  (b) gross profit as a percentage of net sales
  (c) operating expenses as a percentage of net sales
  (d) net income (after income taxes) as a percentage of net sales

If some of the measures are favorable and others are unfavorable, it will be difficult to decide on granting a loan. But if all the measures are favorable, you will probably recommend a loan, or if all the measures are unfavorable you will probably not recommend a loan.

All of this indicates that these measures give you some information, but they are only simple analytical techniques which point out danger signals; the actual situation would, of course, be more complex.

FINANCIAL STATEMENT	MEASURE	PURPOSE OF MEASURE	FORMULA	MEANING OF THE RESULTS OF COMPUTATION
for BALANCE SHEET analysis	Working Capital	Measures the amount of cash left if all current assets were sold at the recorded price and all current liabilities were paid	Current Assets minus Current Liabilities	Negative number here is bad; positive, good. Too large an amount may mean assets are inefficiently used
	Current Ratio	Measures how many times the current liabilities could be paid if all assets were sold at recorded costs	Current Assets divided by Current Liabilities	If this ratio is less than 1-to-1, the business is in bad shape. An ideal might be 2-to-1
	Acid-Test Ratio	Measures how many times the current liabilities could be paid if all assets were sold at recorded cash (except inventory, assumed zero)	(Current Assets minus Inventories) divided by Current Liabilities	If this ratio is less than 1-to-1, the business is in bad shape; if more than 1-to-1, in good shape
for INCOME STATEMENT analysis	Cost of Goods Sold as a Percentage of Net Sales	Measures the relationship between the cost of goods given to customers in relation to net sales	(Cost of Goods Sold divided by Net Sales) times 100%	These vary according to the type of business. Trade association and public statistics give an idea of percentage by industry
	Gross Profit as a Percentage of Net Sales	Measures the relationship between gross profit in relation to net sales	(Gross Profit divided by Net Sales) times 100%	
	Operating Expense as a Percentage of Net Sales	Measures the relationship between operating expenses and net sales	(Operating Expense divided by Net Sales) times 100%	
	Net Income (after income taxes) as a Percentage of Net Sales	Measures the business profitability in all its revenue	(Net Income after Income Tax divided by Net Sales) times 100%	In corporations this is used to notify stockholders of business profitability

2. Let's consider the measures we can use from data on the Balance Sheet. One measure is called <u>working capital</u>. This measure tells the amount of cash left if all current assets were sold at the recorded price and all the current liabilities were paid. To compute <u>working capital</u> we subtract current liabilities from current assets. In other words,

$$\text{working capital} = \text{current assets} - \text{current liabilities}$$

We are generally satisfied if the business can pay its current liabilities with current assets.

Whiz-Bang Corporation's current assets are $17,900. Its current liabilities are $10,300. What is Whiz-Bang's working capital? (a) $_____

Can we be satisfied that Whiz-Bank can meet its debts? (b)_____
(yes/no)

– – – – – – – – – – – – – – –

(a) $7600; (b) yes

3. Bugaboo Surfboard Company has current assets of $35,070. It has current liabilities of $17,530. What is Bugaboo's working capital? (a) $_____

Can we be satisfied that Bugaboo can meet its debts? (b)_____
(yes/no)

– – – – – – – – – – – – – – –

(a) $17,540; (b) yes

4. A second measure used to evaluate the ability of a company to meet its debts is called the <u>current ratio</u>. To compute the current ratio, current assets are divided by current liabilities. In other words,

$$\text{current ratio} = \frac{\text{current assets}}{\text{current liabilities}}$$

Many persons would say that a 2-to-1 (2/1) ratio is healthy, but many businesses operate successfully with a less than 2-to-1 ratio. Applying this measure to Bugaboo Surfboard Company whose current assets were $35,070 and current liabilities were $17,530, the current ratio is _____.

– – – – – – – – – – – – – – –

2-to-1

5. Consider Indian Rugs, Inc. It has current assets of $35,000 and current liabilities of $18,000. Calculate its working capital and current ratio.

(a) working capital: $_____

(b) current ratio: _____

– – – – – – – – – – – – – – –

(a) $17,000; (b) 1.9-to-1

6. A third evaluation developed from data on the Balance Sheet is called the acid-test ratio. To compute the acid-test ratio, current assets minus inventories are divided by current liabilities. In other words,

$$\text{acid-test ratio} = \frac{\text{current assets} - \text{inventories}}{\text{current liabilities}}$$

If this ratio is 1-to-1 or greater, the business is assumed to be able to pay all its current liabilities if pressed. (Current assets minus inventories are called liquid assets.)

Current assets of the Whiz-Bang Corporation are $17,900, and current liabilities are $10,300. Part of Whiz-Bang's current assets consists of inventories valued at $6500. (Incidentally don't go beyond one decimal place on any of these calculations.) The acid-test ratio for Whiz-Bang is

(a) _____. Are you satisfied it could meet its current liabilities if

pressed? (b)_____
        (yes/no)

- - - - - - - - - - - - - - -

(a) $\dfrac{17,900 - 6500}{10,300} \approx \dfrac{11,400}{10,300} = 1.1\text{-to-}1;$ (b) yes, acid-test ratio is more than 1-to-1

7. Consider the case of Fab Foods, Inc., a distributor of gourmet food items. Fab Foods has current assets of $11,000 including $5000 in inventories. Its current liabilities are $3000.

    (a) working capital is $_____

    (b) current ratio is _____

    (c) acid-test ratio is _____

    (d) Could Fab Foods meet is current obligations if pressed? _____
                                         (yes/no)

- - - - - - - - - - - - - - -

(a) $8000 (11,000 − 3000); (b) 3.7-to-1 (11,000 ÷ 3000);

(c) 2.0-to-1 $\left(\dfrac{11,000 - 5000}{3000}\right)$; (d) yes

8. A condensed Balance Sheet for Ace Card Corporation is shown on the following page. Study it carefully and then calculate the answers to these questions:

    (a) What is Ace's working capital? $_____

    (b) What is Ace's current ratio? _____

    (c) What is Ace's acid-test ratio? _____

ACE CARD CORPORATION

Balance Sheet
January 1, 19--

ASSETS

Current Assets

Cash	$ 550
Marketable Securities . . .	500
Accounts Receivable (net) .	660
Merchandise Inventory . .	1500
Supplies.	60
Total Current Assets	$3270

Long-Term Assets:

Equipment	$ 850
Less Accumulated	
Depreciation	50
Total Long-Term Assets . . .	$ 800
TOTAL ASSETS	$4070

LIABILITIES

Current Liabilities

Accounts Payable	$ 560
Notes Payable	1260
Salaries Payable	200
Taxes Payable.	80
Total Current Liabilities .	$2100

OWNER'S EQUITY

Owner's Capital	$1970

TOTAL LIABILITIES
AND OWNER'S EQUITY . . $4070

(a) $1170 (3270 − 2100); (b) 1.6-to-1 (3270 ÷ 2100)

(c) $0.8\text{-to-}1 \ (\dfrac{3270 - 1500}{2100})$

9. Now let's look at the four measures that can be developed from the data on the Income Statement. The first of these measures is called cost of goods sold as a percentage of net sales. This measures the percentage of net sales derived from the cost of merchandise sold. The formula is:

$$\frac{\text{cost of goods sold}}{\text{net sales}} \ \text{x } 100\%$$

The Acme Supermarket had net sales for the year of $450,000 and the cost of the merchandise for the same period was $360,000. Acme's cost of goods

sold as a percentage of net sales is _____ %.

$\dfrac{360,000}{450,000}$ x 100% = 80%

10. By reading Acme's statement, you can tell how this business compares with other businesses in the same industry. If this percentage is higher than the industry average it means that the business is selling its products for less than the competition (it is not marking the products up enough) or else that the business has paid more for its goods than the industry average. Among supermarkets in the area where Acme is located the cost of goods sold percentage (the short way of saying cost of goods sold as a percentage of net sales) is 79%.

What can be said about Acme Supermarket? _____ .

_____

- - - - - - - - - - - - - - -

It is either selling its products for less or it is paying more for the goods it buys than its competition.

11. Another measure developed from the Income Statement is called <u>gross profit as a percentage of net sales</u>--sometimes referred to as <u>gross profit margin</u>. Gross profit is net sales minus cost of goods sold. So the gross profit margin measures what percentage of the net sales was left after the cost of goods sold is subtracted from net sales. The formula is

$$\frac{\text{gross profit}}{\text{net sales}} \times 100\%$$

In the Acme Supermarket the gross profit was $90,000 ($450,000 - $360,000). Acme's gross profit margin is $_____.

- - - - - - - - - - - - - - -

$$\frac{90,000}{450,000} \times 100\% = 20\%$$

12. Note that the gross profit margin can be computed by the formula given above or by subtracting the cost of goods sold percentage from 100%. In the supermarket business in the area where Acme is located the gross profit

margin is _____%.

- - - - - - - - - - - - - - -

$100\% - 79\% = 21\%$

13. Another measure developed from the Income Statement is called <u>operating expenses as a percentage of net sales</u>. This measures what percentage of net sales was used for operating expenses (selling expenses and administrative expenses). Since operating expenses subtracted from the gross profit gives operating profit, the smaller the operating expenses, the larger the operating profit. The formula is

$$\frac{\text{operating expenses}}{\text{net sales}} \times 100\%$$

The operating expenses of Acme Supermarket are $87,750. The operating

expenses as a percentage of net sales is _____%.

- - - - - - - - - - - - - - -

$$\frac{87,750}{450,000} \times 100\% = 19.5\%$$

14. In the area where the Acme Supermarket is located the average supermarket has an operating expense percentage (a short form of operating expense as a percentage of net sales) of 20%. What conclusions can you come

to concerning Acme Supermarket? _____

_____

– – – – – – – – – – – – – – – –

   Acme has a favorable operating expense percentage as compared to the
   average supermarket in this area.

15. Remember that when the operating expenses are subtracted from gross
profits, we get the operating profit. We concluded in Frame 14 that Acme
has a favorable operating expense percentage as compared to the average
supermarket in this area. As compared to the average supermarket in the

area, Acme is doing (a)_____ the average.
                          (not as well as/as well as/better than)
(b) Show by comparison with the average supermarket why this is true.

– – – – – – – – – – – – – – – –

   (a) not as well
   (b) comparing Acme with the average supermarket:

	Acme	Average
Net sales	100.0%	100.0%
Cost of goods sold	80.0	79.0
Gross profit	20.0	21.0
Operating expenses	19.5	20.0
Operating profit	0.5%	1.0%

Note that even though Acme had a lower operating expense percentage,
the cost of goods sold percentage was greater, leaving a lower operating
profit percentage.

16. Businesses compare such percentages as those mentioned in Frame 15 to the percentages of the industry for the same period, or to their own percentages for a prior period. Fill in the percentages below:

	Year 19-5		Year 19-6		
Net sales	$600,000	100.0%	$700,000	(a) _____	%
Cost of goods sold	420,000	70.0	500,000	(b) _____	%
Gross profit	180,000	30.0	200,000	(c) _____	%
Operating expenses	150,000	25.0	165,000	(d) _____	%
Operating profit	$ 30,000	5.0%	$ 35,000	(e) _____	%

- - - - - - - - - - - - - - - -

(a) 100.0%; (b) 71.4%; (c) 28.6%; (d) 23.6%; (e) 5.2%

17. Note the change in year 19-6 as compared to 19-5. The cost of goods sold percentage was higher and the operating expense percentage was lower, resulting in an increase of 0.2% in the operating profit.

As to the higher cost of goods sold percentage: The additional sales may have resulted in a line of products that have a lower gross profit margin than the sales of 19-5; or the prices the business paid advanced faster than the prices charged to the customers.

As to the gross profit margin: The same reasons as above.

As to the operating expense percentage: The operating expenses increased at a lower rate than sales increased. The rent and utilities expense may not have increased at all, for example. A detailed analysis of operating expenses, which we cannot make with the figures given but which management can make by looking at the detailed accounts making up operating expenses, might be made to note how certain costs move with increased volume.

18. A corporation, since it is a legal entity separate from the owners, pays income taxes on its profit. Let us look at the Income Statement of Central Sales, Inc. for the year 19-3.

Net sales	$800,000
Cost of goods sold	630,000
Gross profit	170,000
Operating expenses	123,000
Net profit	47,000
Federal income tax	23,000
Net income after taxes	$ 24,000

What remains after federal income tax is the profit that is available to the owners for dividend. Therefore, the earnings after taxes is important. The last measure we are going to consider that can be developed from the Income Statement is net income after taxes as a percentage of net sales. The formula is:

$$\frac{\text{net income after taxes}}{\text{net sales}} \text{ x } 100\%$$

In the case of Central Sales, Inc., this percentage is _____%.

– – – – – – – – – – – – – –

   3%

19. Summarize what you now know by filling in the following chart:

FINANCIAL STATEMENT	NAME OF MEASURE	PURPOSE OF MEASURE	FORMULA
for BALANCE SHEET analysis			
for INCOME STATEMENT analysis			

Compare your answers with the chart in the Chapter Overview on page 294.

SELF-TEST

This Self-Test will show you whether or not you have mastered the chapter objectives and have completed this text. Answer each question to the best of your ability. Correct answers and instructions are given at the end of the test.

1. From the Balance Sheet below develop:

   (a) Working capital: $_____

   (b) Current ratio: _____

   (c) Acid-test ratio: _____

NEIGHBORHOOD HARDWARE

Balance Sheet
December 31, 19--

ASSETS		LIABILITIES	
Current Assets		Current Liabilities	
Cash	$ 1,000	Accounts Payable	$ 15,000
Accounts Receivable . .	4,500	Accrued Salaries	3,000
Merchandise Inventory .	40,000	Accrued Taxes	5,000
Prepaid Expenses	1,000	Total Current Liabilities .	$ 23,000
Total Current Assets . . .	$ 46,500	Long-Term Liabilities . .	63,500
		TOTAL LIABILITIES	$ 86,500
Long-Term Assets (net) . .	90,000		
		OWNER'S EQUITY	$ 50,000
		TOTAL LIABILITIES AND	
TOTAL ASSETS	$136,500	OWNER'S EQUITY	$136,500

2. From the Income Statement on the next page develop:

   (a) Cost of sales percentage: _____%

   (b) Gross profit percentage: _____%

   (c) Operating expense percentage: _____%

```
┌──────────────────────────────────────────────────┐
│                                                    │
│              NEIGHBORHOOD HARDWARE                  │
│                                                    │
│                 Income Statement                   │
│            Year ending December 31, 19--           │
│                                                    │
│                                                    │
│      Net Sales . . . . . . . . . . . . $212,000    │
│      Cost of Goods Sold . . . . . . . .  162,200   │
│      Gross Profit . . . . . . . . . . $ 49,800     │
│      Operating Expenses . . . . . . .    37,400    │
│      Operating Profit . . . . . . . . $ 12,400     │
│      Other Income and Expenses . . .        400    │
│                                                    │
│      Net Profit. . . . . . . . . . . . $ 12,000    │
│                                                    │
└──────────────────────────────────────────────────┘
```

3. The Gold Value Corporation has net sales for the year 19-- of $123,000.
After paying income taxes of $5600 it has an after-tax income of $6700.
What is the after-tax income as a percentage of net sales?

Self-Test Answers

Compare your answers to the Self-Test with the correct answers given below.
If all of your answers are correct, you have completed this book. If you
missed any questions, study the frames indicated in parentheses after the
answer. If you miss many questions, go over the entire chapter carefully.

1. (a) $23,500 (46,500 − 23,000) (Frames 2, 3, 7, 8)
   (b) 2.0-to-1 (46,500 ÷ 23,000) (Frames 4, 5, 7, 8)

   (c) 0.3-to-1 ($\frac{46,500 - 40,000}{23,000}$) (Frames 6-8)

2. (a) 76.5% ($\frac{162,200}{212,000}$ x 100%) (Frames 9, 10, 16, 17)

   (b) 23.5% ($\frac{49,800}{212,000}$ x 100%) (Frames 11, 12, 16, 17)

   (c) 17.6% ($\frac{37,400}{212,000}$ x 100%) (Frames 13-17)

3. 5.4% ($\frac{6700}{123,000}$ x 100%) (Frame 18)

APPENDIX

Computerized Accounting for Small Businesses

Once a business gets beyond a certain size, it can benefit from a computerized accounting system. Today's small business computers and desktop computers are priced low enough so that all but the smallest business can afford the price of the hardware (the computer and other support devices such as a printer) and the software package (the programs that perform the accounting functions).

But, being able to "afford the price" of a computerized accounting system and being able to <u>justify</u> such a system are two different considerations. Many businesses have leaped fervently into the computer revolution only to discover that the costs of installing the system and getting it to meet the particular business needs far outstrip the costs of the hardware and software.

This appendix gives a general overview of the processes of selecting, setting up, and using a computerized accounting system.

SELECTING A SYSTEM

To select and implement even a small computerized accounting system, you first need to complete three essential studies:

1. A thorough evaluation of your current accounting needs (and possibly a reorganization of the current system, if there is one). This is to determine whether a new system is needed at all.

2. A thorough evaluation of the available hardware and software. This is to determine whether there are any systems that may meet your needs and, if so, which is the best.

3. A plan for installing the system and learning to use it.

In many cases, you may need to secure the services of an experienced computer consultant as well as an experienced accountant.

Having made the choice of the right hardware and software, you can go about setting up and using the system.

SETTING UP A COMPUTERIZED ACCOUNTING SYSTEM

Setting up a computerized accounting system takes about the same effort and time as setting up a paper-and-pencil system. Most of the modern accounting software packages for small business computers give specific instructions for gathering the information you need and entering it first onto worksheets and then into the computer. While the information you need to gather will differ from system to system, you probably will have to accumulate at least the following:

- The names, numbers, and balances of your General Ledger accounts.
- The customers that buy from you on credit, as well as their account balances.
- The vendors from whom you make purchases on account, as well as your balance with each.

The computer system will use this informtion to create a set of "electronic books," which are usually magnetically recorded on disks.

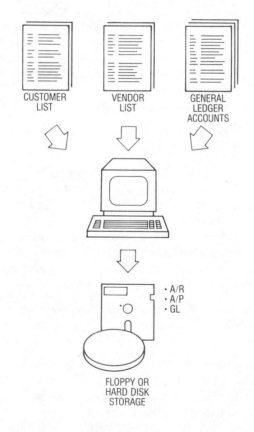

Figure 1: SETTING UP THE SYSTEM

USING A COMPUTERIZED ACCOUNTING SYSTEM

When using a small computerized accounting system, you follow a regular routine, just as with a paper-and-pencil system. Depending on the business activity, you can choose to enter transactions daily, every other day, or even weekly.

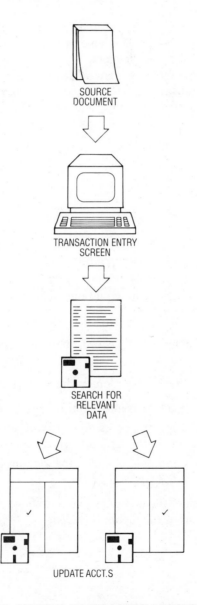

SOURCE
DOCUMENT

TRANSACTION ENTRY
SCREEN

SEARCH FOR
RELEVANT
DATA

UPDATE ACCT.S

Figure 2: GENERAL TRANSACTION PROCESSING

First, you need to gather important source documents for the transactions you want to enter. These may include receipts, invoices, check registers, and so forth.

Then, working with the system, display an appropriate transaction entry screen—a screen that is specially formatted to record the details of a specific transaction type. Entering transactions on the screen is similar to journalizing transactions. The system you use will probably have different screens for cash disbursements, cash receipts, sales, and purchases, as well as other types of transactions.

After you enter the transactions, the computer automatically looks up the appropriate account numbers and makes entries to the ledgers—the general ledger as well as the relevant subsidiary ledgers.

The sections that follow show the general sequences of events that occur when you process common transactions. Remember, these events will vary with different computers, accounting packages, and, of course, different businesses.

PROCESSING SALES TRANSACTIONS

Here is the sequence of events you would most likely follow when entering sales transactions.

1. You gather documents that record sales on account (e.g., invoice register entries).

2. You enter each sales transaction on the Sales Transaction Entry Screen.

3. For the debit side of the transaction, the computer automatically:
   - looks up the customer's name and account number and then enters the amount of the sale in the Accounts Receivable Subsidiary Ledger; and,
   - totals the sales entries and enters the amount in the Accounts Receivable account of the General Ledger.

4. For the credit side, the computer enters the total of all sales entries into the Sales account of the General Ledger.

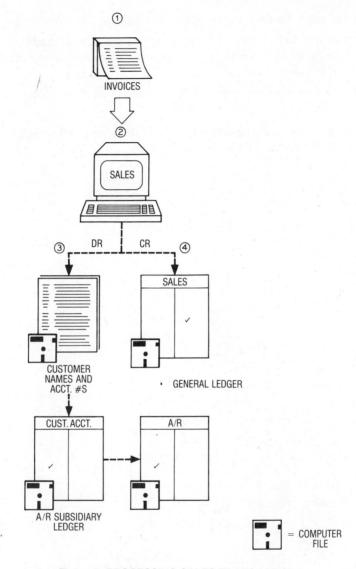

INVOICES

SALES

③ DR   CR ④

SALES

CUSTOMER
NAMES AND
ACCT. #S

GENERAL LEDGER

CUST. ACCT.

A/R

A/R SUBSIDIARY
LEDGER

 = COMPUTER
FILE

Figure 3: PROCESSING SALES TRANSACTIONS

PROCESSING CASH RECEIPTS

With many accounting packages you will follow a sequence like this to record cash receipts:

1. Gather documents that record cash receipts (e.g., checks received from customers).

2. Enter each cash receipt on the Cash Receipts Transaction Entry Screen.

3. To process the <u>credit</u> side of the cash receipt, the computer:

    - looks up the customer's name and account number and then enters the amount of the receipt in the customer's account in the Accounts Receivable Subsidiary Ledger; and

    - totals the receipts and enters the amount in the Accounts Receivable account of the General Ledger.

4. For the <u>debit</u> side, the computer enters the total of all receipts entries into the Cash account of the General Ledger.

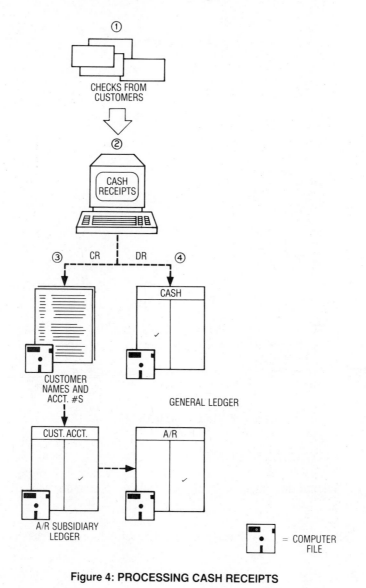

Figure 4: PROCESSING CASH RECEIPTS

PROCESSING PURCHASES TRANSACTIONS

To process transactions dealing with purchases from vendors on account, you can follow a procedure like this with many accounting packages:

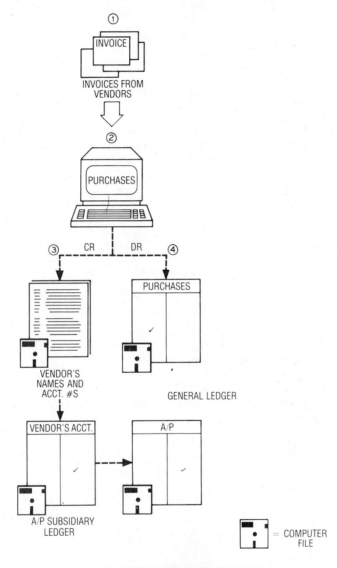

Figure 5: PROCESSING PURCHASES

1. Gather documents that record purchases on account (e.g., invoices from vendors).

2. Enter each purchase transaction on the Purchase Entry Screen.

3.   For the <u>credit</u> side of the transaction, the computer automatically:
  * looks up the vendor's name and updates the vendor's accounts in the Accounts Payable Subsidiary Ledger; and,
  * totals the purchases entries and enters the amount in the Accounts Payable account of the General Ledger.

4.   For the <u>debit</u> side, the computer enters the total of all purchase entries into the Purchases account of the General Ledger.

PROCESSING CASH DISBURSEMENTS

Here is a generic procedure for processing cash disbursement transactions that is similar to what you would follow with many computerized accounting packages.

1.   Gather documents that record cash disbursements (e.g., your check register).

2.   Enter each cash disbursement on the Cash Disbursements Transaction Entry Screen.

3.   To process the <u>debit</u> side of the cash disbursement, the computer:
  * looks up the vendor's name and account number and then enters the amount of the receipt in the vendor's account in the Accounts Payable Subsidiary Ledger; and
  * totals the receipts and enters the amount in the Accounts Payable account of the General Ledger.

4.   For the <u>credit</u> side, the computer enters the total of all disbursement entries into the Cash account of the General Ledger.

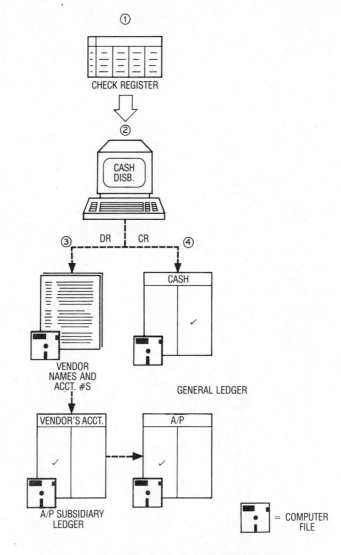

CHECK REGISTER

CASH
DISB.

DR   CR

CASH

VENDOR
NAMES AND
ACCT. #S

GENERAL LEDGER

VENDOR'S ACCT.

A/P

A/P SUBSIDIARY
LEDGER

= COMPUTER
FILE

Figure 6: PROCESSING CASH DISBURSEMENTS

Index–Glossary

Account, 44, 47-51: a bookkeeping device used to record the increases or decreases of a specific type of asset, liability, or owner's equity item brought about by a business transaction. There are five major classifications of accounts: (1) asset accounts, (2) liability accounts, (3) owner's equity accounts, (4) revenue accounts, and (5) expense accounts.

Accounting, 2, 6-7, 9: a study which includes bookkeeping and also deals with the analysis and interpretation of events that affect the financial condition of a business and with establishing bookkeeping systems.

Accounting cycle, 42-43: a bookkeeping process that occurs during each accounting period. It begins when business transactions are recorded in the General Journal and includes posting to the Ledger, preparation of a Worksheet, preparation of a Trial Balance, adjustments to the ledger balances, the preparation of the financial statements, and the closing of the books.

Accounting period, 42, 46-47: the period of time that elapses between the preparation of subsequent financial statements.

Accounts payable, 33-36: a subdivision of current liabilities that refers to money owed by a business to an outside creditor for goods or services it has received.

Accounts receivable, 33-36: a subdivision of current assets that refers to money owed to the business by someone to whom the business has given goods or services on credit (or on account).

Accrual basis accounting, 91, 94-95: an accounting system that accounts for all business transactions that have occurred during an accounting period, whether or not cash was actually received or disbursed.

Acid-test ratio, 296: (current assets − inventories) ÷ current liabilities, or liquid assets ÷ current liabilities.

Adjustments, adjusting entries, 91, 92-99, 110-14: the updating of the ledger account balances at the end of the accounting cycle. Adjustments account for (1) the expiration or prepaid expenses, (2) the apportionment of unrecorded income, and (3) the apportionment of unrecorded liabilities

cash payments.

Cash Receipts Journal, 159, 173-85: a record of the receipt of cash.

General Journal, 45, 51-59: a chronological record of all business transactions not recorded in special journals.

Sales Journal, 159-60, 165-72: a record of sales on account.

Purchases Journal, 160-61, 185-90: a journal to record purchases on
account.

Last in - first out (lifo), 212, 217-220: method of determining inventory
costs in which the most recent costs are charged against revenue first.

Ledger: a group of accounts.

Posting to the Ledger, 45, 59-67: copying data from the General Journal
onto individual accounts.

Subsidiary Ledgers, 157-59, 166-72, 176-85, 187-90, 192-96: the General Ledger, the Accounts Payable Ledger, and the Accounts Receivable
Ledger.

Liabilities, 3, 8-9, 22, 33: the debts of a business.

Long-term assets, 22, 32-33: assets that are expected to be consumed or
disposed of in a fairly long time, usually more than a year.

Long-term liabilities, 22, 31-32: debts that are to be paid off in a period of
time greater than one year.

Lower of cost or market method, 212, 221-23: a method of valuing inventory
in which costs are compared with market price (i.e., the cost of replacing the merchandise on the date of the inventory) and the lower of the two
figures is used.

Net income after taxes as a percentage of sales, 299: (net income after income tax ÷ net sales) x 100%.

Net worth: see Owner's equity.

Notes payable, 33: a subdivision of liabilities that refers to money the business owes to a creditor evidenced by a note.

Notes receivable, 33: a subdivision of assets that refers to money owed to
the business evidenced by a note.

Operating expense percentage, 298: (operating expense ÷ net sales) x 100%.

Owner's capital account, 47, 49: an account that lists the increases and decreases in capital that an owner has invested in the business.

Owner's drawing account, 47: an account that shows the owner's withdrawals
of cash from the business.

Owner's equity, 3, 9: the owner's claim against the assets of the business
after liabilities have been deducted. Also called capital, proprietorship,
or net worth.

Payroll register, 264, 277-87: a form used by a business for computing
taxes which that business must pay on the wages of its employees.

Periodic inventory, 211, 214-15: a general system of inventory accounting
in which only the costs of sales are recorded; no entries are made at the
time of sale that charge profit or loss with the cost of merchandise sold.
All adjustments are made at once at the end of a period (usually the yearly accounting period).